Alastair Campbell

Alastair Campbell

New Labour and the Rise of the Media Class

PETER OBORNE

AURUM PRESS

First published in Great Britain
1999 by Aurum Press Ltd
25 Bedford Avenue, London WC1B 3AT

A catalogue record for this book is available from the British Library.

ISBN 1 85410 647 3

10 9 8 7 6 5 4 3 2 1
2003   2002   2001   2000   1999

Printed and bound in Great Britain

To Martine

CONTENTS

Acknowledgements

Alastair Campbell has not cooperated with this book. There is a danger here to the writer. If friendly sources will not talk, hostile witnesses or those with an axe to grind can come to hold too much sway.

I have strenuously sought to avoid this outcome and from the start have been determined to write a fair-minded and generous-hearted work. There are very few who have refused to talk to me. A number agreed to see me despite Campbell's discouragement of the project. Their intention has been to help me write an accurate and objective account which does justice to the subject. I hope and believe that I have not let them down. I also hope that this work will cast a sharp new light on the way that Britain is being governed under New Labour.

I have incurred an enormous number of debts in writing this book. In the course of researching it I spoke, in depth, to more than two hundred people. My gratitude to each and every one of them cannot be overestimated. I would ideally thank them all by name but for the fact that some have requested anonymity and I suspect that others would prefer it.

There are a number of specific debts. Tom Roberts worked for two months as my researcher: the book might not have been ready in time without his splendid efforts. Nick Fleming of the *Express* carried out an exemplary investigation into Campbell's early career. *Express* journalists Matthew Mervyn Jones and Lucy McDonald helped out generously. Paul Brown, of the *Scottish Daily Express*, accomplished some diligent work on the Campbells of Tiree. The freelance journalist Mark Lister trudged the streets of Keighley in search of traces of the former Campbell presence in the town. For thirteen days there was no sign: on the fourteenth he struck gold. The Page One Press Agency in Nottingham carried out painstaking work on Campbell's Leicester schooldays; my thanks go out to Carl Fellstrom and Simon Wheeler. Mark Mason, researcher extraordinary, was generous with his time and efforts. I am also indebted to James

ACKNOWLEDGEMENTS

Temple-Smithson, Alex Slater, Alex Evans, Anthea Lee of *New Nation* and the staff of Cambridge University Library.

Joe Haines, Campbell's predecessor both as political editor of the *Mirror* and as Downing Street Press Secretary, granted me a fabulous insight not merely into the latter job but into recent political history: lunch with Haines in Tonbridge ought to be an obligatory part of the training of every political reporter. Joe Saumarez Smith undertook some magnificent sleuthing into Alastair Campbell's career as a professional croupier: I am intensely grateful. Paul Routledge, biographer of Gordon Brown and Peter Mandelson, gave invaluable advice about how to research a book of this sort. It made all the difference. It is also a pleasure to record two particular debts in the parliamentary lobby: to Charles Reiss, political editor of the *Evening Standard*, for whom I worked as an understudy for several years; and to Simon Walters, my comrade in arms at the *Sunday Express* for three years. They are both masters of their art, although it may be that Walters' art is blacker than that of Reiss. Stephen Pollard, Patrick O'Flynn, Jeremy Brock and Mark Jones very kindly read the manuscript and their comments were greatly appreciated. The enthusiasm and commitment of my publisher, Sheila Murphy, and her assistant Hannah Tausz has been immense, and the same applies to Antony Wood, the book's editor. Above all, I owe an immeasurable debt to my wife and family who have had to put up with me while the book was written, an even greater tribulation than usual.

P. O.

Chapter One

SPIN CYCLE: THIRTY-SIX HOURS IN THE LIFE OF ALASTAIR CAMPBELL

What a total nonsense this business about image is.
Sir Alec Douglas-Home, 1965

Shortly after 6 a.m. the alarm clock goes off in the modest North London terrace house that Alastair Campbell shares with his partner Fiona Millar and their three children. Campbell rises and gets dressed at once. Ever since he suffered a drink-induced breakdown in the 1980s, he has spurned alcohol and cigarettes. He never wakes up with a blurry head or a hangover. He is clear-thinking and ready for action, the perfect fighting machine for the complex and demanding job that he does.

While in the bath he carefully reads the summary of the day's press which has been faxed through to his home overnight. This version relates only to the first editions. An updated document, incorporating changes as a result of late-breaking stories, will await him when he arrives at his large Downing Street office. While leafing through the press summary, Campbell listens carefully to the 6.30 a.m. news bulletin. If the running order is not to his satisfaction – which can mean that it is not as set out in the news grid laid down weeks before by the Downing Street communications team[1] – Campbell will take action. Some BBC producer will receive a sharply worded call of protest from a Downing Street or Labour Party aide. Normally that is sufficient to correct the direction of the bulletins.

If it is not, and the matter is important, Campbell will take it up at a much higher level. One of his great skills is the knowledge, born of many years' ex-perience both as a journalist and as a press spokesman, of exactly where to pitch complaints and whether or not to do so in person. The government infor-mation machine which Campbell controls[2] is by far the most powerful and

---

1. This sets out the dates of future government announcements in detail. It is designed to ensure that two big events do not clash on the same day and that the news media is never without its dripfeed from the government machine. The Strategic Communications Unit, which prepares the grid, is a New Labour innovation. It operates out of the 10 Downing Street office which used to be set aside for paperwork relating to the appointment of bishops.

2. Mike Granatt is Head of the Government Information and Communication Service. Campbell

1

coherent in British peacetime history. The attention to detail is awesome. No stone is ever left unturned so that the government can get the message it wants across to the British voting public.

Campbell normally leaves his home at around 7 a.m. to make the 25-minute drive to Downing Street. More often than not he will use the family Renault Espace or take a cab. Fiona Millar, who also works in Downing Street, will follow later under her own steam. Campbell is a man with little time for the trappings of power: this indifference marks him out from his great friend and rival Peter Mandelson.

In the car or perhaps earlier at home, Campbell will most likely have talked to Tony Blair. Nobody outside the Prime Minister's immediate family, and at times not even they, talks as often or as intimately to Blair as Campbell. The two men discuss the tone of the morning papers and much else besides. Campbell is much more than a Press Secretary, potent though that position is. He is the Prime Minister's main adviser on politics. He is his closest and most trusted friend in government. Many Cabinet ministers and senior civil servants view Campbell, and not John Prescott, as the real Deputy Prime Minister.[3] No important decision is ever made without Campbell's knowledge: few without his direct involvement.

His job, in part, is to protect Tony Blair and to enable his mind to range free on the really big decisions. Not long after the 1997 election, two BBC journalists[4] travelled up with the Prime Minister to Worcester where he was to make a major announcement about juvenile crime. The statement had been released overnight and was prominent on the BBC news bulletins. On the train journey west the journalists approached the Prime Minister and asked him about the speech. Tony Blair looked blank. Campbell stepped in at once. 'I haven't told you about that yet,' he said.

He will arrive at his Downing Street office shortly after 7.30 a.m. It is a large office on the ground floor of Downing Street, to the left of the policeman guarding the front door. He has made himself at home in this room; numerous drawings by his three children, Rory, Calum and Grace, are displayed. Framed on the wall is an article attacking Campbell and the government in the most

has wisely decided not to take direct charge of the GICS. Nevertheless, it is in effect answerable to him. See *Ministerial Code: A Code of Conduct and Guidance on Procedure for Ministers*, Cabinet Office, July 1997, p. 30.

3. See article by Romola Christopherson, who retired as Director of Information at the Department of Health at the beginning of 1999, *The Sunday Times*, 10 January 1999.

4. Jon Sopel and Nicholas Jones.

lurid and vicious terms by the *Sun* columnist Richard Littlejohn,[5] a *Newsweek* cover story about Tony Blair, and a New Labour election poster in the colours of his favourite football team, Burnley. The day's newspapers are spread out on a table in the centre of the room and over in a corner is a television set. At every fresh news bulletin, Campbell stops whatever he is doing to make a mental note of the significance and slant attached to each item.

From his desk he takes calls from selected journalists. Charles Reiss, political editor of the pro-government *Evening Standard*, will often call at this time. Campbell will take Reiss through the agenda of the day, give him a steer on upcoming announcements, and help him out where possible. London's *Standard* is taken very seriously by Downing Street because it helps set the agenda for the national papers the next day. Robin Oakley or John Sergeant, the two BBC political heavyweights, often phone in: they will get the same thorough and helpful service.

Campbell also uses his first moments in the office to prepare for the daily 9 a.m. meeting.[6] This event is chaired by him and attended by key officials from 10 Downing Street as well as representatives from the Treasury, the Foreign Office, the Labour Party and other government departments. It was inaugurated by Michael Heseltine, then Deputy Prime Minister, in the dying days of the last Tory government. Heseltine saw the need for a forum that would give daily focus and a political cutting edge to the government message. Heseltine's idea failed, partly because the government he served no longer had a message to convey.

But New Labour has made Heseltine's invention work. Campbell has used this 9 a.m. meeting in a far more effective way than the Conservatives: to set the government line for the day, to resolve the problems that lie ahead and to impose discipline on ministers and government departments. It is used as a vehicle for enforcement. The key business is carried out by Alastair Campbell, Policy Unit Chief David Miliband and the handful of other Downing Street officials who pull the strings in Tony Blair's government. 'These people are very bright, very clinical. You do not want to be the problem at the 9 a.m.' says one minister with a shudder. 'You definitely do not want to be the problem.' As a rule, however, ministers do not attend this meeting.

Today, Wednesday 28 July 1999, Campbell varies his routine and misses the 9 a.m. Parliament has risen, and Whitehall is grinding to a halt ahead of the August summer holidays. He and Miliband have worked out a rolling

5. Presented to Campbell by Littlejohn himself.
6. Though known as the '9 o'clock' it is often held at 8.30 a.m.

programme of meetings with national newspapers. Today they have agreed to meet a small group of senior journalists and executives at Express Newspapers. Since newspapers' hours are more relaxed than Downing Street's, this gives Campbell a little more time to sleep in. It is 8.05 a.m. when he leaves his front door in North London and gets into a waiting taxi-cab, 8.30 a.m. when he walks into the *Express* Conference Room.

Campbell is a tall, commanding, well-built man, ruggedly good-looking. When he was younger he was very attractive indeed to women, who would sometimes stop and stare as he passed them in the street. Even though he is now in his early 40s, women say that he still radiates a strong sexual magnetism. He has not yet entirely lost the open-faced good looks of his youth, but they have been mellowed by the maturity and confidence that come with the exercise of power. He is smartly dressed, in the way that high-quality tabloid journalists – he used to be political editor of the *Daily Mirror* – are taught to be. The suit is not well-cut, but it is clean and immaculately creased. His black shoes are shiny clean and his white shirt spotless. He wears red cufflinks and his black tie is criss-crossed by irregular white bars. He automatically commands the room, even when he is not speaking. The Americans have an expression for men like Campbell: Alpha Male.

In all recent governments David Miliband, as head of the Downing Street Policy Unit, would have outranked the Press Secretary. Not in the Blair administration. It is at once clear from the posture and demeanour of the two men that Miliband is the junior figure. Campbell likes to refer to him as 'Brains', a patronising remark. In the Blair government the spin-doctor counts for more, much more, than the policy boss. This is not to say that Miliband, the son of the famous Marxist thinker Ralph Miliband,[7] is an unimpressive figure. That is far from the case. He is simply less impressive than Campbell who, with a sweep of the hand, allows him the floor to give an account of the achievements and objectives of the Blair government.

'Most Labour governments have failed,' Miliband kicks off. 'Certainly they have failed to get re-elected. They have come unstuck on the gap between expectation and reality.' He speaks without emotion in a classless, transatlantic drawl. He looks as if he has come straight out of the Harvard Business School. 'Our job is to explain the bigger picture so that the gap between expectation and reality does not grow.'

7. Ralph Miliband, author of *Parliamentary Socialism: A Study in the Politics of Labour* (1972) and *The State in Capitalist Society* (1973) among other works. Another son, Ed Miliband, works as a Special Adviser to Chancellor Gordon Brown at the Treasury.

Methodically, dispassionately, carefully, Miliband goes through the running of the government machine. He explains how Downing Street has agreed objectives with every Whitehall Department, and each Cabinet minister is held responsible for those targets being met. 'In the DFEE[8] there is a named official responsible for every target,' says Miliband calmly. 'If we don't drive these changes through they will never get done.' He explains how Tony Blair regularly calls in each Cabinet minister and his permanent secretary and monitors progress. 'Everybody knows his head is on the block,' he says. There has been nothing like it in Whitehall before.

It is noticeable, listening to David Miliband, that he does not talk about issues, he talks about 'stories'. He speaks of the 'need to keep the core narrative clear in the blizzard of government initiatives.' In Tony Blair's Downing Street, the policy man even speaks and thinks like a spin-doctor. This is no coincidence. New Labour does not believe that policy and presentation are two separate functions, but indivisible parts of the same seamless process.

A question comes from the floor. Is there still a role for Cabinet government in the face of this central control? 'In the past,' replies Miliband, 'Cabinets were important when governments were factionalised and divided.' This government, he adds, is neither. Campbell wholeheartedly concurs: 'When they had big cabinets, they spent their day doing one of two things: tearing lumps out of each other or writing diaries.'

It could not be plainer: the job of Cabinet ministers in Tony Blair's government is to do what they are told by Campbell, Miliband and one or two others at the heart of government. It is true that their authority comes from the fact that they speak for the Prime Minister. Nevertheless, the fact that so much power is concentrated in the hands of a clique of unelected officials causes unease with many MPs and ministers. But that is one of the simple things which New Labour is all about: exercising power from the centre.

Campbell says that one of Labour's biggest problems is the weakness of the Tory opposition. He claims that Labour has done some 'massive radical stuff' but that it is given 'no definition' because of Tory incoherence. 'We have to try and get the dividing lines back,' he says. Campbell explains that he sees Labour's 'core vote' as the people who voted for the party at the last election. He wants to set out the difference 'between that and a right-wing Conservative Party.'

When the two men emerge into the street from the air-conditioned cool of the

8. The Whitehall acronym for the Department for Education and Employment.

newspaper offices, the heat is stifling. Just walking from the door of the building to the waiting car raises a muck sweat. The view down the Thames towards Whitehall is obscured by a rippling haze. In the Palace of Westminster the Catalpa trees have burst into bloom. When their sickly sweet smell fills the courtyards outside the Commons it is always a sure sign that the dog days of summer have arrived and that it is time for the Commons to rise and for MPs to disperse to Greek islands and Tuscan villas.

Just one delicate task awaits Campbell and Tony Blair, however, before they too can escape. That is the government reshuffle. For weeks the political press has been full of speculation about how the Prime Minister will wield the axe. This subject, of little interest to the wider public, is a matter of obsession in the narrow worlds of Westminster and Whitehall. Ulster Secretary Mo Mowlam, Health Secretary Frank Dobson and Jack Cunningham, the jovial Cabinet 'enforcer', are all said to be in the Prime Minister's sights. Today the *Financial Times* is boldly reporting that Dobson's job is to be given to Alan Milburn, the Treasury Minister. Dobson will become Leader of the House of Commons at the expense of Margaret Beckett.

All afternoon ministers, MPs and journalists wait in the fetid heat for news from Downing Street. It is all speculation and innuendo. Only a tiny group of men and women know what is going on – the Prime Minister, his chief of staff Jonathan Powell, Tony Blair's aide Anji Hunter, his Political Secretary Sally Morgan, and Alastair Campbell. The five of them quietly finalised most of the details at a Downing Street meeting the previous day. The Chancellor, Gordon Brown, seems as much in the dark as anybody: his aides spend the afternoon exchanging gossip about who is going where. So – until very late in the day – is John Prescott, who is to emerge as the big loser. For the last four weeks the Deputy Prime Minister has been the victim of a series of vicious anonymous attacks. Some of Prescott's friends blame Campbell for failing to stifle this whispering campaign. At 5 p.m. rumours of the impending reshuffle begin to harden into fact. A Downing Street civil servant tells a minister that the reshuffle has started; he obligingly passes on the information to a journalist. At six o'clock Campbell steps out of his office and calls in a group of waiting reporters.

Downing Street has made sure that representatives of the three big television networks are there – John Sergeant of the BBC, Michael Brunson from ITN and Adam Boulton, the political editor of Sky News. Bob Roberts, deputy political editor of the Press Association, is present. Tom Baldwin, deputy political editor of *The Times*, who has been standing by outside Downing

Street, joins the select group. Campbell does not invite them back to his room but briefs them in the large Downing Street hallway. He reveals that the reshuffle is now taking place. 'We will let people know in our own way,' says Campbell. 'Those contacted first will be those leaving the government.'

Then he drops his bombshell. 'The Prime Minister has been clear for some time that there will be no change in Cabinet ranks.' In other words, only junior ministers are involved: the political lobby has been taken for a ride. All the talk about Mowlam, Dobson and Beckett was for nothing. Baldwin is the first to respond. 'What chances are there of any further changes after the summer?'

'For fuck's sake, Tom,' snarls Campbell. 'You have written enough crap about the reshuffle already. You can't start speculating about the next one.'

The talk descends to the logistical chat which takes up so much of the time of television reporters, about what shots will be available of which ministers walking up Downing Street.

Campbell's meeting with the full lobby waits until the reshuffle has been completed the following day. (This is a special lobby meeting, called to announce the reshuffle. Downing Street press briefings are ordinarily held at 11 a.m. each day, but only when Parliament is sitting.) By the early afternoon of Thursday 29 July, when he strides into the compact briefing room in the Downing Street basement where reporters await his arrival, every minister has learnt his fate. The underground room holds 50: there are 80 present. Reporters lean against the walls, crouch on the floor, sit on tables. Even though it is the end of term, with the prospect of release for the summer holidays, there is a sour mood. The lobby has been made to look foolish.

Today's meeting will be a stand-off, a battle of wits. The reporters blame Campbell for letting the speculation run. Campbell basks in the lobby's humiliation. He dislikes political journalists with an intensity bordering on hatred. Though he is the Prime Minister's Press Secretary he does not believe his job is to serve the press. Indeed, he will do all he can to make life difficult for the lobby – unless it serves Tony Blair's interest to help them, in which case he will happily do so. He was a political reporter himself for a decade, and it was during that period that he learnt to despise his colleagues so much.

When he worked on the *Daily Mirror* he watched the Tory press destroy his friend and hero Neil Kinnock. Now the press has turned: most papers are friendly to New Labour. It has not made Campbell love the lobby any more. Indeed, being in Downing Street has deepened his hostility. He believes that political journalism in Britain is trivial, rancid and destructive. One of his objectives is to weaken, if not destroy, the parliamentary lobby. It is a form of self-hatred, for he too is a creature of the lobby. He understands exactly how the lobby works, spots the hidden meaning behind every question, knows with the intuition of genius the rhythm and longevity of every news story. There are many things to be said about Alastair Campbell, what he does and how he works. But it should never be forgotten that he is a master of his trade.

Thursday 29 July is even hotter than the day before. Campbell is jacketless. He sits down in one of two chairs placed at the front of the room. His deputy[9] sits in the other. Sitting in the front row, nearest to Campbell, are his two closest allies in the room: Philip Webster of *The Times* and Tony Bevins of the *Express*. As far as he trusts any political reporter, he trusts them. Kevin Maguire, political editor of the *Daily Mirror*, also sits at the front. Maguire is disliked by Campbell on the grounds that he is a friend and supporter of Gordon Brown. George Jones, political editor of the *Daily Telegraph*, one of only two daily papers to retain a pro-Tory line, is also in the front row. Campbell ignores Jones, who is sitting next to John Deans of the *Daily Mail*, the only other daily paper that can in any way be described as Conservative. In the second row back sits Robert Peston of the *Financial Times*. Peston is no Tory, but his stories have a way of causing deep embarrassment for the government. Campbell rarely misses an opportunity to ridicule or diminish him.

For twenty minutes Campbell concerns himself with names: who is up, who is down, who is out. He dwells on the promotion of Patricia Scotland, who has become Britain's first black woman minister. He doles out praise to the reshuffle winners, passes quickly over the losers. 'I don't make any political point here but there are fourteen leaving the government who are men,' says Campbell. He is signalling that there is a story here. The following morning, most of the morning papers will run special pieces on how the reshuffle has boosted women.

The other story – one that Campbell plays down, but not too hard – is the humiliation of John Prescott. There are questions about why John Prescott met Tony Blair earlier in the day. The lobby is suddenly interested, aware, sniffing at a row. There has been talk that the Deputy Prime Minister raised a scene, even threatened resignation, at the way his team of ministers was shot to pieces. Campbell plays the meeting down. 'Because it's Thursday and there's a bilateral[10] with the Prime Minister every Thursday.'

It is Tony Bevins who raises the issue of the day, the issue that is eating away

---

9. Godric Smith, a career civil servant, liked by the lobby, expert at playing a dead bat.
10. Grand Whitehall jargon for a meeting involving two principals.

at the vitals of every lobby correspondent in the room – who was to blame for all the speculation about the reshuffle that never was. 'Could you tell us,' ventures Bevins, 'how you reply to the charge that ministers too were sucked into this speculation?'[11]

'I've lost count of the number of times I've told you that the stories that have been written about this reshuffle are nonsense. It's the easiest thing in the world, having written all that nonsense, to say that we should have told you that nothing was going to happen.'

Bevins points out that Campbell isn't answering his question. Campbell ignores him. He is going strong now. He has got his point and he is determined to make it. 'You asked me how I answer the charge that ministers were sucked in. All I'm saying is that the Prime Minister runs the country, runs the government, according to the country's interests. He thinks the Cabinet is doing a good job. It remains the policy that there is no point in me, as the Prime Minister's official spokesman, engaging in any of the nonsense that gets written about reshuffles. I want the message to get around. I never do it.'

Campbell never does properly answer Bevins' question about ministerial complicity in the reshuffle speculation. It gets drowned out. He is in control. And as journalists make to leave he does something which emphasises just how much in control he is. He hands out prizes. There is an award – a signed copy of Campbell's recent speech on government relations with the media – for a leader writer on the *Independent* who called for Scottish Secretary John Reid to enter the Cabinet, overlooking the fact that he had already joined it. There is a CD from the group Garbage for George Jones of the *Daily Telegraph*, whose paper predicted that Paddy Ashdown, the outgoing leader of the Liberal Democrats, was to be appointed Secretary of State for Northern Ireland. And there is a bottle of champagne for Campbell's old adversary, Robert Peston. 'What we were pleased about with Robert was the way that he just never gave up. Even yesterday he was saying that Dobson was going to be Leader of the House.'

The lobby roars with laughter. There is nothing it enjoys as much as the discomfiture of one of its own. Peston pretends to smile. Campbell is indeed a master of his art. He despises the parliamentary lobby, but he knows how to play it like a violin. It has not yet found a way of playing back.

After the session is over, Campbell's briefing to journalists is typed up and then circulated around ministerial offices and Whitehall departments. Ministers

---

11. Both Mo Mowlam and Frank Dobson had made public statements that they intended to hang onto their jobs.

await its arrival with impatience. The note of each day's lobby briefing is viewed as a sacred text, providing ministers with their line for the day and their best clue as to what they should say and do. The following day the Tories claim that Tony Blair's failure to carry out a wider reshuffle shows that he has become a prisoner of his Cabinet. It is a ludicrous claim. No Prime Minister has ever paid his Cabinet so little attention. Ministers are fond of remarking that the only meaningful reshuffle would be if Campbell left Downing Street for the private sector, and there is precious little sign of that.

Campbell's power stretches well beyond the press, his formal area of influence, into Whitehall. There he is known as PMOS – the Prime Minister's Official Spokesman. Civil servants love him for his accuracy, his hard work, his good judgement and, above all, for the fact that he speaks so precisely for the Prime Minister. It is a very confident minister indeed who does not regard him with fear and trepidation. Campbell is a prodigious figure, a towering presence at the very heart of Tony Blair's government and one who is coming to be resented on an ever-larger scale by the Prime Minister's ministerial colleagues. It is impossible to understand the Blair administration and how it works without grasping the role that Campbell plays within it. And it is impossible to understand Campbell without knowing about his varied and complicated background. As a young man he worked as a busker, as a writer of soft pornography, and as a croupier, and claimed to have made a living as a gigolo in the South of France. He made a successful career in tabloid journalism. He fended off alcoholism, lived through a nervous breakdown, and emerged all the stronger for it. He was a member of the tiny group that masterminded the brilliant election campaign of 1997. Now he is Tony Blair's chosen instrument of political power. He is one of the most extraordinary men in Britain today.

Chapter Two

FAIR AND FALSE LIKE A CAMPBELL

Much may be made of a Scotsman, if he be caught young.
Samuel Johnson on Lord Mansfield
[*educated, like Campbell, in England*]

The name is all-important. To an Englishman the name Campbell is merely an indication that its possessor hails from a nation which has been in turn invaded, plundered, pacified and neglected but never quite absorbed in the course of a thousand years of frequently bloody encounters. To a Scot, and in particular a Highland Scot, the name Campbell is pregnant with a different kind of significance.

All Scottish Highland clans have a history of treachery. But the clan of Campbell, led for centuries by the Dukes of Argyll, has a uniquely treacherous history. Their defining moment came on the morning of 13 February 1692 when, acting on the orders of the king, they massacred the Macdonalds of Glencoe, their hosts throughout the previous two weeks. The crime counted, under Scottish law, as 'murder under trust', an extreme form of murder on a level with treason. No Campbell was ever prosecuted, however, because the clan enjoyed the protection of the hated King William III. The story has all the Campbell hallmarks – betrayal, barbarity, a careful determination to keep in with the government of the day, and an enviable capacity to end up on the winning side. These four characteristics have stood Campbells in good stead ever since.

In 1707 the English government turned to the Campbell clan to enforce the Act of Union between the two countries. The Dukes of Argyll, as ever, were happy to barter their support. The second Duke hastened home from the battlefield – he was serving under the Duke of Marlborough in the War of the Spanish Succession – and demanded instant promotion to major-general, an English peerage,[1] and command of the scrappy militia that passed for a government army. As petitions flooded in from Scottish boroughs and shires against the

---

1. Ever mindful of family interests, he also demanded a Scottish peerage for his younger brother Archibald, who was made Earl of Islay.

Union, Argyll ignored them: he suggested they should be turned into paper kites.

In the course of the eighteenth century most Highland clans joined the doomed Jacobite rebellions of 1715 and 1745. The Campbells ensured that they remained in good standing with the Hanoverian dynasty. The Dukes of Argyll and their followers were well-rewarded with honours and land, often at the expense of Highland rivals who had sided with the Jacobites. They stood apart from the other Scottish clans: machiavellian, duplicitous, wholly without scruple, and guiding all with a cold-hearted eye fixed only on the calculation of their own interests. In the terms of *1066 and All That*, they had a settled policy of being Right but Repulsive rather than, like most of their Highland fellows, Wrong but Romantic. Perhaps Macaulay, in his *History of England*, best illustrates the widespread view of the Campbell character: 'A peculiar dexterity, a peculiar plausibility of address, a peculiar contempt for all the obligations of good faith were ascribed, with or without reason, to the dreaded race. "Fair and False like a Campbell" became a proverb.'

It is doubtless going too far to burden the Prime Minister's Press Secretary with this savage Argyll inheritance. But he is still a Highlander above all else: even today those who share his Gaelic blood say they often know what words he will utter, even before he has opened his mouth. These things run deeper than we know. There are certain traits in Alastair Campbell that would have been instantly recognised, and richly approved, by the Dukes of Argyll as they assured their survival in the shifting sands of Scottish politics: a capacity for barbarism; a profound clannish instinct and ruthless loyalty to his family and those he has chosen to be his friends; an ability to enter into the most unlikely alliances. Most of all, however, they would have noted a strong vein of worldly pragmatism. All appearances to the contrary, Campbell is a man who finds government congenial. He has possessed from a relatively young age the gift of ending up on the winning side. He is a brilliant politician, in large matters as in small, with the true politician's gift for making friends. Only in one part of the United Kingdom is Campbell disliked with any real violence – Scotland. Before the Scottish Assembly elections of summer 1999 he was obliged to make, alongside the Prime Minister, a series of trips north of the border to advance the case for the Union. The visits were marred by unseemly scenes and verbal abuse as the Scots turned against Tony Blair. They saw him – for all his education at an Edinburgh public school – as an English impostor. They resented Campbell, the Prime Minister's hatchet-man, as a turncoat. Who can say that John Campbell, the second Duke of Argyll who sold out so profitably to the English in 1707, was not chuckling to himself from whatever resting place Highland chieftains go to when they die, and smiling sardonically at the characteristic actions of his distant kinsman?

Campbells today are scattered all over Scotland as well as further afield. But Alastair Campbell's own line traces easily and directly back to the very Argyll heartland. For generations his family lived on Tiree, a Hebridean island of heart-stopping beauty whose inhabitants for centuries owed their fealty to the Dukes of Argyll. It is sometimes known as 'the land below the waves', on account of the fact that it is almost entirely flat, and treeless. It is a simple matter, using the magnificently maintained archive in the General Records Office in Edinburgh, to trace Alastair Campbell's direct line back to the early 1800s. Hector Campbell, a farm labourer, was born in Tiree around 1820. His son Donald, a crofter, was born, also in Tiree, in 1853. He married Mary Macdonald in January 1878. Lachlan Campbell, Alastair's grandfather, was born six years later. They were all simple farming folk, but there is perhaps a sense of quiet ambition and steady progression through the generations: farm labourer, crofter, farmer. Today Alastair Campbell must have scores of cousins on the island. Though he has never lived there, Tiree is a central part of his blood and his heritage.

It was Campbell's father Donald who broke away from the Hebrides. Like so many Highland Scots, he benefited from a superb education system to abandon the hard life of his forefathers and find his way to the Glasgow Veterinary College. There he made firm friends with a fellow Scot, Murdo Ferguson, and this friendship was to prove decisive in the life of the young vet.

A vet's life in Keighley

Not long after the war, Ferguson was offered the position of assistant in a veterinary practice based around the mill town of Keighley in the West Riding of Yorkshire. He happily made the journey south and took up employment at the Aireworth Veterinary Centre. Very shortly afterwards Hubert Holland, the owner of the practice, decided to retire. Unable to purchase Aireworth on his own, Ferguson appealed to his old friend Donald Campbell to join forces with him. They bought the practice together and for a few years they were partners.

It was a happy and fulfilling time all round in the life of Donald Campbell. Not only was he experiencing the rewarding sensation of building up his own business, he brought with him to Keighley his bride Elizabeth. She fitted in easily with the local Yorkshire folk. George Crabtree, who soon joined Donald

Cameron in the veterinary practice, remembers her as a 'great lass, charming and very lovely'. (During the 1997 General Election campaign Tony Blair was introduced to Betty Campbell. 'You can't be Alastair Campbell's mother. You're nice', he said.) There is no question that the Campbells were an attractive and popular couple in the Keighley area. They threw themselves into local life. 'Donald worked hard and he played hard,' recalls Crabtree. 'If the work was done and he was off-duty he would go out partying with Elizabeth or enjoy a few drinks with his male friends.'

Donald Campbell, as befitted a man of professional standing in the community, was an active member of the local Conservative Club. You did not have to be political to belong to the Tory Party of the 1950s. It was more a state of mind, a statement about the kind of person you were. In a decade when there was little else available in the way of entertainment, Conservative Clubs provided an important social hub for the communities they served. They were places to drink, to meet members of the opposite sex, to do business, to go when there was nothing else in particular to do. They were emphatically not places where people went to discuss politics. George Crabtree says of his partner: 'Donald was a member of the Conservative Club, but he was not particularly interested in politics. We would go there once every fortnight to play snooker and chat to the other members. It was a good social scene. Neither of us was particularly good at it.'

There were hundreds of Conservative Clubs in Britain in the post-war period. They flourished because professional men like Donald Campbell and his partner George Crabtree found them congenial to go to, even if it was only for the snooker and the beer. They were an important part of the hold that the Tory Party had over the British people in the era of Churchill, Eden and Macmillan. It is just one symptom of Conservative decline that for the last decade they have been closing down all around the country.

It is possible that young Alastair's earliest memory of the Conservative Party was of a mysterious place where his father went after work and from which he occasionally returned reeking of alcohol, late for dinner and in disgrace. It is very doubtful whether Elizabeth Campbell approved of the Keighley Conservative Club as much as Donald Campbell did. Alastair may have noted that, and taken heed. From such small matters great consequences flow.

Not long after arriving at Keighley the young couple set about rearing a family. For several years the children came thick and fast. To friends it seemed as if Elizabeth gave birth every few months. Donald, Graham, Alastair and

Elizabeth – the only daughter – were all born about eighteen months apart. Alastair was born on 25 May 1957, at the Victoria Hospital, Keighley.

The West Riding was a stimulating, in some ways an ideal, place for a young child to grow up. Alastair's parents lived in Oakworth, a small industrial town outside Keighley. The family had a stone-built house called 'Lydstep' at the end of Station Road. The house has long since been demolished, but the railtrack at the bottom of the road remains and is now in the hands of the Keighley and Worth Valley Railway, whose preserved steam trains still lumber up and down the valleys of the West Riding and form an inevitable part of any holiday taken in the region. In 1974 the station at the bottom of the road gained a modest kind of fame when *The Railway Children* was filmed there.

Just as important as the town itself were the Pennine Hills which surrounded it. The hill farms of the area provided much of the work for Donald Campbell's veterinary practice. Anyone wishing to gain some insight into Alastair Campbell's early life should study James Herriot's sequence of novels about the life of a peripatetic vet on the Yorkshire Dales, which paint a gripping and surprisingly unsentimental picture of the daily dramas facing any veterinary practice: the battles for payment with impecunious hill farmers, the sudden midnight calls, the difficulties of access in winter to snow-bound hill farmers, the tedious but profitable triviality of dealing with domestic pets. Serving the domestic pets belonging to the urban dwellers of Keighley was the part of his practice Donald Cameron liked least. They failed to absorb him either emotionally or intellectually. What he loved was travelling into the hills to sort out the farmers' problems – on many occasions with young Alastair or one of the other boys in tow.

James Herriot himself, a veterinary surgeon whose real name was Alf Wight, was an acquaintance of the Campbell family. His prodigiously successful books are based on the very post-war years when Donald Campbell served the isolated communities of farming people in the North of England, and draw on experience which must have been very similar to Campbell's. George Crabtree tells how Donald Campbell and Murdo Ferguson were called to treat a sick cow at Hebden Bridge. The owners were amateur farmers, who were utterly baffled by the illness, unlike the vets, who promptly realised the animal was suffering from milk fever.

'The animal was unable to get up and would have eventually fallen into unconsciousness and died if not treated with an injection of calcium,' recalls George Crabtree. 'Donald and Murdo had a wicked sense of humour and were secretive about the treatment to the farmers, who were all stood around the cow.

Soon Murdo realised the cow was ready to get up and asked all the assembled to place their hands on his and he would miraculously cure the animal. They all stood around with their hands on the animal, when Murdo said "Abracadabra" and nudged the cow with his knee, and with the pain the cow got up. The owners did not realise that it had been a joke and, I'm sure, believed the vets from Keighley had magical healing powers.'

Another anecdote from this period also contains the Herriot flavour; it is easy to imagine it making its way into a Herriot story. The vet was called to a remote farm to castrate a herd of twelve bull calves. This simple business, though momentous as far as the bull calves were concerned, was a routine matter for Donald Campbell. He would go along the line of animals, injecting them all with anaesthetic, then wait a few minutes for the drug to take effect before walking back down the line and cutting off the testicles.

On this occasion he was forced into a small variation of routine. After castrating the first bull calf, he threw the testicles on the ground in the corner of the cow-shed, where they nestled amidst the mud and sawdust. At this point the old farmer intervened. 'Eh, don't throw them away, veterinary. I'll 'ave them for me tea.' So Campbell put the testicles in a bucket, carried on with the other eleven animals, and thought nothing more of it. Later that evening he received an alarmed telephone call from the farmer, who huskily enquired why his mouth had gone numb and he was finding it hard to talk and eat. The vet replied that it would have been wiser to have allowed the anaesthetic to wear off before cooking.

The successful television series made from the Herriot stories have fostered a delusion that life in the Dales was some rustic idyll. But for Donald Campbell and his partners, it was hard and sometimes dangerous work. George Crabtree recalls seven-day weeks and nineteen-hour days. Even though theirs was a successful and well-run practice, it was difficult to break even because of missed payments. 'I used to dread the annual book-keeping,' recalls Crabtree. 'We would be depressed for days after the annual accounts.' There is some evidence that the Campbells were occasionally forced to take in lodgers to help make ends meet: when Alastair was born, one Wilfred Waterhouse is recorded as living at their address.

All this took an undoubted toll on the members of the Aireworth practice – as indeed it did on Alf Wight in Thirsk, who suffered from a debilitating form of depression all his life. A short history of the practice recently disclosed that a former partner took his own life by cutting his throat. Murdo Ferguson, Donald Campbell's friend from college days, was struck down by a heart attack while returning from a house call five miles away. He died in 1956. In due course it all became too much for Donald Campbell as well. Ironically, the event that caused the Campbells to leave Keighley – and which nearly cost Donald his life – took place while he was doing his beloved farm work.

It was a routine job. After a sow has given birth to piglets, the vet is called to castrate the males. Donald had carried out the task thousands of times. On this occasion it went horribly wrong. It is vital, when performing the operation, to keep the sow well away from the litter. Unforgivably, she was allowed to escape. The furious beast charged at Donald, and smashed him to the ground before sinking her teeth deep into his leg. As the vet lay on the ground, blood gushing from his wound, the farmer's young daughter bravely intervened to pull the angry animal away.

Donald was obliged to spend six weeks in hospital, and at least as much again recovering at home before he could go back to work. He was never again quite fit enough to cope with the demands of his arduous practice: he retired in 1969 and the family moved south to Leicester where Donald Campbell managed to secure a very much less physically demanding administrative job with the Ministry of Agriculture.

The accident must have had a traumatic effect on the young Alastair Campbell. It happened at an age when any young boy is very dependent on his father, regarding him as a hero figure. The prostration of Donald Campbell would have smashed through the comfortable certainties of a happy childhood. At an almost identical age, the Prime Minister suffered a similar though far more traumatic affliction when his own father – a man of high talent who was poised on the verge of a possible parliamentary career – was struck down by a massive stroke. Happily Donald Campbell needed just three months to recover. It took Leo Blair three years to regain the power of speech: the effect on the future Prime Minister cannot be overestimated. The two men share a common awareness of tragedy, gained at too young an age; it is one of the things that bind the two men together.

Keighley gave Alastair Campbell much. His early years were spent among solid northern country folk. For a man whose professional life has been devoted to the cultivation and conquest of a rootless metropolitan élite, this has been no bad thing. Keighley plays a role in Campbell's personal mythology similar to that of Hebden Bridge for Sir Bernard Ingham when he was Margaret Thatcher's Press Secretary. Sir Bernard felt that the lessons Hebden Bridge (which lies in the Pennine Hills, and near enough to form an outlying part of Donald Campbell's practice) had to offer were so profound that to celebrate his ten years in Downing Street he invited thirty valued colleagues to join him there for the weekend. Alastair Campbell's acknowledgement to the town of his childhood is – thus far – less demonstrative. His single tribute is to have accepted the Presidency of the Keighley branch of the Burnley FC supporters' club, an honour that has been duly noted in his otherwise sparse *Who's Who* entry.

Burnley Football Club

The most tangible legacy of Alastair Campbell's Keighley years is his enduring devotion to Burnley FC. Anybody brought up in Keighley in the early 1960s had a choice of several football teams to support – Leeds, Bradford City or Burnley, to name three. Leeds lies 25 miles away to the east; Bradford is the nearest big city; while Burnley is more romantically positioned, 20 miles across the wilds of Keighley Moor to the west. In the early 1960s, when Alastair was a young boy – the age when decisive choices are made in these matters – there was not a great deal to choose between the two teams of Leeds and Burnley. With the benefit of hindsight it is possible to see that Burnley was the declining force, its years of greatness behind it. Tucked away in a hidden corner of England, the once important Victorian town of Burnley was going nowhere much, neither commercially nor in footballing terms. Leeds by contrast was a bustling place. Great things were about to happen: the town was on the point of producing one of the finest League teams of all time: Don Revie's ensemble, which dominated English football in the late '60s and early '70s.

It is inconceivable that the Alastair Campbell of today could for a moment have contemplated the decision the youthful Campbell made thirty-five years ago. Assessing matters with his customary pragmatic and unsentimental eye from the Downing Street bunker, he would have plumped, without a moment's reflection or regret, for Leeds. New Labour is ruthless with losers. Burnley's famous past would have counted for nothing: he would have been careful to buy into Leeds' glorious future. But as a small boy he was completely unable to read the clear signs which, even in the mid-1960s, indicated that the club was doomed to collapse into respectable oblivion. And even more important, family loyalty lay with Burnley – friends remember that his elder brothers already supported the club. Thus Alastair Campbell's long association with the little East Lancashire football club was forged.

The boundless depth of Campbell's life-long devotion to Burnley FC could be read as a clear sign of derangement – were not the condition shared with hundreds of thousands of other young men who, in other respects, lead ordinary lives. Even today, burdened as he is by one of the most demanding jobs in the country, the No. 10 Press Secretary will go to extreme lengths to attend a Burnley home game. Burnley games take precedence over practically every-thing else. It was natural, for instance, for Campbell to cite the necessity to watch his favourite team play as the reason why he could not attend Peter Mandelson's 40th birthday celebration.[2] 'Alastair will drive the 240 miles up to Burnley,' observes political columnist and fellow Burnley supporter Chris Buckland, 'watch them get beat and then drive all the way back.'

Campbell is nowadays a revered figure on the Burnley terraces, where he normally chooses to sit in the Bob Lord stand, opened by Edward Heath when he was Prime Minister and, according to Buckland, 'a Tory stand through and through'. He is beloved of all Burnley supporters, and after four decades supporting the Club, known to most of them personally. And the Burnley directors have become friends and some get invited down to Campbell's rare parties in London. Campbell takes a close and active interest in team affairs. From time to time the Prime Minister's Press Secretary, having dealt with some important matter of state, will pick up the phone in his Downing Street Office and dial the number of Burnley Football Club. Then, claims Buckland, he will issue lucid instructions about 'who to put in the team and important insights into tactics'. His views are listened to with respect, even if they are not always acted on with the same promptness and thoroughness Campbell has come to regard as normal in other areas of his life.

The Burnley obsession remains intense, yet it is paltry compared to the devotion Campbell accorded the club as a younger man. Vast tracts of his student days were spent in making the lengthy train journey across central England from Cambridge to watch Burnley play. It is a journey of almost absurd inconvenience, involving numerous connections in desolate midland towns. To be sure of reaching Burnley in time for the game meant leaving university before breakfast-time. Even then, such was the truculent inefficiency of British Rail that arrival in time for the game could not be guaranteed or even expected. Many were the occasions when, thanks to some derailment or signalling problem, the student Campbell would be left kicking his heels in the buffet at Blackpool, Crewe or Rugby, listening on his portable transistor to the Radio Two football commentary, hoping against hope for some shred of news

2. It is possible, of course, that the fixture was simply being used as a convenient excuse. If so, it did not work. Mandelson was upset.

about the Burnley performance. Even on the rare occasions when the commentator paused to bring scores from the lower divisions, the news from Burnley's
Turf Moor headquarters was likely to be unpalatable. The team of his dreams
had already embarked upon that melancholy gyration among the lower League
divisions which has been their characteristic movement over the past three
decades.

By the time he reached Cambridge Campbell's bottomless love for Burnley
FC had become a symbol of failure at every level: moral, personal, intellectual,
social and above all emotional. The syndrome is far from uncommon. Nick
Hornby's brilliantly original *Fever Pitch* has shown how the preoccupation with
a football club can ruin personal relationships, hinder professional advancement, and become a metaphor for failure to communicate in an adequate way
with the outside world. That is what Burnley came to represent, at a certain
stage of his life, for Alastair Campbell.

Hornby describes how he found his redemption when a goal deep in extra
time against Liverpool secured Arsenal a famous League Championship win in
1989. He suddenly realised football didn't matter quite so much after all. For
Campbell, a supporter of lowly Burnley, salvation through his club's sporting
success was never an option. For him it would come in a different way, by
finding alternative objects of adulation: through the Labour Party and tabloid
journalism. It was through Burnley Football Club, however, that he first discovered a meaningful identity that enabled him unreservedly to escape from
himself.

Leicester Highlanders

The Campbell family moved south to Leicester in the late 1960s and settled
into a house in 11 Welland Vale Road. This was just half a mile away from the
City of Leicester Boys' School, which Alastair entered half-way through the
1968/9 academic year.[3] As at Keighley, Alastair's parents quickly made themselves popular in the neighbourhood. There is a pub at Thurnby, The Rose &
Crown, which is no more than three miles from the Campbell family home.
Even today, though it is more than ten years since the family left the area, the
mere mention of Donald Campbell raises a roar of approbation among the
locals. To say that he is vividly remembered would be an understatement.

It seems that the further south Donald Campbell – 'Old Man Donald' as he

3. According to Bill Mann, Alastair Campbell's physics teacher and head of the lower school.

was coming to be known – went, the more Scottish he became. He never lost his links with his native Tiree and for many years he and Betty Campbell would load the four children – and their pet West Highland Terrier – into the back of their Morris Traveller and trundle all the way back up to the remote Scottish isle for the annual two-week holiday every August. Old Man Donald was a Gaelic speaker and for a number of years he contributed a column, discussing the latest developments in the language, to the *Oban Times*. At The Rose & Crown he is still remembered for the way that, dressed in the correct manner, he would pipe in the haggis on New Year's Day. On Sunday afternoons he would teach his sons the bagpipes. Neighbours still recall the colossal din that would emerge from the back garden of Welland Vale Road as the practice sessions got underway. But complaints were rare, and once they got used to the noise, locals came to quite look forward to their weekly entertainment. The eldest son, Donald, showed such facility with the bagpipes that he eventually joined the Scots Guards as a piper. Alastair, too, was an accomplished player. It is still remembered how he once took the pipes with him to school and amazed everybody with his dexterity on the instrument during break. Later in life, the instrument became his trade-mark and has been unveiled at the most unlikely times in the most unlikely places: those who have never seen Alastair Campbell in full flow upon his beloved pipes have missed a very splendid sight.

The ability to play the pipes was the most noteworthy of the gifts that Old Man Donald bequeathed to his son. But there was much else besides that Alastair inherited from this magnificent man: the capacity for hard work, a warmth and depth of character, a deep-seated enjoyment of life, an easy, conspiratorial charm. In short, Campbell inherited numerous amiable characteristics from his esteemed father; the barbarism, brutality and worship of power are his own.

Campbell was not happy at Leicester. Writing about the town in his early twenties, he took his revenge on the place. 'Leicester, like its people, is dull,' he announced. 'To sit in a Leicester bus, listening to incomprehensible conversations trundled out in an accent that makes David Bellamy and Lorraine Chase sound delectable, is to be nauseated.'[4]

It probably wasn't quite as bad as that. The young Campbell was an apt pupil. 'As a small boy he was fairly enthusiastic about whatever he did,' recalls Bill Mann, his physics teacher. Mann says that Campbell was an eager rugby player, and recalls the day when he had to drive the boy to hospital with a

4. 'The Laid-back University of Liesexter', *Forum*, June 1980.

broken arm. Once again, the episode shows the innate good manners of the Campbell parents. 'About two or three days later,' as Bill Mann recalls, 'during my physics lesson, Alastair handed me a package from his dad, Donald. In the package was a charming note which said something to the effect that he was glad his son was in the right hands at the school and hoped that the enclosed package was the right sort of poison. It was a packet of fine pipe-smoking tobacco.'

Whatever his subsequent complaints about the city, Campbell flourished at the City of Leicester Boys' School. Talented academically, he was one of the relatively few boys at the school to gain a place at Cambridge University: it was a formidable achievement and justly celebrated in the family home. Sadly, Alastair Campbell's four years at Cambridge, reading Medieval and Modern Languages (French and German), were to include some of the most miserable of his life.

Cambridge party pooper

There were a number of brilliant undergraduates up at Cambridge with Alastair Campbell in the mid-to-late 1970s who – it was obvious even at the time – were destined to become distinguished national figures. At Trinity College, a select coterie congregated around Charles Moore, who already bore the air of high moral seriousness and Christian virtue that has made him such an anomalous figure in Fleet Street. It was perfectly obvious, from the moment he walked through the Trinity gates for the first time, that he would one day be a distinguished editor of the *Daily Telegraph*. There were admirers who thought him a natural candidate for the premiership as well: Moore disappointed them by turning up his nose at the prospect of such a worldly distraction.

Moore consorted with men like Oliver Letwin and Noel Malcolm. Letwin emerged after the 1997 General Election as the MP for West Dorset and a brilliant member of the rising generation of Tory MPs. There are those who now view him as a future Tory leader, but to achieve this aim he needs to overcome the treble obstacle of high intelligence, Jewish blood and an Eton education: a hopeless prospect. But most brilliant of all in this extraordinary troika was Noel Malcolm, also from Eton. Malcolm learnt languages with the ease with which some men pick up women. Two decades later he was to try the patience of his friends by writing a long and prodigiously learned work about a faraway place no one wanted to know about. Perhaps he was the only scholar in the Western world capable of mastering the complex dialects of the province of

Kosovo as well as understanding the deadly politics of the era. The work, appearing two years in advance of the war, was brilliantly timed, brilliantly written and brilliantly informed. His diagnosis – that Kosovo should become an independent or at least autonomous state – guided the strategy of NATO's high command during the ten-week conflict in the spring of 1999.

Alastair knew none of this glittering circle at Cambridge. It is just as well that he did not. He would have hated them with the bitter and venomous hatred a state-educated lad from Leicester at odds with the world would naturally reserve for the gilded youth of his generation.

At Selwyn College Robert Harris, who became one of Campbell's closest allies in the fetid lobby politics of the 1980s before converting himself into an accomplished thriller-writer, was feeling his way. Harris, from as modest a background as Campbell, coped better. He edited the university paper and became President of the Union. Another contemporary of Campbell's who managed the leaden progression to Union President was Andrew Mitchell. A decade later, in a celebrated article, Campbell was to pluck Mitchell – by then a Tory MP – out of the hat as one of six hand-picked rising political stars destined for greatness. Mitchell was the one dog that did not bark: the other five were Tony Blair, Gordon Brown, Mo Mowlam, Michael Portillo and John Major.[5]

On the Footlights scene a brilliant generation of comedy stars was being formed: Stephen Fry and Hugh Laurie arrived at the university while Campbell was there, and so did a promising young actress called Emma Thompson. A bearded youth, Andrew Marr, whom Campbell would one day try to get sacked as editor of the *Independent* for criticising Tony Blair, appeared at Trinity Hall. Soon he plunged into student politics, taking up a post selling left-wing litera-ture to baffled locals.[6]

Campbell did not know any of these people. They, in turn, remained unaware of him. Adair Turner, an ambitious Cambridge Union member who has since staged an inevitable, well-planned ascent to the Director-Generalship of the CBI, was for two years at Gonville and Caius College with Campbell. Despite the cheek by jowl physical proximity, he cannot conjure up the faintest recol-lection of his college contemporary. Keith Vaz,[7] now a rising member of the government in which Campbell plays such a luminous, if non-elected, role was

5. *Sunday Mirror*, 11 September 1988. Even so, the selection did not manage too badly. Mitchell was on the fringes of the Cabinet when he lost his seat in the 1997 General Election landslide.

6. The author is grateful to the cartoonist Martin Rowson for this information.

7. Known as Nigel when he was at Cambridge. The change of name has never been satisfactorily explained.

also at Caius at the time. He has only the haziest memories of Campbell. A look of panic spread over Vaz's broad, beaming face when he was recently asked about his fellow student. 'Of course I remember him,' Vaz at length replied. 'I remember him *very positively indeed.*' The truth is that the larger university world remained a mystery to Campbell from the day he arrived at Cambridge to the day he left.

He confined himself to the narrower sphere of college life. Gonville and Caius was a modest establishment in the centre of town with powerful links to Midland schools. Kenneth Clarke, the former Tory Chancellor, went on to Caius from Nottingham High School. Socially undistinguished, the college had a reputation for turning out brilliant history scholars. Fellow undergraduates recall Campbell vividly, some with a shudder of horror. In their minds he is irrevocably associated with the college late night bar – the LNB as the place was colloquially known.

At an Oxford or Cambridge college there is something almost shameful about too frequent attendance at the college bar. The brightest of each genera-tion are to be found elsewhere. It is the plodders, the nonentities, the socially inept, the terminally dull, those with nowhere else to go and nothing else to do – in short, the losers – who drink at college bars with regularity. Campbell made it his daily pastime. Though he made no measurable impact in any other area of university life, he became a legend at the college bar. 'I avoided Campbell like the plague because he was pissed out of his mind. By 11 p.m. he was on the floor of the LNB,' recalls one Caius contemporary.[8] 'He was a loud, drunken, football-playing thug,' he adds.[9]

Laudably perhaps, Campbell made no attempt to conform to the conventions of university life. Campbell was the only student of Gonville and Caius to turn up for the matriculation ceremony for first-year students wrongly dressed. In what can only have been an act of deliberate provocation, he posed for the photograph without a tie. Later, when Campbell had risen to prominence, an aggrieved former fellow student wrote to the *Daily Mail* to complain about this act of subversion: 'This tieless rebellion, together with the conspicuous

8. In Campbell's time the bar was open late into the night. After he left, the college authorities, fearful that intellectual standards were being undermined, imposed strict limits on its hours of operation. Caius' standing in the academic rankings immediately rose.

9. The source here, who craves anonymity, perhaps needs to be treated with caution, though not because he is in any way an unreliable witness or felt any personal animosity towards Campbell. He subsequently became a Tory councillor. However, the weight of testimony that Campbell was regarded as a menace to passing traffic at the Caius bar is overwhelming.

positioning, constituted an unwelcome blot on a unique academic memento for myself and around 120 other undergraduates.'[10]

Campbell's sartorial approach was highly distinctive. 'He was smartly dressed, after the style of the football hooligan of the day,' recalls John Morrish, a Caius contemporary. 'It was after the era of the skinheads and the suedeheads. His Burnley scarf would be done up very tightly at the neck so as to look like a cravat. He wore straight, stay-pressed trousers. His hair was cut like Rod Stewart's – high on top and cut close into the neck. This, remember, was the seventies, the era that fashion forgot. Alastair didn't look like the rest of us. He looked like a football hooligan, a lad from the town. He spent all his time at the Caius late night bar, a notorious den of drunkenness, and played football for the college football team. That was all he did.'

Not quite all. Fellow students recall a girlfriend, who came up at weekends from Leicester and produced a mellowing effect on Campbell's character. There are no reports of romantic affairs with fellow students. Indeed, the absence of female undergraduates at the university was one of those subjects about which Campbell felt particularly strongly. He would ruminate angrily about the shortage when, as was so often the case, he was in his cups at the college bar. A few years later, writing for *Forum* magazine, he would address the subject of student romance at Cambridge. There is no mistaking the tone of aggrieved frustration. 'Sex at Cambridge,' he announced,

is like sex in no other place on earth, thank God, because two Cambridges would be too much for anyone, especially for anyone who wants to use some of his student years to learn a few things about sex. The main problem, put in unromantic terms, is one of supply and demand.

Those who go to university to stave off the rat-race for a few years find another rat-race awaiting their arrival – the race for sexual conquest. I dropped out after a term, happy that I could go home every weekend to a girlfriend free of the pretensions that belong to a beautiful woman in a man's world. Any pretty woman in Cambridge is likely to have scores of men itching to get inside her, and she knows it, so she can lie back and take her pick. Parties in Cambridge are more like rugby scrums than jovial social events, and it's usually the same men that are picked – the rich, the handsome, and the intelligent and, unfortunately for Mr Average Student, there are still a few who are all three. Others turn to excessive working, excessive sport, or heavy drinking.[11]

This sounds like a belated attitude-statement of the student Campbell: angry, baffled and resentful that he's not part of the glamorous university scene. Later

10. Quoted in *Sunday Business*, 28 July 1996.
11. 'Sex at Cambridge is a Disgrace', *Forum*, March 1980.

in life, looking back on his university career, Campbell happily acknowledges that he made a mess of things. 'I could not hack it,' he admits. 'I hated first year. I was too young and too chippy. I drank too much and stayed away – going to football matches to see Burnley play.[12] I didn't work hard enough.'[13] Lonely and baffled, he would sit at the bar, drinking and brooding. Occasionally Campbell and a few cronies might sally forth into the town, on the look-out for a fight, preferably with an Old Etonian.[14] There is ample testimony to his hatred of Old Etonians, who symbolised in Campbell's eyes much that was wrong not only with Cambridge, but with the world in general. This generalised loathing continues to the present day. Campbell is quite capable of interrupting a Downing Street meeting with a sudden, outspoken tirade against the pernicious influence of OEs in British public life, though these days there is less likelihood that this prejudice will express itself through a violent physical manifestation.[15] There is no question, however, that as a young man Campbell was prepared, and perhaps at times eager, to use his fists. Upper-class accents and military uniforms in particular inflamed him. When Campbell was at Cambridge there

12. Travelling to Burnley's home ground of Turf Moor took immense dedication. To be sure of reaching the town in time for the game meant leaving Cambridge on the 7.03 a.m. train to King's Cross. Campbell then had to change to Euston, from where he would catch the 9.45 a.m. train to Preston, arriving at 12.34 p.m. The 13.27 p.m. from Preston got Campbell into Burnley Central at 14.24 p.m., just in time to make a run for the stadium and arrive in time for the 3.00 p.m. start. I am grateful to Philip Atkins of the National Railway Museum for this information. Atkins stresses that there were other equally tortuous routes, avoiding London, which Campbell may have taken. The return journey to London was even more fiendish, involving arrival back at Cambridge after midnight, probably after missing the last ten minutes or so of the game. Campbell may of course have chosen to stay overnight in the area. Nor was the cost of the journey negligible. In September 1975 the second-class return between the two towns was £14.16, rising to £19.46 by January 1978. As a student, however, Campbell would have paid less.

13. Campbell has given half a dozen interviews to journalists since taking on the job of Press Secretary to Tony Blair. He always speaks revealingly, openly and honestly about past problems, in striking contrast to the fog of obscurity and bombast in which he is capable of veiling current political events. The above quotation is taken from a long, perceptive and important portrait of Campbell by Kevin Toolis (*Guardian Weekend*, 4 April 1998). Campbell has spoken in similar terms about his university days to Roy Hattersley in another highly illuminating and sympathetically written newspaper profile. He told the former Deputy Leader of the Labour Party that as a student he had been 'a bit chippy, against things. Anti-politics' (*Observer*, 2 February 1998).

14. Campbell told Hattersley that he 'drank too much and got into too many fights' (*ibid.*).

15. Alastair Campbell's subsequent career was to abound in gratuitous attacks on OEs. For a particularly vicious assault, see his *Today* newspaper column of 9 May 1994. More striking still was his address to 500 senior Whitehall officials, many of them OEs, at the Business Design Centre in Islington not long after Labour won power. Speaking of the Foreign Office Campbell said: 'At times we do get these Old Etonians and I think, "My God, are they speaking for Britain?"' (see *Daily Telegraph*, 16 October 1998).

was a boisterous group of officer trainees. On generous army scholarships, they possessed an ample supply of money, flash cars and pretty women. Speaking in loud, braying voices, they wandered round Cambridge as if they owned the town. It is forgivable if Campbell would from time to time lay down his glass, look dispassionately around the bar, and announce that he was off to beat up 'an upper-class twit.'

Nevertheless, he does not emerge as an unattractive figure at this time. There is a certain raw humanity about the undergraduate Campbell that marks him out as worthy of respect. This life of a lost soul, unhappy at Cambridge, has an uncertain, existential quality. Once, heavily hungover, Campbell was shaken out of his drunken stupor by a friend. 'What is it?', groaned Campbell. 'I've got it!' replied the friend, who had been reading the works of Samuel Beckett for the last three days, and after two sleepless nights had finally mastered them. 'I understand Beckett! I understand Beckett!', he announced.

'Excellent,' replied Campbell. 'Now I want to go back to sleep.'

His fellow student explained his idea. Beckett, he observed, was in the daily habit of taking his breakfast in a certain café in the Latin Quarter of Paris. It was now imperative that Campbell should get up at once (it was already lunch-time), that the two should catch the overnight ferry and make their way to Paris. There they would track down Beckett and have breakfast with him.

Campbell reluctantly rose from his bed. The two undergraduates made an overnight journey to the French capital, a longer and more difficult matter then than it is now, and tracked down Beckett's café. There, seated at his usual table, drinking coffee and reading the previous day's edition of *The Times*, was the renowned playwright. Campbell and his friend approached him and explained that they were students who had come all the way from Cambridge University specially to discuss his work. Beckett, surprisingly, asked them to sit down with him.

This was the moment Campbell's friend had been waiting for. Nervously and at some length, he expounded his new insight into the meaning of Beckett's work. Beckett listened closely. In due course Campbell's friend reached the end of his exposition. 'That's right then?' he asked. 'That's what your plays are all about?'

'No,' said Beckett. 'They are not about that at all. What you've just said is rubbish. Fuck off!'

Crestfallen, the two undergraduates rose, thanked Beckett for his attention, and wandered away. They did not know what to do next. They set off to the Père Lachaise cemetery, which contains the last resting-place of Balzac. There the two literary enthusiasts shuffled around, visited Balzac's grave, and made tracks back to Cambridge.[16]

Campbell took his final-year exams in May 1979. It was the month Thatcher led the Conservative Party back to power in a General Election whose epic importance few realised at the time. It is doubtful whether Campbell bothered to vote. He took no interest in politics, student or national. He has this in common with Tony Blair who was up at Oxford five years before. Both of them had other ways of spending their time. It is only obsessives who get drawn deeply into politics while still students: people like Gordon Brown and Peter Mandelson. It is arguably the case that the primary reason why Tony Blair is Prime Minister, and not Gordon Brown, is that Blair has an understanding of what it takes to be an ordinary voter with aspirations to lead a reasonable life. There is nothing difficult or profound about this kind of knowledge, which does not concern the wellsprings of political philosophy, in which direction the Chancellor is if anything over-endowed. Just an intuitive sympathy with the banalities of everyday life will do, and a grasp of why they matter so very much. Blair and Campbell possess this: Brown and Mandelson, for all their brains and phenomenal political expertise, do not.

Campbell took a 2:1. In some cases this class of degree, which is handed out in too great an abundance by the university examiners, can be read as an unmistakable sign of mediocrity. Campbell's upper second was a minor miracle, an indication that if he had worked at all hard he could easily have achieved first-class honours. Needless to say, he had made no plans and barely given any thought to what to do with the rest of his life.

16. I am indebted to Mike Molloy for this anecdote, which Campbell recounted when he was a young reporter. It has doubtless grown with the telling.

Chapter Three

BUSKING WITH BAGPIPES

He rather hated the ruling few more than
he loved the suffering many.
Caroline Fox on James Mill

The type of aimless drifting to which Campbell devoted the next year and a half
had gone out of fashion a few years before. In the 1960s and the first half of the
1970s it was customary for undergraduates to take a detached view of future
prospects. Jobs were plentiful, and in any case, in the decade of flower power
and fun-revolution there were deemed to be more important things than jobs.

By 1979 the Keynesian post-war economic spurt which had made all this
self-indulgence possible was over. A new gravity descended on the student
population that made it both more boring and more amenable to adult employment. Most of Campbell's college contemporaries scuttled off into safe jobs in
the professions. This trend horrified and baffled Campbell. He set off on a life
of Rabelaisian adventure. For the next eighteen months or so, until he joined
the Mirror Group trainee scheme, Campbell was without a regular job. It is not
easy to establish exactly how he spent his time. Nine years later, when *Sunday
Mirror* editor Eve Pollard was trying to convert her talented reporter into a star,
she allowed a brief account of his life and times to be published in her
newspaper. This version does not skirt round the fact that he 'first worked for a
year as a busker after leaving Cambridge University'[1] but it is by no means the
full story. A complete account of Campbell's eighteen months out would also
have had to include a failed attempt to become a professional croupier. Most
significant of all, Campbell took his first faltering steps as a professional writer.

On assignment with *Forum* magazine

Nowadays Campbell, when questioned about his career as a contributor to the
pornographic *Forum* magazine, dismisses the matter as little more than a joke.

1. *Sunday Mirror Magazine*, no. 5, 11 September 1988. This number contains Campbell's famous
account of six rising political stars, which included Tony Blair, Gordon Brown and John Major.

In September 1994 he told a reporter from the *News of the World* – which, with characteristic speed and professionalism, was chasing the story within hours of his appointment as press adviser to Tony Blair – that it was down to 'youthful exuberance'.[2] Campbell went on: 'It was partly a way to make some cash. The whole thing started as a laugh with a bloke I knew when I was living in France. We had this bet about who could first get into print. He was going to write for sports magazines and I thought there would be an insatiable market for this kind of tripe.'

The fact is that *Forum*'s importance in the life of the young Alastair Campbell can hardly be overestimated. It not only gave him his first experience of paid journalism, it enhanced his battered self-confidence and gave him some sort of mission in life. For the best part of two years it partly provided him with a living. When the time came to move onto a broader stage with Mirror Group newspapers, it was the experience with *Forum* that helped convince his next employers that he was capable of doing the job.

All of us can look back to two or three moments that changed our lives and set us on a new course. Alastair Campbell, whose life has been crowded with far more drama than most, can look back on six or seven or even more. One of them came when, as a third-year undergraduate idly leafing through *Forum* magazine, he spotted the word 'COMPETITION' in an advertisement inviting readers to submit articles, luring them with the prospect of a cash prize. It read as opposite.

Alastair duly submitted his entry, forgot about it, and was amazed, a few months later, to learn that he had won. His submitted work was duly published under the catchy title of 'Inter-City Ditties.'[3]

Every writer who has ever lived can remember his first published piece. It is an important moment of recognition, a vital rite of passage, rather like the loss of virginity. It shows what one can do, removes doubts, opens the way to an

2. *News of the World*, 11 September 1994. The phrase 'youthful exuberance' played its full part in the downfall of Jeremy Hanley, then chairman of the Conservative Party. Hanley, interviewed that morning on the *Frost Programme*, was questioned about violence that had erupted the night before at a boxing match between the British super-middleweight champion Nigel Benn and the Paraguayan Juan Carlos Jiménez. Hanley's answer, dismissing the affair as 'exuberance', failed to catch the right tone and was fiercely criticised. He had been leafing through the Sunday papers in the studio earlier, and it may be that he was unconsciously copying the phrase used by Campbell to explain his contributions to *Forum*. That was certainly Campbell's own view. He later claimed credit for Hanley's débâcle.

3. 'Inter-City Ditties' was published in *Forum*, May 1978. It was followed by 'Elsie's Jackpot' (September 1978), 'Busking with Bagpipes' (February 1980), 'Sex at Cambridge' (March 1980), 'Sex at Oxford' (April 1980), 'The Riviera Gigolo' (May 1980), 'The Laid-Back University of Leisexter' (*sic*) (June 1980), and 'Casino Toil' (August 1980). For the first nine months of 1980 *Forum* must have provided a substantial component of Campbell's income.

entire new range of opportunities and experiences. Campbell's first articles were introduced with some fanfare. 'These two stories have been written by a young man from the Midlands,' proclaimed the standfirst. 'He is still only 21 – and we believe they show great promise.'

COMPETITION

WHY DON'T YOU WRITE FOR FORUM?

There's nothing stopping you. In fact we'll make it rather easier by offering cash prizes for the five best articles received by the closing date of our super new Autumn competition.

ALL YOU HAVE TO DO

is write an article of not less than 2000 words and not more than 3000 words for publication on any subject you feel should be included in *Forum*. The theme may be medical, sexological, human, social, political or erotic as you wish and the competition will be judged by the Editor of *Forum* together with three members of the Board of Editorial Consultants.

1st Prize – £75   2nd Prize £50   3rd Prize £35
and two prizes of £25 each plus free *Forum* subscriptions

The judges will be looking for bright, exciting, stimulating, intelligent and readable pieces. Penalty marks will be given for pomposity, jargon and clichés. Closing date: December 1st 1977. Judges' decision absolutely final.

DON'T DELAY – WRITE TODAY

The future tabloid man still had a lot to learn about the need for a grabby 'intro'. 'Train journeys are rarely very interesting,' he began. 'Any survey of how most people spend their time on trains would undoubtedly reveal that the vast majority of passengers in transit pass a large period gazing out of the window.' After this, however, the action moves on rapidly, culminating in a sexual encounter between two complete strangers in the train lavatory. Campbell takes twenty short paragraphs to get them ready for action. This first published piece carries some of the hallmarks of his later journalism. It is clear, unpretentious, has a sense of humour, and gets to the point in a thoroughly businesslike and professional manner.

'Inter-City Ditties' was the foundation for a long and successful association between Alastair Campbell and *Forum* which took off in the first months after he left university. During this period few editions of the monthly magazine were without one of Campbell's sharp and snappy contributions. For a brief time he was one of the magazine's most prolific and valued contributors. There is no question that *Forum* set him on his career in journalism.

It was Phillip Hodson who talent-spotted Alastair Campbell.[4] Today he lives in Hampstead and works as a psychotherapist and management consultant. He is still fiercely proud of the paper he edited, arguing that it stood at the cutting edge of the sexual revolution and was far more than a mere pornographic rag. Besides the young Campbell, contributors included Germaine Greer, Rosie Boycott and Auberon Waugh, who was notorious for demanding the highest fee.[5] Clifford Longley, the religious affairs correspondent of *The Times*, elevated the tone of the magazine with a learned 2,000-word article. Chad Varah, the founder of the Samaritans, was a contributor. Varah's own philosophy that Jesus Christ's teaching about love had a profoundly physical dimension chimed well – or so Hodson claims – with the beliefs and practices of *Forum*.

Shortly after Campbell came down from Cambridge, Hodson sent him on his first journalistic assignment. He was told to travel round Britain reporting on sex at various universities. These articles – a passage from one of which was quoted in the second chapter – are an uneasy mixture of ribald personal anecdote and austere sociological research. They alternate between interviews with solemn figures such as members of student counselling services and lusty accounts of Campbell's own more personal investigations.

Riviera gigolo

Campbell wrote two types of piece for *Forum*: short fictional pieces and factual accounts based on his own experiences. At first glance, his most controversial piece for *Forum*, 'The Riviera Gigolo',[6] falls squarely into the factual category. It is written under Campbell's name, in the first person. Anyone perusing the piece was given every reason to assume that it was either true or a deception on the reader. It tells how, as a young *assistant d'anglais* teaching English in a French school, he developed a profitable and enjoyable sideline selling his services to mature French women of independent means.

One half of the story is clearly accurate. Campbell had indeed worked as an assistant in a French school, as many modern language students do during their third year of university studies. It is the accuracy of the second half of Campbell's account that is open to question. Campbell describes how Madame Rinaudo, 'a forty year old attractive Mediterranean' type, meets him at a

4. Hodson worked for many years as agony uncle on *Woman's Journal*. In June 1999 the management sacked him to make way for Margaret Cook, the former wife of the Foreign Secretary.

5. He was paid £400, a prodigious sum which is still etched in Hodson's memory.

6. See note 3.

reception and invites him to dinner, 'an offer I accepted with pleasure for my interest in older women was a lively one and in any case, I was still finding my feet in a strange country. We were halfway through a bowl of marinated mussels when it became transparent that Mme Rinaudo had a more than purely personal interest in me.'

Campbell describes how he comes to perform stud duties for a wide circle of women, 'the majority of whom were rich, beautiful and in love with sex.' One such from Beaulieu paid him 1,000 francs – more than a week's salary at his school – and 'held my testicles firmly from behind, a slight pain preventing ejaculation, then let go as her orgasm approached.' The '37 year old wife of a fat and pompous German financier . . . paid me 2,000 of his easily earned francs to spend three days on one of her husband's yachts, moored on the harbour at Saint-Jean-Cap-Ferrat.' There was a 'lady lecturer at the University of Nice, who, in return for a handful of orgasms, helped me to write my thesis on Racine and Corneille.' And so forth.

Campbell today insists that 'Riviera Gigolo' was a work of fiction. He told a *Times* reporter that it was all 'totally in the imagination.'[7] But that is not how his editor saw it at the time. 'We were very keen on realistic and fact-based copy,' Phillip Hodson insists. 'He told me that everything was true and I believed him. I still do. He had no motivation to lie to me.'[8] Hodson insists that he discussed all Campbell's pieces with him before they were written, and that it was clear to all concerned they were based on his real life experiences. And it is not only Hodson who was taken in by Campbell if, indeed, his piece was not what it claimed to be. So was the *Sun*.

Campbell's article on being a gigolo was straight up the *Sun*'s street. It is likely that Hodson, who was alive to the commercial possibilities of the articles which appeared in *Forum*, played some part in introducing Campbell to the newspaper. On Friday 9 May 1980, a photograph of Campbell appeared in the *Sun* alongside the headline: 'Wanted – Men for hire'.

He was quoted at length. 'One evening at a recreation for the English students,' Campbell told the *Sun*,

a woman came up to me and asked me out to dinner with her. At the dinner she asked whether I would be interested in becoming a gigolo. The way it worked, she said, was that she gave parties in the afternoon, which women attended for a fee. At these parties, there would be a selection of young men, all available for hire, so to speak. Your job

7. *The Times*, Diary, 10 September 1994.
8. Conversation with the author, June 1999.

was to entertain them and put yourself at their disposal. You would talk, have dinner, make love. In return they would give you money or gifts. The women I met were mainly between 35 and 50 and wanted a young man who would make them feel good. It was all done very discreetly. It was completely civilised and there were very few risks. Only once did a husband turn up unexpectedly.

Often these women didn't even want to have sex. More than anything they wanted an intimate companion – for pillow talk, for affection, to make them feel desirable. The most I got paid was £250 for one night. The least was £12.

Campbell claimed that

there are men in the South of France who turn it into a profession and become very rich. You can be successful between the ages of 20 and 28. After that, you are less in demand. But think of the advantages – you choose your own hours, have a high standard of living, no ties, and all your clients are upper class, rich and civilised. It's never hard work, but the women do expect a high standard of performance.

The story about Campbell the gigolo was filed by a *Sun* reporter called Liz Hodgkinson. Hodgkinson still writes regularly for newspapers, but devotes the greater part of her energy to her career as an author and has had nearly forty books published. Scarcely older than Campbell himself, she vividly remembers the evening they spent together at the Orange Tree pub in Richmond. 'He told me that he had acted as a gigolo in the South of France,' she recalls, 'and that all those middle-aged women down there were gagging for it and he was providing it. He was having a wonderful time and they paid for everything. I had no reason to disbelieve him.'

Hodgkinson is also happy to admit that she had every incentive to trust what he was telling her. She had been dispatched to write a story about gigolos, and gigolos were hard to come by, at any rate ones prepared to spill the beans to the *Sun*. Here was a gigolo, talkative and large as life. It would have been perverse to have questioned Campbell's credentials too closely. 'I wanted to believe him,' she admits, 'because we were doing a story about him.' Campbell, too, had every motive to spin Hodgkinson along, if that was what he was doing. He was being paid handsomely – one or two hundred pounds was the going rate. Either way, everyone was happy.[9]

It is impossible now to say whether or not the Press Secretary to the Prime

9. The *Sun* story has a curious sequel. In May 1996 Jasper Gerard, then editor of the *Sunday Telegraph* Mandrake column, obtained a copy. He rang Campbell who said: 'It was youthful fantasy. I had a bet with a friend who could get into print first.' Pressed further, he claimed: 'I can't remember.' Gerard recalls that Campbell 'grovelled' and pleaded with him not to use the story and went to the

Minister worked the Côte d'Azur as a gigolo twenty years ago. His own account of events is contradictory and of little use. Twenty years ago he had a strong financial and perhaps even professional incentive to inform the *Sun* and Phillip Hodson that he did. The necessity, after he had been appointed to Tony Blair's team, to tell *The Times* it was all 'totally in the imagination' may have been just as strong.

Croupier

Long ago, over a leisurely, drink-sodden summer lunch in the South of France, Campbell explained to an entranced group of friends that it really was possible to make a profit playing roulette. He set out in detail a complex system that tilted the odds very slightly in favour of the punter and against the casino.[10] 'How do you know all this?' he was asked. 'Because I was once a croupier,' came the instant reply.[11]

Campbell's brief stint as a croupier was his first serious attempt to get anything resembling a real job after leaving Cambridge. All the signs are that he would have persevered with it, for a while at least, had he not fallen out with the casino management. He was certainly committed enough to endure six weeks training at the Golden Nugget casino in the West End. But he survived for only four days dealing American roulette on the tables as a professional croupier; according to the records at the Golden Nugget, he was dismissed because of 'failure to meet the required standards'.

John Galvani, now a senior executive with the casino group London Clubs, which owns the Nugget, remembers Campbell reasonably well. He says that he responded to an advertisement in the *Evening Standard* that the casino placed each week. According to Galvani, the Nugget was – and remains – 'a training casino where people go and learn their skills. Going out on the casino floor is a bit like going out on stage and some people freeze. There are subtleties in

lengths of offering another instead. Gerard accepted the alternative story and used both (see *Sunday Telegraph*, 5 May 1996). The *Sun* article is now hard to find. According to Gerard, who now works for *The Times*, it has disappeared from News International files.

10. Gus O'Donnell, John Major's Press Secretary, was also fascinated by roulette systems. He claimed to have found a formula which guaranteed a profit. On foreign trips with the Prime Minister, he would break away from the official party as soon as he could in order to see whether it worked in the local casino. It invariably did, but with a profit so small as hardly to justify the prodigious consumption of time and effort involved. But it made O'Donnell, a Treasury man both by training and by nature, very happy indeed.

11. Mike Molloy in conversation with the author, February 1999.

dealing with customers that you can't replicate in training and obviously if there are going to be mistakes then we'd prefer to see them at that end of the market. The supervisory staff are used to seeing people struggle. Alastair struck me as being pretty confident but not cocky. He didn't suffer from stage fright and beyond the reason listed in our records I honestly don't know what went wrong.'

Shortly after he left the casino Campbell wrote an account of his experiences for *Forum*.[12] It is interesting to compare his own version with Galvani's and indeed the company records. Campbell's *Forum* article is perhaps the weakest of the pieces that he wrote for the magazine. It is embittered and filled with venom against the company management. 'From the moment one spots the gaudy advert in the *Evening Standard*,' he records, 'it's evident that the growing casino chains in London and elsewhere are trying to sell a false mystique based on the quasi-erotic aura of illicit gaming, enticing those of us who drift and thrive on excitement to become croupiers, entering a world where, with any luck, Al Capone and his merry band of psychopaths might suddenly burst onto the premises to profit from a business as sordid as their own.'

Campbell records that 'I answered the advert for various reasons. Chronic insomnia was one of them, another the desire to work through the night and use the day for a modicum of sleep and a maximum of writing.' He also records that 'I had been hoping to get some good quality gigolo work to supplement my other earnings.'

Campbell claims that he started work on 20 March 1980, and that 'twenty-nine hours later, I was sacked by a gaming executive.' This account is at variance with the company record which states that he started dealing on 10 March and lasted four days on the casino floor. Campbell was clearly baffled and angered by his expulsion. He writes that 'I was told by a fellow dealer that I was very good indeed.' His own speculation, and it may not be far from the truth, is that the management got nervous about employing a part-time writer. But, as he pointed out, he had informed the management that he wrote before he joined. More likely still, there was something unfathomable about his attitude which made them nervous.

Busking with bagpipes

It is doubtful whether Alastair Campbell would have had anything to learn from Laurie Lee's *As I Walked Out One Midsummer Morning*, one of the most

---

12. 'Casino Toil', *Forum*, August 1980.

illuminating texts on the busking business ever written. From all reports, he knew every trick. 'I think he discovered, during the time that he was teaching at Nice, that any time he needed money he only had to play the bagpipes,' recalls Mike Molloy, an old friend who once saw him in action. 'It was almost like Picasso, paying for his dinner by sketching on a napkin.'

Something about this tall, magnetic young man, in his Campbell of Argyll tartan, captured the imagination of the peoples of Europe. During this period he became a fabled figure. British holiday-makers brought back stories of a strange piping Scotsman from the South of France and elsewhere. They compared notes about him at dinner parties. Some of them recall him even today. A photograph survives of Campbell playing the bagpipes. Dating from 1980, it shows him – still with that Rod Stewart haircut – playing his pipes in the centre of a crowd of good-humoured shoppers.[13] A sexy girl in jeans and tight-fitting tee-shirt is collecting the money. Campbell was never again to be at the centre of so much concentrated attention until he addressed lobby briefings in the seclusion of Downing Street two decades on.

'Busking with Bagpipes'[14] is Campbell's most accomplished work for *Forum*. This is partly because it is his third piece for the magazine: there is a growing assurance about his style. He is also writing about a subject he knows off by heart. 'I won't bore you with finance,' he proclaims in his preamble. 'Suffice it to say that during 10 months as a busker, I have lived comfortably, indeed very comfortably. Nor will I give details of busking techniques. I'm good at it, that's all you need to know.'

He travelled all round Europe. Campbell hated Italy, where he fell victim to predatory advances from homosexuals. 'Never, ever go to Italy,' he advised. 'The Catholic Church is viciously strong, the Italian lira pitifully weak. The women are virginal and coy, their men frustrated and obscene. Riding in a busy tram in Milan, the kilted busker realises that Italian men really DO fancy anything in a skirt.'

Holland was highly satisfactory ('If Dutch women want something they ask for it. Her impeccable English told me to keep my kilt on. She gave me a leather belt. Her head disappeared and the next I knew of her was a gentle lick along my penis, which responded and rose. "Tie me in," she ordered . . .'). So was France, where a Parisian businessman paid Campbell 400 francs to play his pipes naked for a night outside his new restaurant in the nudist town of Cap

13. First published in *Forum*; see page 2 of the picture section.
14. *Forum*, February 1980.

d'Agde. Sweden, however, was a severe disappointment. 'The men were long and thin, the women insipid and straight-laced. Sweden, like Amsterdam, has far too many sex shops and not enough sex.' Best of the lot, to Campbell's mind, was Norway. In Oslo he met a man, 'a very nice Norwegian man', who offered him food, lodging and unlimited access to his sixteen-year-old daughter Marit for a week. 'Our love-making seemed to last forever,' recorded Campbell. 'We were fast asleep when Marit's mother came in with a cup of tea and an old copy of the *Daily Telegraph*.'

The words and phrases are beginning to flow in 'Busking with Bagpipes'. Furthermore, Campbell is starting to get savvy about the press. He gives details of his first ever spin-doctoring operation. 'Even a busker needs public relations backing him,' reveals Campbell. 'I let the press do mine. Go to a town, find a busy bar, find a journalist, preferably pissed. Buy him a Bloody Mary, tell him you love his town; the morning paper does a nice article and for a day or two you're a local celebrity.'

Campbell was growing up. Something was telling him that it was time to drop his free-wheeling, easy-riding life and get serious. In a moment of clarity, he applied for a traineeship with the *Mirror*, then as now one of the great newspaper groups with a chain of local papers as well as the flagship *Daily Mirror*, *Sunday Mirror* and *Scottish Daily Record*. Every year nearly 5,000 ambitious young journalists would apply for the dozen or so places that were made available on the *Mirror* course. It was recognised by everyone in the trade as the best training any young aspiring journalist could possibly get.

Mirror Group trainee

Campbell has had many pieces of good fortune in his life, but none greater than the fact that James Dalrymple was Director of Mirror Training when he made his application. Dalrymple is a tough, working-class Scot, proud of his roots; with it all a lovely writer. He has worked for most Fleet Street papers at one time or another and spent the summer of 1999, often in dangerous conditions, reporting on the Kosovan conflict.

It was Dalrymple who weeded Campbell's job application from the thousands that flooded into the *Mirror* offices. They were all written on two sides of A4. One side provided the regulation details about education, family life and so forth. On the other, applicants were asked to give a 500-word feature describing themselves. 'I set great store by this part,' says Dalrymple today. 'The thing that hit me about Alastair's was that it was a well-written vignette, full of humour. It intrigued me.' Nothing was held back. It told how he had busked around Europe and written for *Forum* magazine. It was enough to ensure that Campbell's name was among the élite group summoned down to London for the interview process.

Although there were thousands of other eager applicants for the course, the interview confirmed Dalrymple's hunch that, despite his unconventional CV, there was something exceptional in Campbell. And he wasn't going to allow this boy, and a fellow Scot at that, to escape his destiny. Dalrymple ranks high among the long list of benefactors who have helped make Alastair Campbell the man he now is.

The scheme he joined had been founded in 1966 when the legendary Hugh Cudlipp still ran the *Mirror*. The paper acquired its group of regional papers in the South-West partly in order to use them as a training ground for young journalists. When Campbell emerged two years later, he was an almost fully-fledged reporter. After a short induction course lasting two months, the trainees were thrown in at the deep end on local papers. Campbell was seconded first, in the autumn of 1981, to the *Tavistock Times*, where he stayed for about a year before being moved to the *Sunday Independent* in Plymouth. Later Campbell enthused: 'It was absolutely fantastic. You went onto local papers and within days you're sports editor, columnist, chief interviewer.'[15]

It was during this period that he started to make friends, in a way that he never had at Cambridge. He met many of the people who were going to mean most to him for the rest of his life. For the first time since childhood, in a way that he never had been at university, he was at ease in his own skin. He had found an occupation that engaged him intellectually and emotionally. He was a born journalist, as James Dalrymple had spotted back in London. He was tough, arrogant, oozing confidence and charm: the ideal personality for a reporter. It had taken courage and bombast to travel all alone round Europe for months on end with just the bagpipes for company, that courage and bombast would do just as well for the foot-in-the-door reporting the *Mirror* was crying out for. Added to that an ease with words and a gift for a phrase: he made something close to the perfect package. What, though, made him absolutely right for the *Mirror* was the chip on his shoulder. He was anti-establishment, an outsider with everything to prove. Campbell must have felt somewhere in his bones, as he joined his fellow trainees for their two-year stint in the West Country, a part of the world he hardly knew, that in some strange way he was coming home.

15. Quoted in the *Observer*, 22 February 1998.

He was already wearing the heavy trench-coat that he made his trade-mark when he joined the *Daily Mirror* as a young reporter a few years later. Sometimes, for a joke, he would turn his head to one side and downwards and engage in imaginary conversations in the manner of an American secret service agent murmuring into his walkie-talkie. He was loud, boisterous and had an unmistakable presence and charisma. He possessed that sexual confidence that some men have who know how to please women: it often flows over into other areas of life. He was very good-looking in a dangerous sort of way. Someone once compared Campbell's physical presence to a 'young Russian goalkeeper' running out onto the football field. It was a felicitous comparison which captured his size – he is well over six foot and well-built – his exuberance, the sense of foreignness that he owes to his Gaelic roots, and the way he has of appearing both concentrated and detached at the same time. For women all this could make a heady cocktail. He was beginning to develop the poise and urbanity that would stand him in such good stead when he moved into political reporting five years later. He had an extraordinary gift, one of which he was probably not yet aware: he could make people, including very important people, feel honoured that he should choose to confer his presence upon them. He was still very dangerous when drunk, and would remain so for some years.

On the training scheme Campbell made the closest friendship of his life. It was with John Merritt, the most brilliant journalist on the course. Ginger-haired and also strikingly good-looking, Merritt, like many talented reporters, was quiet and softly spoken. A Roman Catholic, he was a journalist who felt the need to do good as well as sell newspapers. Some colleagues saw him as 'almost saintly'.[16] He seemed destined to go to the very top in journalism.

Campbell not only met his best friend that first day in Plymouth: he also met the love of his life. Fiona Millar, the daughter of *Express* journalist Bob Millar,

---

16. An expression used by Michael Prescott, political editor of the *Sunday Times*. 'Saintly' or not, Merritt was sharp as a razor. During the 1987 General Election Prescott, then working for the Press Association, and Merritt, for the *Mirror*, were among the team of journalists on the Margaret Thatcher campaign bus. The party stopped off at a factory. As the Prime Minister was introduced to workers on the production line, Denis Thatcher was seen chatting away meaningfully to the commercial director. After the Prime Minister's consort had been summoned back to the official party, Merritt wandered innocently up to the commercial director and engaged him in conversation. As the journalists boarded the bus at the end of the visit Prescott turned to Merritt. 'What was Denis talking to the commercial manager about? It looked to me as if he was trying to sort out a bit of business.' 'That is exactly what he was trying to do,' replied Merritt. 'And I've got it all on tape.'

was another of the select band of trainees. It was love at first sight. Cedric Pulford, who was running the *Mirror* scheme at the time, remembers taking the new recruits on an induction tour of Plymouth on the second day. As part of the tour he took them to the roof-top viewing platform of the civic centre. He still vividly remembers one moment: 'I was just looking around making sure nobody was falling off the balcony or something and I caught a look between Alastair and Fiona which was totally electric. I've never seen such a look of mutual attraction between two people before or since. Alastair was in those days certainly classically handsome. He really was like the Grecian ideal of male beauty. He's over six foot, she's verging on the petite. Whether they were seeing each other for the first time I don't know. I would not describe the look as lascivious. I did not think that on either part it was a look of lust, it was more what they call a cow-eyed look of dumb adoration.' Pulford recalls that 'there was never any question from that moment onwards it was Alastair and Fiona.'

By a striking coincidence, John Merritt also met the love of his life on the first day of that training scheme. She was Lindsay Nicholson, who is now the editor of the magazine *Good Housekeeping*. The two couples became inseparable. They went on holiday together. When they all moved to London a few years later, they were so close that they chose to live in the same street in North London. They started up families at the same time in the late 1980s.

It was around that time that things started to go terribly wrong for John Merritt and Lindsay Nicholson, who has been obliged to cope with the most unimaginable tragedy. When her daughter Ellie was just eighteen months old, she learnt that her husband, at the very height of his powers as a reporter, and aged only 32, had contracted leukaemia: he died of a haemorrhage in August 1992. Five years later she learnt that their little daughter Ellie had the disease too: she died in June 1998.

Today Lindsay Nicholson can barely find words to describe the way that Alastair Campbell and Fiona Millar rallied round. When Ellie was ill Alastair Campbell, already under huge strain in Downing Street, took on as much of the burden as he could. He visited the little girl, who adored him, at least once a week as she lay in Great Ormond Street Hospital. He threw his weight behind a national campaign to find a matching donor for a bone marrow transplant. As all this was going on Lindsay Nicholson made a public pronouncement of sorts about Alastair Campbell. She told Roy Hattersley, who was doing a profile of the No. 10 Press Secretary for the *Observer*: 'In times of trouble there are those who will be there and those who won't. Alastair is always there. Doing anything. Twice a week at the hospital. Driving me home. Talking to Ellie about her father as only he can.'[17]

In June 1999, in an interview with Catherine O'Brien of the *Daily Telegraph*, Lindsay Nicholson poured out her heart even further. She described how Alastair Campbell and Fiona Millar had drawn her deep into their circle of friends: 'They call themselves "the Team"', she said, 'and they really are the most well-oiled machine. When John became ill and died, they worked out who did what best and swung into action. Ever since, they have coordinated between themselves to make sure there is always someone there for me.' Besides Campbell and Millar, the 'team' includes Cherie Blair and government minister Tessa Jowell. Some time before Ellie died, she was allowed home for Christmas: Tony and Cherie Blair immediately invited her up to Chequers.[18]

Fiona Millar

If being interviewed by James Dalrymple was a huge stroke of luck, meeting Fiona Millar at this juncture was an even bigger one. Fiona, a devastatingly pretty and charming blonde, has been the solid rock in Campbell's life ever since. He in return has been utterly devoted to her. Whatever dalliances he may have been involved in as a red-blooded single man – and it is unlikely that the encounters described so graphically in *Forum* had no basis whatever in fact – all concur that they came to a halt the moment he set eyes on Fiona. The parliamentary lobby, where Campbell went on to spend so many years, is one of the most efficient gossip factories in the world. Not a whiff of scandal has attached itself to his name. Today he takes a disapproving attitude to what he would now see as sexual misconduct. At one overseas summit during the days when John Major was Prime Minister, a woman was spotted leaving the bedroom of a renowned political editor in the early hours of the morning. This incident soon became the talk of the British press corps as they sat around waiting for news of the next inevitable calamity to strike the beleaguered Tory premier. Campbell made known his scorn and disapproval.

There have been many temptations for this good-looking and also powerful man, doubly attractive to women. But he has steadfastly resisted them. At a Conservative Party conference in Brighton nearly ten years ago, Campbell

17. *Observer*, 22 February 1998.

18. See Catherine O'Brien's revealing interview with Lindsay Nicholson, 'Cherie and Alastair are Incredible', *Daily Telegraph*, 29 June 1999.

discovered a young female Scandinavian journalist of striking good looks and intelligence. On further enquiry into her circumstances, it emerged that such was the poverty of the girl's newspaper that she was unable to afford accommodation in Brighton, but was travelling down daily from London, where she had secured temporary accommodation. Campbell, then political editor of the *Mirror*, made it his urgent business to remedy this unhappy state of affairs and soon secured her free use of one of the many rooms booked in the Metropole Hotel for the use of *Mirror* executives. The girl felt an effusive gratitude for his kindness. She found it hard to believe that such generosity came without a corresponding obligation, an obligation, it was intimated, she would not be averse to fulfilling. Campbell's behaviour was the complete model of propriety. Several weeks later a postcard arrived at the *Mirror* offices thanking Campbell for his kindness. 'You know a great deal about British politics,' it read, 'but very little about Scandinavian morals.'

There is no doubt, in Campbell's mind or anyone else's, that but for Fiona Millar's love and boundless support he would not now be Press Secretary in Downing Street and one of the most powerful men in the land. Things had begun to look up for Campbell when he met Fiona, but there were some desperately hard times ahead. Without her, there is every possibility that he would never have pulled through. It is easy to imagine Campbell today as one of those drink-sodden, self-pitying, charming unemployables who can usually be found in any pub or wine-bar where journalists gather, still much loved by their friends, who remember how amusing and promising they once were, but of no consequence whatever to the outside world. He has every reason to be thankful to her. But he too deserves some credit: for allowing her to save him from the abyss. Forgiving one's benefactors is sometimes the hardest thing of all.

On the *Tavistock Times* Campbell did all the things that local reporters are supposed to do. He reported council meetings, flower shows and court cases. He developed an accurate shorthand note. He learnt how to file clean copy to a tight deadline. He knocked on the doors of grieving relatives who had just suffered a newsworthy bereavement.[19] He gradually mastered the weird, convoluted craft of writing news stories. It is an ugly, soulless and mechanical job which demands the total abandonment of literary pretensions. A-level English is an impediment: a degree in English literature a disqualification.[20] A good,

19. The 'grieving rellies', as they are known on the road. They are often surprisingly glad to talk.

20. English graduates do, however, find employment as diarists and in the features department, scornfully referred to by newsdesks as the 'shallow end'.

precise reporter has far more in common with a competent neighbourhood plumber or a reliable carpenter than a flowery weekly essayist.

As Campbell made all these strange and surprising discoveries, he was also practising how to be a spin-doctor, although the phrase had not then become current. Still more surprising, the man he practised on – the prototype for Tony Blair two decades on – was a Tory.

Robin Fenner, Auctioneer

Robin Fenner is the sort of man who used to join the Conservative Party as a matter of course – but rarely does today. He is founder and senior partner in Fenners, one of the leading West Country auctioneers. He is one of the most respected members of the Tavistock commercial community, for two decades served part-time as a local councillor, and was mayor of the town in 1984. Like Alastair Campbell's father, Fenner used to be a member of the local Conservative Club and like him he went along at least partly for the snooker. Fenner saw himself as a 'one-nation Tory': he was a member of the left-leaning Bow Group. He was never to be more at ease in the Tory Party than in the 1960s, when Edward Heath was party leader and the local MP for Tavistock was Michael Heseltine: he left the party in the 1980s.[21]

In 1980 Fenner, in his role as local councillor, played a prominent part in launching the Tavistock community recycling scheme. It was an innovative idea, the first ever to be sponsored by a local council. In the wake of the launch the auctioneer was surprised to be rung up by a local reporter: the reporter expressed his admiration for Fenner's brainwave and asked if he could come and see him. Fenner readily agreed. That is how he met Alastair Campbell for the first time.

In Fenner's office the future Press Secretary to the Prime Minister got straight down to business. The basic idea for a community recycling scheme – called Tavistock Wastesavers – was good, he said. But the presentation had been poor. Fenner, he said, needed a good press officer. And Campbell was volunteering for the position. The auctioneer was enthusiastic. The two men shook hands. For the next few months Fenner had the benefit of the advice of a

21. By coincidence Fenner worked for Heseltine's Haymarket Group in the 1960s. He describes the Tory politician as 'the best employer imaginable'. While Fenner was recovering from a serious car crash Heseltine paid his wages for thirteen months, providing him with a cleaning lady into the bargain. This while Heseltine was still building up a small business: Haymarket had not become the large, prosperous enterprise it is today.

man who, he became ever more convinced, was a brilliant manipulator of the press. Campbell, in return, was in the place where he always wanted to be: at the centre of events, whether the events in question were going on in Westminster or sleepy Tavistock. He was not just a journalist observing the passing scene from the outside. He was also deep on the inside of Tavistock politics, with privileged access to information and the key personalities who ran the West Country town. As Fenner says: 'He had his finger on the button within a few days of arriving in Tavistock. He became very well aware of what made the place tick.' It was an almost obsessive pattern of behaviour that would repeat itself again and again during Alastair Campbell's remarkable rise to power.

'He acted as my spin-doctor for one and a half years,' Fenner now recalls.[22] Together the ambitious young reporter and the Tory politician wrote speeches, arranged press conferences and devised stunts designed to promote Wastesavers. For a brief period Fenner's star, under this mesmerising new influence, shone brightly on the West Country scene. A press release drafted by Campbell grabbed the attention of the *Grapevine* programme on BBC2. They came down and made a programme about Wastesavers. Thanks to Campbell, Fenner was invited to lecture on environmental projects in the United States. But today he has no doubt who was the most important member of the team. 'I was the mouthpiece. He was planting the ideas.' Many of the ideas were planted at the bar of the Tavistock Conservative Club, where the two men went to play snooker.

Fenner has no doubt about Campbell's skills: 'He never took no for an answer. It was obvious who and what he would become. I have never known any journalist who could pen any story as quickly. He wanted to hit it on the head. If you look at his Fleet Street journalism, that was his trademark: he gets to the point.'

Fenner claims that many of the techniques Campbell uses today in Downing Street were first tried out on him. 'I am convinced,' he says, 'that two-thirds of every major speech by Tony Blair is Alastair's. He would help me put together speeches. I can still see Alastair saying to me: "We should put emphasis on this." There are certain terms I have heard coming from the Prime Minister's lips which I would have used in my speeches after talking to Alastair.'

There was one further trait that Campbell has kept from that day to this. He

22. Fenner's memory may be deceiving him here. It seems unlikely that Campbell spent eighteen months in Tavistock.

has always been prepared to fall out, if need be savagely, with his boss. On one occasion Fenner, outraged by some local vandals, called for the return of the stocks. 'It rankled with his nibs,' Fenner now recalls. 'Alastair was totally opposed. I said: "I've had people calling me all through the night." And he just said it served me right. I've never forgotten that.'

The Bob Edwards incident

At the end of the two-year course, all the trainees wanted a job with one of the Mirror Group titles. It came as no surprise, and caused not the slightest resentment, when the first to get a job with the flagship title – the *Daily Mirror* – was John Merritt. Campbell followed him shortly afterwards. As ever with Campbell, the circumstances surrounding his appointment were far from simple and even now remain shrouded in a certain amount of mystery. What is certain is that Campbell took it into his head to publicly abuse and, according to some versions, physically manhandle one of the most senior and powerful Mirror Group executives.

The incident took place at the Green Lanterns restaurant in Plymouth at a dinner hosted by Colin Harrow. Harrow had recently taken over from James Dalrymple as training manager: today he is the managing editor of the *Sunday Mirror*. Guest of honour at this occasion was Bob Edwards, a celebrated Fleet Street hand then approaching the end of a long career. He had edited some of Britain's finest papers, and was currently nearing the end of a record-breaking thirteen-year spell with the *Sunday Mirror*. In retirement he went on to write one of the finest autobiographies by a newspaperman. His *Goodbye to Fleet Street* gives a memorable portrait of a vanished age.

Edwards had come down to Plymouth to address the trainees. After such occasions it was Harrow's custom to use the Mirror Group's famously lavish expenses to invite the guest and a few others to dinner. On this occasion he suggested that Alastair Campbell and Fiona Millar – by now an established couple – should attend the event, mainly because Fiona's father Robert Millar was an old friend of Edwards. Also present was John Theobald, a *Mirror* executive who was editor of the *Sunday Independent* in Plymouth for several years.

Campbell and Edwards did not hit it off, and it is easy to imagine why not. Campbell was young, hot-headed and arrogant. He felt no automatic respect for title or rank, if anything rather the reverse. By this stage of his career Edwards had perhaps become slightly pompous. He had a splendid record in newspaper journalism, and felt that he deserved to be listened to with respect and even reverence, a feeling that Campbell did not share. It is possible, though at this distance of time difficult to say for sure, that sexual friction may have played some role in the incident. As an old friend of her family Edwards may have felt entitled to take a proprietorial or even gently flirtatious attitude towards Fiona. Any such move, however innocently intended, would have been deeply resented by Campbell, and served to inflame his in any case volatile temper.

As the evening progressed Campbell found it more and more difficult to conceal his irritation towards Edwards, and was less and less inclined to do so. Drink played its full part in the dénouement, which was sparked by an argument over the Afghanistan War. Campbell, it emerged, was angered by the way a story about the conflict had been hidden away at the back of the newspaper. He believed that it should have been given greater prominence towards the front. Edwards, for his part, was not inclined to pay a great deal of attention to the views of a young and inexperienced reporter. He may have indicated in a patronising manner that he found Campbell's stridently expressed opinion naïve. Whatever the rights and wrongs of it all – and Edwards was surely right to insist that Afghanistan was of little or no interest to the vast bulk of *Mirror* readers – everyone is agreed on one thing: Campbell was needlessly and brutally offensive to one of the most eminent men in Fleet Street. When he woke up the following morning, he had every reason to assume that his career as a *Mirror* reporter was over before it had even begun.

But Campbell had chosen exactly the right person to pick a fight with. Bob Edwards was not a popular man in the *Mirror* empire. For one thing he came from a foreign culture. Fundamentally, he was an *Express* man, reared in the Beaverbrook empire. More important, his great days were coming to an end. He was no longer the power in the land he once was. The vultures were beginning to circle. It may even have been that Campbell, whose nose has always been highly attuned to the tiniest nuances of power, could sense some of this and that there was an element of calculation in his savage attack.

So the following day when news reached Holborn Circus of a fracas involving the editor of the *Sunday Mirror* and a young, unknown reporter, there was considerable interest in that young reporter. Opinion at the 'Stab-in-the Back', the disgusting pub standing at the foot of the imposing *Mirror* building (its real name was the White Hart, but no *Mirror* journalist ever called it that), was firmly on his side. The story had, as they say in the trade, got legs. Soon reports were circulating round the Stab that the two men had come to blows, with Edwards coming off the worst. According to another report, equally without foundation, Campbell's nose had been put out of joint when he discovered Edward making a sexual pass at Fiona.[23] A new generation of thrusting executives, impatient with the existing hierarchies, was emerging at the *Mirror*. They noted down the name Alastair Campbell and, whenever they saw Edwards, which was far too often for their liking, thought of him with warmth and something resembling affection.

Whether or not the Bob Edwards incident can be held responsible, Campbell was not invited to apply for a job at the *Mirror* at the end of the course. Fiona Millar, however, was. Several months later Campbell accompanied Fiona to London when she went for her interview. While he waited for her to return from the interview, he dropped in at the Stab-in-the-Back for a few pints. Kingsley Amis, in his book *Stanley and the Women*, describes a Fleet Street pub in the following fashion: 'Like all newspaper pubs it was nothing like the nicest in walking distance, not even the nicest a minute away, just the nearest. Inside, the noise from the people almost drowned the music. There was nowhere to sit, and there seemed to be nowhere to stand either.' Amis's description conjures up the Stab-in-the-Back as it was in the days before Mirror Group Newspapers moved to Canary Wharf, with a deadly accuracy.

Word spread rapidly round the *Mirror* building in Holborn that 'the man who had thumped Bob Edwards' was to be found in the vicinity. *Mirror* journalists never needed much of an excuse to go to the pub, especially during working hours. There was a general move towards the Stab to inspect the prodigy.[24] After the paper had been put to bed Richard Stott, then an assistant editor on the *Daily Mirror* and a rising star who was in due course to assume the editor's chair, dropped down to the Stab. Stott, who became an important influence in Campbell's career, liked what he saw. He asked Campbell why he had not been

23. This story has a certain general plausibility. 'It was not uncommon,' recollects one former *Mirror* man, 'for senior executives to go down to Plymouth in the hope of a shag off one of the female trainees.' That was certainly not Bob Edwards' intention, however.

24. Some details of the account given here of the row with Bob Edwards and Campbell's subsequent entry into Fleet Street are drawn from a profile by Kevin Toolis (*Guardian Weekend*, 4 April 1998). Lesley White's profile in the *Sunday Times* (11 December 1994) is also helpful; it quotes Richard Stott saying: 'He really caught our attention as a potential *Mirror* reporter when we learnt that he gave an editor a smack round the chops in the West Country. That seemed to suit our style.' Bob Edwards, the alleged victim, who now lives in retirement in Banbury, is adamant that no fight occurred: 'The story of us having a punch-up has become a legend and I honestly can't remember what happened that day but it definitely didn't come to blows. It wasn't wise of him to row with an editor, but I am not vindictive and it didn't stop him getting a job on the *Daily Mirror*.' Edwards is even generously prepared to concede that 'you could say it was a good thing to stand up for his beliefs even if to a Fleet Street editor' (private conversation).

called up for interview. Campbell shrugged his shoulders. Stott told him: 'Give me a ring tomorrow and I'll fix you up with a shift.'

This was an amazing stroke of luck. Campbell was being offered casual work – an opportunity to break in through the back door. Even so he made an effort to evade his destiny. He did not call the following morning. Stott, furious about this, tracked him down and effectively ordered him in.

Campbell, just 25 years old, was launched.

Chapter Four

IN WHICH OUR HERO'S FORTUNES SINK VERY LOW

I always say that if you've seen one Gentleman of the Press having delirium tremens, you've seen them all.
    P. G. Wodehouse, Bachelors Anonymous *(1973)*

The Fleet Street Alastair Campbell joined as a *Daily Mirror* reporter in the early months of 1983 was irretrievably squalid: lecherous, boozy, back-stabbing and brilliant. It fitted Campbell like a glove. He arrived in the dying days of the hot metal era. The characteristic sound of a news-room was the clatter of typewriters as reporters spewed out their stories, to be grabbed by copy-boys and raced to the sub-editors, who would mark them up before dropping them down a chute to the compositors, who would expertly but laboriously set up the type. Fleet Street newspapers in those days were like ocean liners. From deep in the bowels of the building came the roar and hum of heavy machinery as the newspapers were produced. Fleet Street was the last surviving centre of manufacturing industry in central London. Late at night articulated lorries would make their way as best they could through the narrow lanes round the great newspaper buildings, be loaded up and set free to hurtle up the nation's motorways bearing their load of sensational stories to an apathetic nation. It was a hopelessly antiquated nine-teenth-century system which modern computerised technology had made redundant decades before. But nobody had yet found a means of overcoming the resistance of the printers' unions, which were corrupt, complacent and all-powerful. The slightest infringement of the rules they dictated to terrified newspaper management led to an instantaneous strike and the consequential loss of a day's revenue. When Campbell arrived at the *Mirror*, reporters were not allowed to change their typewriter ribbons. A union man had to be called to carry out the task. He would invariably take hours if not days to arrive. Any protest at his procrastination caused offence: he performed his derisory function with the air of a man bestowing a huge favour, which in a sense he was. Salvation was round the corner in the shape of Tory employment legislation, then being roundly denounced as oppressive by – among others – Tony Blair, the promising young MP for Sedgefield. Undeterred by Labour threats of retaliation, Rupert Murdoch and Eddie Shah were poised to take advantage.

For the moment, however, the *ancien régime* survived – and prospered. Thanks to their massive circulations, Fleet Street papers could be hugely profitable. Journalists' salaries, compared to today's, were meagre. But they were rewarded liberally in kind. Expense accounts were prodigious. Senior management provided itself with large cars, expenses-paid holidays, first-class travel and lavish lunches. Of nowhere was this more true than the *Mirror*. In 1984 Clive Thornton, formerly a building society manager, was appointed Mirror Group chairman. It was not to be a long-lived appointment. The first thing he did was to bury his head in the *Mirror* accounts. Several days later he emerged. 'Do you know,' he declared in his nasal northern whine, 'the annual profits of this company are less than the sum *Mirror* journalists spend taking each other out to lunch. Not contacts out to lunch. Not people who could possibly give them stories or be of use. Taking *each other* out to lunch.' Thornton had lost his leg – in the war, it was thought. Inevitably the cry went round Fleet Street: 'In the land of the legless, the one-legged man is king.'

It was a cocksure, macho, boozy culture. *Mirror* men lived high on the hog.[1] They felt themselves, with less justification than they realised, to be the governors of Fleet Street. They were a close-knit lot. They stuck together, drank together, ate together and conspired together. When they went to parties *Mirror* men tended to form themselves into little huddles as if it was lowering to mingle. As time went on, the paper began to read like that too. It had got stuck at a fixed point in the 1960s. Unlike its wide-awake mass-market competitor the *Sun*, the *Mirror* failed to spot that the world was moving on. This was the paper that took Alastair Campbell to its heart.

Doorstepping celebrities and rooting through dustbins

When he arrived at the *Mirror* Campbell was greeted with rapture by John Merritt, by now well on his way to becoming an established reporter. Merritt gave him two pieces of advice: always sit within earshot of the newsdesk so that you know what they are talking about; and always keep something up your sleeve so that 'if the bastards give you some boring rubbish to work on you can trump them with something better.'

1. When Anne Robinson, then a widely admired columnist, later to become famous as a television presenter, arrived at the *Mirror* she enquired how much she had to spend. 'No budgets here, blossom,' came the astonishing reply.

Campbell proved himself very quickly indeed as a reliable, accurate and lively reporter. Since he has been Press Secretary to Tony Blair, he has frequently enjoyed contrasting the rancid triviality of today's newspapers to the serious, idealistic *Mirror* of his own day. There is a small measure of truth in this. Back in 1983, there were a number of names on the *Mirror*, such as Paul Foot and John Pilger, who were there to inform rather than entertain. Writers like Keith Waterhouse gave the paper style and class. But none of this had anything to do with Alastair Campbell. Nothing he contributed in the early days at the *Mirror* was ever likely to be a submission for the Pulitzer Prize.

Early on he established a monopoly on the Miss World competition: 'Twenty year old Frédérique Leroy from Bordeaux has attracted heavy betting. Brown-haired and brown-eyed, she's been charming all week with a typically French, cute, sexy smile…' 'Barnarda, Miss Yugoslavia, has been photographed in a variety of erotic poses, including topless shots.'

Another Campbell staple during his days as a tabloid reporter was small animals. These, accompanied by an affecting picture, were perhaps a tribute to his early days trundling around the Yorkshire Dales in the back of his father's Morris Traveller. It would be possible to fill a small zoo with the animals Campbell wrote stories about during his time at the *Mirror*: it would include swans, badgers, rooks, frogs, golden labradors, foxes and mink. He has never lost his eye for an animal story. One of the memorable images of the Blair years in Downing Street, published in practically every paper, was of a mallard duck taking her ducklings for a walk in front of the steps of No. 10 Downing Street.

There were the inevitable celebrity stories. A gallant Campbell lent Selina Scott his Wellington boots ('this was sophisticated Selina as you'd never seen her before') on a day out on the beach at Southend.[2] Royal stories were important in Campbell's early career. Prince Andrew's girlfriends served him well. He made a splash with a story about 'glamour girl Vicki Hodge' and her affair with Prince Andrew.[3] He was one of the team which doorstepped 'beautiful Katie Rabett' as she left home the day after her romance with the Prince had become public knowledge.[4] Campbell and his fellow reporter

2. *Daily Mirror*, 14 August 1984. The young Campbell invariably took advantage of the month of August to get his stories into the paper, while the big hitters were away on holiday. Later, he became an assiduous holiday-maker in August himself.

3. 'Vicki: I'm a foolish bitch', *Daily Mirror*, 21 May 1984.

4. *Daily Mirror*, 22 February 1984. The three reporters on this story, Alastair Campbell, John Merritt and Chris Gysin, were all on the training scheme together.

Christian Gysin reported the birth of Sara Keays' baby daughter. It was probably Campbell who doorstepped Cecil Parkinson outside his Potter's Bar home the following day. Parkinson, who has always been civil to reporters and liked in return, paused on the way out to apologise for inclement weather conditions. 'I advise you to find some more interesting news,' he said to the assembled journalists, and was on his way.[5] Campbell developed a line in gangsters and earned himself a rare front-page exclusive with a story about how the 'the notorious Kray twins were secretly reunited for their 51st birthday yesterday.'[6]

Some of his stories might today be accounted intrusion. He secured a page five lead with a piece on Cliff Richard's love life. 'The man who has lived with pop star Cliff Richard for 19 years,' reported Campbell, 'denied yesterday that they are lovers.'[7] Campbell was also involved in the team that harassed Martina Navratilova during Wimbledon 1984 over rumours about her relationship with her friend Judy Nelson.[8] Having neglected to get into the tournament by conventional means, he resorted to a typical piece of chutzpah. 'I had neither tickets nor accreditation,' he recalls. 'So I put on a tracksuit with lots of logos on it, carried a few rackets under my arm, signed a few autographs for queuing students who hadn't the faintest idea who I was, and the chap on the gate let me in.' Navratilova and Nelson hit back by calling him 'scum'.[9]

These were the stories all tabloid reporters do, which Campbell later described as a 'phase of rooting through dustbins and hanging around outside celebrities' homes'. There is no sense that Campbell was a heavy foot-in-the-door merchant, or any more unscrupulous than his contemporaries at the time. And it was not all trivia. Campbell was, for example, a junior member of the reporting team that dealt with the aftermath of the Brighton bomb.

One of his articles stands out. At the start of the 1983 football season, he was commissioned to write a special report on soccer hooliganism. Not without personal risk, he infiltrated West Ham's feared Inter City Firm to produce a piece that revealed how apparently chance encounters between rival groups of supporters were actually engineered well in advance.[10] Campbell had learnt a great deal about the craft of writing journalism since his faltering first piece for *Forum*.

5. *Daily Mirror*, 5 January 1984.
6. 'Kray Twins' Secret Treat', *Daily Mirror*, 10 October 1984.
7. 'I'm not gay says Cliff's live-in pal', *Daily Mirror*, 22 January 1985.
8. *Ibid.*, June 1984.
9. *Today*, 23 June 1994.
10. 'Soccer's Sickness,' *Daily Mirror*, 5 September 1983.

He was made for tabloid reporting of this type. 'He was great fun to work with,' Rupert Morris, who worked with Campbell two or three years later when he was on *Today*, records. 'He had this fantastic enthusiasm and dynamism. He was really passionate about his work. Almost like a boy scout.' From the very start his pieces for the *Mirror* communicate a directness and confidence. He clearly had no difficulty getting his copy into the paper and was accepted within a short space of time into the beery *Mirror* culture.

Most people become tedious when drunk – repetitive, boorish and increasingly pathetic. Alastair Campbell did not fall into this category. During the relatively few years that he was a drinker – he gave up around his 29th birthday – he turned drunkenness into an art form. Until the very latest stages of the evening he remained hypnotically funny or, when he wasn't being amusing, dangerous. The prospect of physical violence was never far away. He was anarchic, clever, witty and an accomplished mimic: a devastating gift which could be used mercilessly against those whom he and his friends wanted to destroy. The Campbell performance was worth travelling miles to see. He was filled with an urge to seize life by the scruff of the neck. You never knew where the evening would end.

What made these evenings with Campbell absolutely extraordinary was the fact that he was genuinely unstable. There was nothing feigned about his graveyard humour, the brooding sense of violence, his sudden bursts of furious outrage. Campbell was beginning to suffer from the illness that would culminate in his nervous breakdown while working for *Today* newspaper in 1986. But having Alastair Campbell as a member of your party in a pub or drinking establishment was an unmistakable badge of honour. There was only one reciprocal obligation. That was to stay with him to the end, and make sure that he returned home safe and sound. Many were the evenings when a kindly fellow drinker at the Stab-in-the-Back shovelled Campbell into the back of a cab, muttered an address, and put a fiver into the cabbie's hand, never failing to demand a receipt to claim back on *Mirror* expenses.

Only those who know what it is to drink and to get drunk on a regular basis understand that it is not as easy as it looks. The real drinking geniuses – the Dylan Thomases and the Jeffrey Bernards – create an alternative reality, a more amusing and arguably saner version of everyday life. Over the years Fleet Street has produced some world-class drinkers, though diminishingly so nowadays. For a brief five-year period, Campbell was to be classed among them. The journalist Rupert Morris, now assistant editor of *The Week* magazine, worked with Campbell at *Today* newspaper in the mid-1980s and was a regular drinking partner. 'Alastair was a great drinker,' he recalls. 'He was absolutely the life and soul. He was a tremendous person to have around. He communicated an electricity that made you want to be part of it all. You had a feeling that no way was life going to be dull. He was a star but completely without any kind of vanity. You couldn't turn down a drink with Alastair because you knew anything might happen.'

The demands of his job were gruelling. There were some dangerous signs from a very early stage that drinking was beginning to intrude upon his effectiveness. One of his colleagues, Paul Callan, was then a well-regarded writer on the *Mirror*. His job was to furnish 'colour' while one of the reporters would perform the more onerous, but less enjoyable and prestigious, task of providing hard facts. On one occasion, Callan recalls, he and Campbell were sent to report on a visit by Prince Charles to a London Hospital. 'Alastair was extremely pissed,' says Callan. 'He wanted to go into one of the wards with the Prince. He wanted to speak with the Prince personally. I said: I wouldn't do that if I were you. I propped him up against a wall and said: stay here. Then I went in to see the Prince. Fifteen or twenty minutes later I came out. He'd slid down the wall. He was a little muddle of limbs on the floor. Alastair was a good journalist,' concludes Callan, 'especially when he was sober.'[11]

Bob and Audrey Millar

The one solid point in Campbell's world was Fiona. And not merely Fiona. As often happens, Campbell had fallen in love not simply with the girl herself but with all the Millars. Like the Campbells, they were originally from Scotland. But they had embedded themselves in the heart of English metropolitan culture in a way his own parents, with a deeper Scottish identity and their provincial roots in Yorkshire and Leicester, had not.

The Millars were a distinctive Labour type: civilised, decent, politically active in North London. The existence of people like them was one of the primary reasons that Labour survived as a political party during the convulsions of the early 1980s. They had nothing to do with the arid and destructive infighting of the period, belonging to an older, wiser, more profound and warmer version of socialism.

Audrey Millar, Fiona's mother, still works most days for the Labour Party.

11. Callan is a skilled raconteur and it is possible that this story might have grown with the telling. He swears to its absolute veracity, however.

She is a living link back to Labour's heroic period, when it was still establishing itself as a mass political party. Frank Field, the Liverpool MP who is a family friend, says of her: 'She is the last of that generation of women who would now have become doctors, lawyers or accountants. But the world was different then and she has devoted herself to voluntary work.'

As a young girl she was a secretary to G. D. H. Cole, the great Labour Party thinker and historian. She worked for a while in the House of Commons and for the Cooperative Movement. According to Bob Edwards – another family friend: the Edwardses and the Millars once took a holiday together in Spain, chugging down to Barcelona together in an aged Triumph Mayflower – she met her husband Bob Millar at Ruskin, the progressive Oxford college which has been responsible for the education of so many trade unionists and Labour politicians. Everyone who knows them says that it was a happy and successful marriage. When Bob Millar died, Alastair Campbell wrote a passionate tribute to him for *Tribune*.[12] Audrey Millar is nowadays to be found regularly in her daughter's North London home, a vital cog in the complex domestic machinery that keeps the show on the road for Alastair, Fiona and their three children.

Bob Millar was one of those extremely rare people for whom no one has a bad word. A very brave man, he served in the RAF during the war. His close friend Wilfred Greatorex, the television scriptwriter, recalls: 'He was a bomber pilot and as a sergeant he had a flight lieutenant as a co-pilot. In the air he was supposed to give him orders and on the ground he was supposed to salute him. I asked him if he did salute him on the ground and he said he'd be buggered if he did.' Upon his return to civilian life, he was a member of that idealistic and confident generation of political activists that rebuilt Britain along socialist lines. For a number of years Millar worked for *Tribune*. Like many *Tribune* writers – Bob Edwards and Michael Foot are prominent examples – he was in due course snapped up by Lord Beaverbrook, the legendary proprietor of Express Newspapers. Beaverbrook took a peculiar and specific pleasure in capturing leading writers on the left and moulding them for his own purposes.

Millar may have gone to work for a right-wing newspaper empire, but he never lost his Labour principles. He and Audrey, members of the close-knit North London Labour squirearchy, knew everyone who was anyone in the movement, and were particularly close to Michael Foot, a near neighbour, and the visionary Aneurin Bevan, founder of the National Health Service. For the

12. *Tribune*, 1 July 1994.

young, raw, drunken Alastair Campbell the Millars were a revelation. Meeting them was a salutary reminder of something that he had at least partly forgotten since leaving his parents' home six years before: that there was more to life than sex, football, pubs, bagpipes and tabloid stitch-ups.

Millar was suspicious, as fathers of pretty girls tend to be, when Fiona first brought her boyfriend home. A number of Fleet Street journalists first became familiar with the name Alastair Campbell in the Bell public house, just across the road from the old *Express* building in Fleet Street. At around eleven most mornings Millar was inclined to drop into the Bell, often in company with the film critic Ian Christie, for many years a close friend and colleague. The two of them would drink White Shield Worthington, a live beer with sediment in it. There was a brief period, in the very early 1980s, when Bob Millar was prone to confide to fellow drinkers at the Bell his disquiet about 'this strange man who was seeing his daughter, who played the bagpipes.'[13]

This period soon passed, and suspicion was replaced by the warmest of friendships. Wilfred Greatorex recalls: 'Bob talked endlessly and Alastair just sat at his feet and learnt.' Campbell could not have hoped for a better teacher. The future No. 10 Press Secretary became so devoted to Fiona's father that he actually took up bowls, the sport to which Millar devoted his declining years, in order to see even more of him.

Campbell came to politics at a very late age. Now in his early 40s indisputably one of the three or four most powerful men in the land, the individual upon whom the Prime Minister leans on more than any other for guidance and advice did not have a political thought of any consequence whatever until he was approaching the age of thirty. Till he came across the Millar family, he knew nothing of politics. He stood on the left, but in an ill-defined way. His political philosophy was pitiful: a kind of incoherent, inchoate, anti-establishment, half-formed anarchism. This is extraordinary for a man with such a brilliantly intuitive sense of how power works and which levers need to be pulled. Meeting the Millars when and in the way he did was a remarkable piece of good fortune. It meant when he finally did learn about politics, it was not the half-baked, hard-left nonsense that was fashionable in the student halls and constituency parties at the time. He learnt about the Labour Party over the dinner tables of Hampstead, with companions of the calibre of Robert and

13. Alan Cochrane, now of the *Daily Telegraph*, was one of those to whom Millar expressed his worries. 'At first I think he was slightly alarmed,' says Cochrane. 'Then I think he was just amused by it all.'

Audrey Millar or Michael Foot and his wife Jill Craigie. He could not have had a more privileged introduction to the Labour Party.

Since that time in the early 1980s, a number of famous and powerful men have loomed large in Campbell's life and helped to form his character. Among them can be counted Neil Kinnock, Robert Maxwell and Tony Blair. None of them was half as important for Campbell as that softly spoken and widely-loved journalist Bob Millar.

Political correspondent

It was partly the influence of Bob Millar that caused Campbell to take his first steps towards political journalism. But Campbell is likely to have made the move anyway. He would have become aware soon after arriving at the *Mirror* that lobby journalists are an élite. The political editor of a national newspaper is a powerful figure. He has direct access to his editor, and very often to the proprietor as well. On many papers he can, and frequently does, pull rank on the news editor. His relationship with the other sections of his paper is very similar to Downing Street's relationship with the rest of Whitehall. An effective political editor has the capacity to move in on practically any story he likes, on the grounds that it has entered the realm of national politics, often to the intense resentment of specialist staff and ordinary reporters. All of this would have been quite enough to draw Campbell, with his acute antennae for power, towards the lobby even if he were not belatedly beginning to take an intelligent interest in national politics.

After his first eighteen months as a general reporter it began to be obvious to anyone who knew Campbell that his inclinations lay in that direction. He started to visit the Commons and cultivate political correspondents. Colleagues remember him hanging round the Press Gallery in the Commons, getting drunk at the Press Bar, always with a Marlboro cigarette in his mouth. He started to travel up to party conferences as a news reporter and get to know politicians as best he could. Wilfred Greatorex remembers being surprised when Campbell turned up uninvited at a private lunch at County Hall hosted by Illtyd Harrington, then deputy leader of the Labour group on the GLC. The episode shows how eager he was to get onto the political scene around this time.

Gradually Campbell was managing to get more Westminster-based stories into the papers. For a period the Tory MP Harry Greenway was Campbell's best – or at any rate most visible – contact. He was one of the few MPs who would give the unknown young reporter the time of day. The two spoke regularly and Greenway still recalls him warmly. 'We had an easy relationship,' remembers the Ealing North MP. 'In his early days he was interested in people who had some character. He was very friendly. I was helpful. It would be wrong to say I took him under my wing because he wasn't the sort of chap who needed that.' Greenway, a popular back-bencher who lost his seat in the 1997 landslide, was renowned as much for the quantity as for the quality of his public pronouncements. His unfailingly populist observations formed useful ballast in Campbell copy. On one glorious occasion the obscure Tory MP even provided him with a coveted front-page story. When it was announced in October 1985 that the Princess of Wales's second son was to be christened Henry, Greenway weighed in with a ringing call for the baby Prince to be known as Harry. 'Henry is too turgid a name for a prince with such exciting parents,' proclaimed the MP, 'Harry is a dashing, robust name which is in tune with the 1980s.'[14] The *Mirror*/Greenway campaign met with instant success. Later on, Harry Greenway was puzzled when Campbell dropped him like a stone. 'I suppose he had more important fish to fry,' he now says, with perfect accuracy and not an ounce of resentment.

He did indeed. It is absolutely typical of Alastair Campbell that within months of setting out to become a political journalist he hooked one of the biggest fish in the sea – Neil Kinnock. The two men met properly for the first time at a *Mirror*-sponsored event. The editor, Mike Molloy, had the idea of inviting the extended Kinnock family – uncles, aunts, nephews, nieces, grandparents, second cousins, the lot – to central London for a family photograph. Molloy hoped that its publication would give the Labour leader a more homely and family-friendly image. He even planned to run a series on the Kinnock extended family around the theme of 'people like us.'[15] The project was a logistical nightmare and a number of reporters were ordered to act as minders for the seventy or so Kinnocks who turned up for this unique occasion. One of them was Campbell. He performed his demanding task with enterprise, humour, tact and loving attention to detail. By the end of it all he was firm friends with every single one of the Kinnock clan, and above all Neil and Glenys. In the words of a colleague on the *Mirror*: 'Alastair fell in love with the Kinnocks. Head over

14. 'Call Him Harry!', *Daily Mirror*, 1 October 1985. Greenway's intervention upset another Tory MP, Henry Bellingham. 'I am very disappointed that people have taken to calling Henry Harry,' he told Campbell. 'Henry, historically speaking, is a regal name, with eight monarchs of that name behind us.'

15. 'We wanted to show what an ordinary family the Kinnocks were,' remembers Molloy. 'There was a great range of ordinary working-class people. They all took a shine to Alastair.' Molloy left the paper shortly afterwards, and his idea was never properly followed up.

heels, bowled over. Besotted.' It was the beginning of a partnership that was to be broken only with Labour's defeat in the 1992 General Election.

It speaks volumes for the sheer force and conviction of Campbell's personality that it imprinted itself so deeply and so quickly on the Labour leader, a busy and important man whose time was heavily in demand. Campbell was a nonentity, a junior reporter of some talent but no standing, with no real political knowledge or experience, not even a member of the parliamentary lobby. And yet everyone who knew Campbell at the time accepts that this was the moment when his friendship with Neil Kinnock was forged.

For Campbell the benefits from the association were immense. In any newspaper the establishment of a direct, personal link to the Leader of the Opposition is a valuable commodity. At the *Mirror*, the flagship of the British left, it was priceless. Campbell's status within the paper doubled overnight: it became inevitable that he would join the lobby. The road that would take him to the political editorship had suddenly become clear. But Kinnock's own attachment to this young, raw, drunken reporter remains hard to fathom. The Labour leader already possessed a wide and amusing circle of friends, as well as plenty of sycophants. The truth can only be that something about Campbell has a hypnotic effect on very powerful men. What is certain is that from their very first meeting in the mid-1980s, Neil and Glenys Kinnock drew Alastair Campbell and his girlfriend Fiona Millar into the very centre of their lives.

The appointment as lobby reporter duly came in the summer of 1985. The political editor, Joe Haines, opposed it. He says that he wanted a woman reporter in his team.[16] That may well have been so. It would also have been natural if Haines was reluctant to employ someone who had a warmer relationship with the Labour leader than he did. His objections, such as they were, carried no weight. Haines was swiftly overruled and Campbell made the switch from Holborn Circus to work out of the cramped *Mirror* office in the Press Gallery in Westminster. He was not to stay there long.

Breakdown

Campbell's decision to accept a job offer from *Today* newspaper in the autumn of 1985 now looks like the first indication of his impending mental breakdown. The move was partly attributable to his frustration at Robert Maxwell's method

16. Haines wanted either Catherine O'Brien, now of the *Daily Telegraph*, or Rosemary Collins, today deputy editor of the *Sunday Times Magazine*, to fill the vacant post.

of running the *Mirror*; he and Merritt were both disturbed by the way the tycoon continually thrust his views and personality onto the pages; they thought he was turning the paper into a joke. Even so, the move was in no sense rational. Campbell was one of the most highly valued young reporters on the *Mirror*. He had just been given one of the most prized jobs on the paper. His prospects were assured. Eddie Shah's *Today* was a bold venture which, though a failure, has an honourable place in Fleet Street history. It brought desperately needed new technology to the newspaper industry and smashed through the labour practices that had hobbled it since the war. And yet it required no great insight to perceive, even at the time, that *Today* was fatally flawed by inadequate management and shortage of capital and that it was at best a highly uncertain prospect. Campbell was jumping off the first-class compartment of an ocean-going liner and choosing instead to bunk down with the crew on a leaky tramp steamer. His readiness to leave the Labour-backing *Mirror* to join the anti-union *Today* is an interesting commentary on the strength of his left-wing views at the time.

Many of his friends tried to dissuade him. Richard Stott, his patron at the *Mirror*, did his best.[17] Joe Haines, despite his initial reluctance to take Campbell on board, went to extreme lengths to keep him. 'He came into the office in the evening,' recalls Haines, 'and said that he had been offered a job on *Today*. I didn't want to lose him. When I asked him why he was going he said he was worried whether he would keep his job under Maxwell. So I went over to see Maxwell who said: "You can assure him his job is safe." By the time I got back Alastair told me he had resigned. I was not pleased. Nor was Richard Stott. I told him that he was not ready to undertake any executive job on any paper, particularly not a new paper, with the stresses and tensions that involves.' There is some confusion today – it may very well be that this reflects confusion at the time – about exactly what role Campbell performed at *Today*.[18] One of the attractions for the ambitious young reporter may have been the prospect of an executive position and the chance to boss others around rather than remain on the receiving end of other people's whims. Doubtless he was flattered to be heavily wooed by another paper for the first time. It is certain that a large salary increase would have formed part of the attraction. Even so, his decision to leave the *Mirror* for such a flaky outfit strongly suggests that his judgement had entirely deserted him.

17. According to Haines.

18. Sue Cameron, political editor of the new paper, recalls interviewing Campbell for a post in her political team. On the other hand, others recall working under him as news editor on *Sunday Today*. It seems that he changed jobs at least once while at the paper.

The paper was a shambles. Nobody knew who was doing what. The launch date was frequently put back. Just opposite the *Today* offices in the Vauxhall Bridge Road was a pub called the Lord High Admiral. It was gloomy, with a painted wood panel ceiling and heavily stained black panelling. It was very dark inside, and the enormous block of flats directly above it added to the already strong sense of oppression. Not surprisingly, very few people visited the place. Campbell promptly colonised the pub, surrounding himself with boon companions. He started going there early in the day, and would return to top up at regular intervals. Once Fiona Millar stormed into the pub, seized Campbell by the scruff of the neck, and dragged him away.

On his desk in the office, which he visited from time to time, carefully placed in a position of honour, was a photograph of Neil Kinnock. He would often admire it ostentatiously. In the absence of a newspaper, there was nothing much to do. There was a limit to the number of dummy copies that could be brought out. For most journalists this was merely an irritant. It gave them extra time to write novels, conduct love affairs, above all drink in pubs. For Campbell, however, the lack of structure in his day was a problem. He insisted on inventing meaningless little tasks for himself. At one point he developed an obsession with Dean Reed, a mysterious American pop-star who had failed in his own country but thanks to some peculiar chemistry turned into a celebrity in the Soviet Union. Campbell would bang on endlessly about Dean Reed in the Lord High Admiral, where fellow drinkers tolerantly viewed his latest enthusiasm as a sign of originality. 'I would have thought that this Dean Reed was a bit of a sad bloke but Alastair was really passionate about him in an almost boy-scoutish sort of way,' recalls a colleague. 'He wanted to know everything about him. Were the KGB after him? Did the CIA want to bump him off? He was planning to take flights to all sorts of weird places to track him down.' Close friends say that he came to believe that British intelligence – thought to have an office in the vicinity – was spying on him and drilling radio waves into his head. One reporter claims that he developed an unusual and striking habit when turning corners. By now Campbell had come to feel his allegiance to the Labour Party so strongly that he felt that it would be disloyal to turn right on any level. So rather than make a simple right turn, he is said to have insisted on making three left turns in order to achieve the same effect before proceeding on his way. On one occasion, very close to his final breakdown, he made his way back to his old stamping ground, the Stab-in-the-Back. He stood at the door, sizing everyone up, muttering incomprehensibly to himself. After a while he made an attempt to advance towards the bar, but an innocent drinker got in his way. Campbell thrust him aside. Shortly after that he left the pub, just as suddenly and mysteriously as he had arrived.

Not surprisingly, things were starting to degenerate in the office, especially after Campbell was given the task of news editor for the Sunday edition. Reporters remember him wandering round with a large notepad issuing incoherent instructions. 'You didn't know if he was telling you what to do or just talking to himself. He would come over, mutter something, then wander away. He was absolutely useless,' remembers one *Today* journalist. 'He was positively the most incompetent newspaper executive that I have ever come across.[19] And he obviously knew it.'[20]

The end of this distressing phase in Campbell's life finally came around the time when he travelled up to Scotland to cover the Labour Spring Conference in March 1986. By this stage it was becoming increasingly difficult to dismiss his behaviour as eccentric: it had become downright peculiar. Julia Langdon, then a senior member of the *Mirror* political staff, recalls walking through Perth on the eve of the conference with Geoffrey Parkhouse, the political editor of the *Glasgow Herald*. In due course they reached the Conference Centre. There they found Campbell just outside the building, involved in a heated altercation with a policeman. Campbell was loudly and abusively demanding instructions to the Centre, and refusing to believe the policeman's repeated assurances that it was just a few feet away. Eventually Campbell spotted Langdon and Parkhouse: he greeted them like long-lost friends. He aimed one last parting shot at the hapless policemen, scathingly informing him: 'It's all right. Don't worry. They'll tell me where it is.'

The three journalists went off to a wine bar to eat some lunch, Campbell talking obsessively about Neil Kinnock. He was in Scotland, he told Langdon and Parkhouse, to write an account of a week in the life of the Labour leader. (Here is a clear sign of the shambles that *Today* had already become even before a copy had been sold. At the time Campbell was a news editor. The job of a news editor is to stay at his desk making decisions and handing out instructions, never to set out on jaunts of his own.) Several bottles later the three returned to the Conference Centre. Campbell was not allowed in. It became apparent that he had failed, once again, to provide himself with press

19. This is a very strong statement: it is a crowded and highly competitive field.

20. As always, Campbell is happy to acknowledge past failures in his personal and professional life. He told Roy Hattersley: 'I was flattered into doing a job which I shouldn't have taken on either professional or political grounds. It was a big tension all the time and it ended disastrously' (*Observer*, 22 February 1998).

accreditation. As the others left him at the entrance, struggling to overcome this fresh and overwhelming problem, Parkhouse muttered to Langdon: 'There is a man who is heading for a nervous breakdown.' Parkhouse was to be proved right.

Only a very few people know exactly what happened to Alastair Campbell in Scotland – his own family, Fiona Millar and some members of the Kinnock entourage. It is a testament to the affection which Campbell inspires that none of them has since talked about the details in an indiscreet way.[21]

A decade and a half later there are various accounts of where the catastrophe occurred: a hotel foyer in Glasgow, a shipyard on the Clyde, and the banks of a Scottish loch have all been cited as the scene of the dénouement. There appears to have been a function involving the Labour leader from which officialdom endeavoured to exclude Campbell, either on the grounds that he was not invited or on the basis that he was drunk, or very possibly both. This rebuff hit Campbell hard. All accounts agree that he started to behave very strangely indeed. Roy Hattersley is one of the few writers who have discussed the breakdown with Campbell himself. The version of events that he gives, in his exemplary 1998 *Observer* profile, goes as follows: 'He was on his way to interview Neil Kinnock in Scotland when the crack-up came. His editor says that he "suddenly lost contact." Campbell was out of touch with more than his paper. Without knowing how he lost consciousness, he woke up in hospital.'

One colleague remembers the reaction among fellow journalists as the news filtered back to London. After brief initial obligatory expressions of sympathy and concern, Campbell's prospects were swiftly written off. 'We all thought: That's it. He's nothing in this business anymore, unemployable. We all thought that he would never work again.' There was nothing personal or vengeful in this assessment: it was the dispassionate view formed by fellow professionals who had seen the same thing happen to colleagues many times before.

21. I have made no attempt to ask them to do so.

Chapter Five

SERVING KINNOCK AND MAXWELL

The whole world's against me. People are out to destroy me.
Robert Maxwell to Alastair Campbell, Brighton, 1991

Campbell was off work for about six months. After a spell in hospital he spent some time recuperating, part of it at the quiet and pleasant country home of Sid Young, a former *Mirror* colleague.[1] His friends rallied round. Years later, at his friend John Merritt's memorial service in St Bride's, Fleet Street, he recalled Merritt coming to visit him while he was still in hospital. Merritt was clutching a handful of marbles. He handed them to Campbell with the words: 'Here are your marbles back. Now don't lose them again.' There are those who still shake their head and wonder how Campbell got to the end of that address.

Today seems to have looked after him in exemplary fashion, making sure that he got proper medical treatment, that he remained on the staff, and that he was put under no special pressure to return to work. But when Campbell was finally fit enough to cope, he chose to go back to the *Mirror*. It is easy to see why. The *Mirror* was his real home and he returned to Holborn Circus in the same spirit that a wounded animal returns to its lair in order to lick its wounds. He asked a friend to make a discreet approach to Richard Stott, by now *Mirror* editor, to see if he would be welcome back. When a positive reply came Campbell jumped at the chance. No one at *Today* ever expressed the slightest resentment that the employee it nursed so generously and well while he was distressed should have abandoned the paper the moment he was fit to return to work.

The first thing that colleagues noticed was that Campbell had changed physically. Gone was the large, confident presence of his first few years in Fleet Street. He had shrunk. He no longer drank. He was thinner, paler, more self-effacing in manner. One old drinking friend remembers meeting up with Campbell and Fiona Millar shortly after he returned to Fleet Street. He recalls: 'Ali had those staring eyes and a hunted look. He was desperately on edge. One

1. In the spring of 1999 Campbell attended Sid Young's leaving party from the *Mirror*, a sign that he had not forgotten his friend's kindness, for he attended very few such events.

feared for him. He knew he had come within an ace of losing it. I looked at Fiona and thought: thank God nurse is there.' It would take him more than a year to regain the dominant, abundant personality that had been so attractive before the breakdown. But it did return. Those who knew him in his early days say that he has become very much the same imposing figure as before. This suggests that the brilliant figure at the Stab-in-the-Back was the genuine Campbell, not some artificial, drink-driven invention.

Campbell threw himself into teetotalism with the same manic enthusiasm that he had once devoted to alcohol. This made him very boring indeed. His old drinking companions recall with distaste how he would take them aside and lecture them about the dangers of strong drink. One reporter remembers Campbell trying – unsuccessfully – to wrestle his pint of beer out of his hand. Paul Callan says that Campbell wandered round the Stab-in-the-Back distributing temperance literature. This was too much even for Fiona, who told Callan: 'I wish you could persuade him to go back on the booze. He's such a pain when he's not drinking.' It is clear that Campbell believed alcohol was the cause of his breakdown, and was endeavouring to save others from the same fate. It may have been important for Campbell to believe that alcohol was the primary cause of his troubles, but it was not entirely true. No one who knew Campbell well before the episode in Scotland thinks that he was an alcoholic. He drank heavily, but there was nothing exceptional about it and no suggestion that he was addicted. Lindsay Merritt, who was as close to him as anybody, states that he drank 'no more than any other young journalist with an expense account.'[2] Others say the same. There is no evidence that he used the secret tricks and devices that real alcoholics are forced to resort to. Campbell was certainly a binge drinker, and giving up drink was the crucial step in helping him get to grips with his problem. But drink was only a part of the problem itself.[3] Campbell's nervous breakdown was brought about as much by his inability to

2. *Observer*, 22 February 1998.

3. Nine years after his breakdown, Campbell talked to Helena de Bertodano about giving up drink (*Sunday Telegraph*, 19 March 1995). He told her: 'I don't think I ever was an alcoholic but the doctor asked me to talk him through a day. So I picked Tuesday, two days earlier, and as I went through the list, it dawned on me that it was a huge amount.' Bertodano asked him how much. Campbell replied: 'Fifteen pints of beer, half a bottle of Scotch, four bottles of wine with David Mellor at lunch.' This quotation has been widely repeated. It deserves examination. First, even Oliver Reed at the height of his powers would have been pushed to cope with those prodigious quantities. Second, Campbell is unlikely to have known Mellor in the days when he drank. Later, when he was an established lobby correspondent, the two men are more likely to have lunched together; they got on well, discovering a common interest in football. But by then Campbell, who liked to taunt Mellor over his occasional switches of footballing affiliation, was on a diet of orange juice.

cope with the demands of his new job at *Today* as by alcohol. To speculate about its deeper nature and causes would be impertinent as well as unrewarding.

Many people who undergo the kind of calamity Campbell suffered in the spring and summer of 1986 never fully recover. They remain haunted, torn in two, in some cases almost literally a shadow of their former selves. With Campbell the opposite was the case. It is as if the breakdown enabled him to solve a mysterious conundrum in his nature, some personal roadblock that prevented him from making headway with his life. From the moment that Campbell returned to work in late 1986, the course of his life became very different. It was no longer the story of a charming, unsettled, itinerant rogue. There was a new steel in his character. It would be entirely wrong to state that before 1986 Campbell was without personal ambition. But it was unfocussed. The fights, the boozing, the pornography, those long railway journeys to Burnley Football Club – all spoke of a desperate and almost suicidal lack of direction. From the end of 1986 there was a cool and precise sense of purpose about the man. He knew exactly where he wanted to go and who he wanted to become. His breakdown turned out in the end to be the springboard for one of the most meteoric rises that Fleet Street has ever seen.

One happy development gave Campbell a new stability and provided a rich source of happiness in his life. In the late 1980s he and Fiona Millar at last set about rearing a family. The birth of their eldest son Rory was followed two years later by Calum, and a few years on, by a daughter, Grace.

Fiona Millar to some extent put her career on hold when the children started to arrive. She had gone straight to the *Daily Express* at the end of the *Mirror* training scheme in 1982. Four years later Paul Potts, then political editor and today Editor of the Press Association, had picked her out to join his team of Westminster reporters. He remembers her as 'hard-working and committed.' There is no doubt in Potts' mind that she would have become a political editor herself if she had wanted to. Potts says that Fiona, though known to be a socialist, was 'professional about the *Express* agenda' at a time when it was trumpeting Thatcherite opinions. Fiona continued to do frequent work for the *Express* on a freelance basis after handing in her notice in 1988. She also profiled MPs for *The House* magazine.

Sunday Mirror political editor

Joe Haines wanted Campbell back on the political desk. But he says that Stott insisted that Campbell must work his passage back and gave him a general reporting job. It cannot have lasted very long.[4] Within a few weeks Campbell had been found a safe billet as deputy to Victor Knight, the veteran political editor of the *Sunday Mirror*. Knight, a respected and knowledgeable political correspondent of the old school, took Campbell under his wing. But he was distracted by domestic tragedy. His wife was ill, and his own health was beginning to fail. Within a year of Campbell's arrival Knight had taken early retirement, prelude to an early death. Always punctilious in such matters, Campbell arranged Victor Knight's memorial service at St Bride's. Knight's family is still grateful to him for putting on a magnificent show. Campbell ensured that the bulk of the British political establishment came to pay their respects to a much-loved figure. James Callaghan was the most senior Labour figure present. Edward Heath, Willie Whitelaw and Francis Pym came for the Tories. Bernard Ingham, Campbell's renowned predecessor as Downing Street Press Secretary, gave a reading from the Book of Proverbs. An account of how the passage in question – highly subversive in the context of the late 1980s – provoked a most unstatesmanlike fit of the giggles from Heath and Whitelaw forms the concluding section in Robert Harris's fine book on Margaret Thatcher's loyal adviser: 'Exalt her, and she shall promote thee: she shall bring thee to honour when thou dost embrace her. She shall give to thine head an ornament of grace; a crown of glory shall she deliver to thee.' Victor Knight's surviving family remain under the impression that Campbell chose this biblical reading. They do not mind a bit.[5]

Campbell was formally appointed political editor of the *Sunday Mirror*, rather sooner than anyone intended, in the autumn of 1987. It was a job that he used, with brilliant effect, as a stepping-stone on the way to the cherished and far more important position of political editor of the *Daily Mirror* only two years later. He was regarded as an outstanding success. Judged by any conventional measure of political journalism, this success simply cannot be explained.

The political editor of a Sunday newspaper has two primary functions. First in order of importance is the provision of fresh, exciting, tasty political exclusives. Any political editor who fails to provide a story which makes a worthy candidate for a front-page splash by the close of play on Friday evening is likely to receive a frosty glance from his editor. If he fails to do so for three or

4. A careful search failed to find any *Daily Mirror* cuttings by Campbell on the news pages in late 1986. The first tangible sign that he has returned to work comes in the *Sunday Mirror*, where he becomes visible as a political reporter towards the end of the year.

5. Victor Knight's son Keir has nothing but good to say of Campbell, who was a frequent visitor to his father's home in the late 1980s.

four weeks in a row the atmosphere is likely to turn icy. Any further dereliction of duty and he is in danger of being invited to an 'interview without coffee'.

During the full eighteen-month period that Campbell was political reporter or political editor at the *Sunday Mirror* he provided just one front-page story. It was a worthy item about the dangers of passive smoking, not something that was going to set Westminster alight.[6] Not only was his presence on page 1 negligible but his page 2 offerings were paltry things, effectively dressed up press releases of the kind that Gordon Brown, the latest rising star on the Labour benches, was already beginning to hawk around town with fatiguing regularity. Campbell supplied a ready market for Brown's shop-soiled commodities: he might not have any decent stories of his own but he could normally guarantee a home for whatever piece of pap the Labour machine was pumping out for weekend consumption.

The second – and subsidiary – function of a political editor is the provision of crisp, well-informed analysis about the week in Westminster. Campbell was provided with the ideal vehicle. His still youthful features beamed out from above a weekly column, given plenty of space, a prominent position on page 6 in the paper,[7] and the imposing heading of 'People, Politics & Power'. Admittedly, few political columns improve when they are reread years later: the self-regarding tendency of well-known journalists to publish collected editions of their daily writing is absurd. Nevertheless, it is fair to say that Campbell's column in the *Sunday Mirror* was unusually poor. It was almost entirely lacking in insight or information, the jokes were weak: it can only be classified as vinegary Labour propaganda.

The reasons for Campbell's failure as a story-getter are not hard to find. He knew hardly any Tories, an omission he was later to remedy but which at this stage of his career prevented him from delivering hard-hitting scoops about the government of the day. His contacts with the Labour Party, by contrast, were good. The trouble is that they were too good. There is every reason to believe that Campbell knew a great deal that was going on in the Kinnock camp. Making use of such information, however, would have killed off the access that enabled him to obtain it in the first place. Campbell had allowed himself to become too close to the subject he was writing about: a debilitating state and an age-old danger in any kind of journalism.

6. Alastair Campbell and Steve Bailey, 'Babies in New Smoking Peril', *Sunday Mirror*, 14 February 1988. Campbell also filed a report on the Bush/Gorbachev summit in December 1989 which made the front page of the *Sunday Mirror*. But by then Campbell's prime responsibility was the *Daily Mirror*.

7. Sometimes the column made its way as far forward as page 4.

His failure as a columnist is more complex and more interesting. There is no doubting Campbell's credentials as a writer. He had already proved himself as a capable tabloid reporter, and had easily mastered the lubricious, cold-hearted argot of soft porn. In years to come he would prove himself as a speech-writer. He would make himself indispensable to Neil Kinnock and Tony Blair by ghosting their newspaper articles. Even today Cabinet ministers marvel at Campbell's facility for turning a complex argument that has baffled Whitehall's finest brains into a form of words that even the meanest intelligence can understand. His speed of delivery is equally impressive. During the long prelude to the 1997 General Election he would often dash off a thousand-word leading article on behalf of Tony Blair in an hour or, if the need was urgent, even less. The copy was invariably flawless, the message exact, the style precisely tailored to the intended audience, the professionalism awesome.

Not so with Campbell the columnist. Columnists must possess a sense of mischief, a relish in the play of ideas, and a mastery of the texture and the rhythms of the English language. They also need to make an impact of personal presence on the printed page. It was asking far too much of Campbell, at the age of thirty, to possess all these qualities. What is so striking is that he possessed none of them.

His writing, while competent and to the point, is barren of texture. He possesses an unmistakable genius for the compelling tabloid phrase, as he proved years later when in the early hours of 31 August 1997 he conjured up the words 'people's princess' in the wake of Princess Diana's death.[8] But he has no real feel for the English language. His range of reference is hopelessly limited. He displays no knowledge of history, ideas or literature. Metaphors are drawn, to a monotonous extent, from the football field. What is most puzzling of all is that Campbell's massive, complicated personality fails to communicate itself to the reader.

Something strange is at work here. Campbell the writer is most effective when he adopts an idiom: whether it is the arid formulae of tabloid news-reporting or the shrill platitudes of the press release. He is happiest of all when he surrenders his identity and allows it to be absorbed into that of someone else: converts himself into his political master of the moment for the purposes of a speech or a newspaper piece. If Campbell had been a painter and not a writer,

8. Julie Burchill was the first to use the phrase in print while Princess Diana was still alive. But it still took flair to launch the phrase into universal use.

he would have been an adequate but unoriginal artist. But he would have been a master forger. That is where his true gift lies.

Given Campbell's astonishing failure to provide a single decent front-page story in the entire period that he was political editor of the *Sunday Mirror*, it is well worth asking how he survived at all and what he can possibly have done to deserve promotion so quickly to a bigger job on the *Daily Mirror*. Part of the answer lies in the fact that Campbell was an office politician of rare talent. By now Bob Edwards had finally been dispatched as editor of the *Sunday Mirror*. His replacement, Eve Pollard, doted on Campbell, luxuriating in the urbane charm which he was quite capable of laying on when circumstances demanded it. When Campbell gave up being political editor he was succeeded by a talented journalist called Peter MacMahon, who found handling Pollard a fraught affair. After one particularly sticky session, he retreated to the Stab-in-the-Back with the paper's chief sub-editor, a man called Andy Howell. MacMahon asked Howell what quality Campbell had possessed that he lacked. Back came the reply from the chief sub: 'Alastair always gave Eve the impression that he wanted to slip her one but was too busy at just that particular moment. And it worked.'[9]

From journalism to politics

But dealing with a temperamental female editor was child's play as far as Alastair Campbell was concerned. He was playing a far bigger game. Well before the end of 1987 he had renounced the trade of journalism, at any rate as it is commonly understood by those who practise it, and turned to something which he found very much more exhilarating: power politics. There are two keys to Campbell's professional success between 1987 and the beginning of 1992. One of them is Neil Kinnock and other is Robert Maxwell, the proprietor of Mirror Group Newspapers. They both needed him almost as much as he needed them.

It is impossible to exaggerate the closeness of the friendship that developed between Alastair Campbell and Neil Kinnock during this period. They had struck up a warm friendship before Campbell's breakdown. It was twice as close afterwards. It would be reasonable to imagine that the victim of the kind of crisis that Campbell had endured would feel a strong reciprocal obligation to

9. This world-class observation was first quoted, unattributed, by Kevin Toolis in the *Guardian* (4 April 1998). It is only proper that its original source should gain the public recognition he deserves.

those who had bailed him out. And Campbell did feel a sense of gratitude. But his benefactors were even more strongly tied to him. The Labour leader had got emotionally drawn into the drama, and liked to imagine that he had played some part in salvaging Campbell from the wreckage. The tale still goes the rounds of how Kinnock came across a drunken Campbell, seized him by the scruff of the neck, and gave him a dramatic warning about the perils of drinking. The account may be true, but cannot be entirely relied upon. The former Labour leader has an engaging reputation for never spoiling a good story for the sake of the truth. It was Kinnock, for example, who claims to have first put about the apocryphal story about how Peter Mandelson mistook a bowl of mushy peas in a chip shop in his Hartlepool constituency for guacamole.[10]

To understand Neil Kinnock in 1987, it is helpful to conjure up the situation of William Hague today. Kinnock is much the warmer, more passionate and emotional individual: therefore more exposed and vulnerable. There is an awesome and slightly chilling detachment about Hague which enables him to emerge from his many rebuffs and humiliations personally unscathed. This was not so with Kinnock, whose leadership of Labour was spent veering between the depths of despair and the heights of elation. The emotional make-up of the two party leaders may have been radically at odds, but their political circumstances were strikingly similar. Kinnock in the late 1980s and Hague in the late 1990s were not merely at the head of unpopular political parties: they themselves were the objects of constant ridicule and vilification. Every speech Kinnock made, every decision he took, was systematically and as a matter of course distorted by the Tory-controlled press.[11] Ten years later Hague finds himself in a similar predicament. But Neil Kinnock felt it harder. It struck home personally and he was open to a new member of his inner circle, a journalist who was ready to offer blind, unconditional loyalty and adulation.

Campbell would do anything for the Kinnocks. He was a mixture of adviser, minder, speech-writer, family friend and manservant. Alastair Campbell – along with Fiona Millar – would babysit the children, pick up the shopping,

10. Or so Kinnock claimed when Mandelson stepped down as Labour's Director of Communications in 1991. It is of course possible that the former Labour leader was improving upon the truth on that occasion as well.

11. Charles Clarke, Neil Kinnock's chief of staff until 1992 and today a rising star in the Blair administration, recalls one telling moment early in the Kinnock period. Bob Hughes, Labour's transport spokesman, unveiled a proposal to abolish road tax and raise the same amount of money by raising petrol duties. The idea, designed to reduce car use, is commonplace today. It was met by screaming front-page headlines that Labour was doing its worst to hammer the motorist. 'Our conclusion had to be,' says Clarke, 'that there was no point in publishing anything. We had no chance of a fair hearing.'

draft a press release, give a view on the handling of a sensitive political problem. The two families went on holiday together. Years later, Campbell would travel to Wales for the funeral of Glenys's mother, while Neil Kinnock went to visit Bob Millar while he was dying in hospital.

The moment that established Campbell's new role as bruiser for the Labour leader can be dated with complete precision. It came in March 1987, a fraction over a year after his breakdown. Campbell was part of the team of political correspondents that accompanied Neil Kinnock on an ill-starred visit to Ronald Reagan at the White House. It was a highly charged time, with just months to go before the General Election. Kinnock was endeavouring to project himself as a statesman on the world stage. Anyone could have told him that this particular attempt was doomed. Denis Healey, the shadow Foreign Secretary who came with him on this visit, had strongly urged him not to go. Kinnock ignored this sensible and kindly-meant advice.[12]

The lobby pack were, as ever, after Kinnock's blood. As Robert Gibson, then the deputy political editor of the *Daily Express*, firmly notes: 'The Tory Press went on trips with Neil Kinnock for one reason only: to watch him fall flat on his arse.' During this journey the Labour leader was doing his best to make their job easy for them. His meeting with the President, unwisely billed beforehand by the Kinnock camp as a weighty discussion between two prominent figures on the world stage, was vanishingly brief.[13] Afterwards, Reagan's Press Secretary Marlin Fitzwater emerged to brief the waiting newsmen. His account of events gave the strong impression that the hapless Kinnock had been hauled over the coals by the US President over Labour's defence policy and his proposals for unilateral nuclear disarmament. It was more than enough. The boys had their story. The travelling party rushed to the phone booths to file their accounts of Kinnock's latest humiliation back to London newsdesks.

According to some of the pressmen who were on this trip, Campbell at first joined the rush. One reporter claims to have heard him filing the same line as everybody else. Later that night, Campbell pulled out at the last moment from a

12. Denis Healey, *Time of My Life* (1990), p. 534. Healey, even then an elder statesman, warned Kinnock that 'since Reagan was bound to see him only as the opponent of his dear friend Mrs Thatcher, there was no way in which he could gain by visiting the White House.' It is a sign of the shambles surrounding the journey that Healey was only brought on board at a few days' notice. President Reagan, already entering the preliminary stages of senile decay, mistook the Shadow Foreign Secretary for the British Ambassador, a man he had met on numerous previous occasions.

13. Seventeen minutes according to most accounts, though not Campbell's. He said twenty-eight, but seems to have reached this figure only by including the time Kinnock and his entourage spent hanging about the White House before meeting the President.

prearranged flight with the rest of the party to New York. Fellow lobby correspondents gained the impression that he had either been told, or decided on his
own accord, to refile a more Kinnock-friendly account of the day's events.[14]
Certainly Campbell's story which appeared in the next day's *Mirror* was more
measured, and appeared under a neutral headline: 'Kinnock and Reagan Clash
on Defence'.

In the following week's *New Statesman* Campbell published his own version
of events. This compelling article amounted to an extraordinary denunciation of
his colleagues in the parliamentary lobby. He called them 'cynical, cowardly
and corrupt' and accused them of colluding with the White House in a bid to
'stitch up' Kinnock. Ignoring the rights and wrongs of the matter – and there is
a respectable case that the lobby in this instance was doing no more than
reporting the facts – this was a commendably bold thing to do. The lobby hunts
as a pack, never more so than on overseas trips. For a reporter as junior as
Campbell to place himself at odds with such a powerful institution showed a
certain presumption, not to say foolhardiness. But Campbell had already made
his decision. He would happily continue to make use of the privileges of the
lobby and the access it provided. But in most essential respects he was from
that moment on a member of Neil Kinnock's private office. Campbell's career
as a Labour spin-doctor did not begin in 1994 when Tony Blair asked him to
become his press spokesman. It really started seven years earlier when – to all
intents and purposes – he went to work for Neil Kinnock.

The first manifestation of this new role came at the Labour leader's press
conferences. The lobby had come to regard these events as a blood-sport. There
was a regular pattern, hallowed by ancient lobby tradition. The boys would roll
up, sit at the front, kick off by chucking in a few deceptively friendly questions,
then move into full frontal attack. Campbell put a stop to that. It seems likely
that he and Kinnock would work out the most dangerous issue in advance.
Campbell would be called first, and raise it. The Labour leader would then
provide a prearranged answer. 'The sting would have been drawn,' one
prominent member of the Thatcherite press moans today, with real sadness and
more than a hint of resentment, as if a favourite toy had been plucked away.
'The tough question would have been asked. The issue would have been dealt
with more neatly than would otherwise have been the case. And we couldn't

14. The account given by Campbell in the *New Statesman* (3 April 1987) suggests that he was originally taken in by the White House spin but changed his tune after a briefing from Kinnock's aide Pat
Hewitt.

really accuse Alastair of being Kinnock's poodle, because he'd asked a hard question.'

Campbell was not merely useful in defensive operations of this sort. He was an invaluable weapon in hostile terrain, where he could be used with brilliant effect to harry the Conservatives. At by-elections he worked in a team of three with two other Tory-tormentors, Vincent Hanna of the BBC and Tony Bevins of the *Independent*. Hanna and Bevins would devote hours working out how to flummox whoever the Tory candidate happened to be – normally not that difficult an operation – and staging stunts designed to show him up in an unfortunate light. The Tory machine, formidable though it was in some ways, had nothing to match the Hanna–Bevins–Campbell troika. Campbell tended to remain one step back from offensive operations, but played an important role in strategy and media advice to the Labour candidate. Many journalists and others assumed from Campbell's behaviour during this period that he was actually working for the Labour Party in an official capacity. The veteran political columnist Alan Watkins is merely the most distinguished in a large number of observers who persist in the belief that Campbell was a Labour Party official in the 1980s.[15] There was every excuse for this belief. Campbell did not merely help out Neil Kinnock and kick the Tories wherever he could. He took especial pleasure from berating pro-Tory journalists. His verbal bullying was invariably accompanied by the threat of violence, always implicit and in some cases openly stated. There are numerous examples.

Liz Lightfoot, now the education correspondent of the *Daily Telegraph*, remembers being abused by Campbell after she filed an anti-Kinnock story for the *Mail on Sunday* during the 1987 General Election. The campaign bus had been following Kinnock on a trip to Wales. The day was carefully arranged by the Kinnock machine so that nothing could go wrong. Nothing did, till Kinnock lost his cool when questioned by the Press Association about some verbal atrocity that Ken Livingstone had recently committed. So Lightfoot – then going out with a Labour candidate and by no stretch of the imagination a Tory stooge – sent a story about how Labour's careful stage management was ruffled when Kinnock lost his temper. It was mild stuff by the standards of the day. Nevertheless, Campbell started to shout at Lightfoot and try to intimidate her. 'That's complete rubbish and totally untrue,' he screamed. 'You shouldn't be

15. Paul Potts, then political editor of the *Express* and now Editor of the Press Association, is another senior journalist who formed the indelible impression that Campbell actually went to work for the Labour machine. He never did so.

filing that.' Somewhat upset, Lightfoot told the *Mail on Sunday* political editor Alan Cochrane about the episode. He raised it with Campbell, who shrugged it off.[16]

On one occasion, when Kinnock was facing heavy flak from political editors, Campbell appears to have allowed his imagination to run riot. Today he claims that his account of how Jill Morrell, the girlfriend of Beirut hostage John McCarthy, was set to run as a Labour MP was the only story he ever got wrong as a practising journalist.[17] Certainly Jill Morrell herself was never consulted about Campbell's claim that she was 'poised' to stand as Labour candidate in the Hemsworth by-election of November 1991. According to lobby colleagues, Campbell steered them away from following up his story even on the night it was run.

Campbell struck up a strong friendship with Glenys Kinnock. The two would flirt openly – though innocently – in public places. The relationship between the two couples was so close that Fiona Millar and Glenys Kinnock agreed to write a book together, an endeavour which led to a rare falling out between the menfolk. The book, published by Virago Press in 1993, was largely made up of a series of interviews with prominent women.[18] Much of the work – according to some accounts, the majority of it – was carried out by Fiona Millar. She conducted the interviews and then converted them into lucid prose.[19] Glenys Kinnock's own connection with the enterprise, besides lending it the full weight of her name and personal authority, was most visibly confined to a lengthy introduction.

When proofs came from the publishers, Fiona felt that her role was not fully acknowledged. She conveyed her irritation to Campbell who, in turn, passed on his own indignation to Neil Kinnock. Kinnock declined to become involved. 'Leave aside the justice of what you are saying,' he told Campbell. 'Glenys is

16. There are endless examples of Campbell attacking and abusing other journalists who filed anti-Kinnock stories. Simon Walters, then the *Sun* political correspondent and now political editor of the *Mail on Sunday*, was one recipient of Campbell's attention on Neil Kinnock's second trip to New York. Campbell approached him, 'angry and snarling', in front of all the lobby journalists with 'I see you wrote your usual Tory propaganda shit in the *Sun*.' Walters, of course, was perfectly capable of looking after himself. Later, when Campbell became Press Secretary, Walters described this encounter in the *Sunday Express*. 'As he leaned towards me with his trademark scowl, four-letter abuse and the veins on his neck bulging with rage, I thought he was going to hit me. I said something rude back, the bus swerved, a colleague intervened and he backed off' (*Sunday Express*, 9 August 1998).

17. Possibly a true claim. No other examples spring to mind.

18. Glenys Kinnock and Fiona Millar, *By Faith and Daring* (1993).

19. Though due credit should be given to Fiona's mother Audrey, who transcribed the tapes, perhaps the most onerous task of all.

my wife.' In the end everything was resolved to the satisfaction of all concerned, an indication perhaps of the strength of the underlying relationship.[20]

There is something striking, indeed verging on the pathological, about the way the Campbell-Millars[21] have served two successive generations of Labour leaders. They are rather like those devoted couples who attach themselves to grand families and get passed on from generation to generation. In time they can come to embody the tradition of the great house to which they are attached more closely than the actual owners. There have been Campbell-Millars in attendance upon Labour Party leaders and their consorts for fifteen years now, with the exception of the brief two-year John Smith interregnum. It is an arrangement that suits all sides. The leader and wife get unrivalled service, while the Campbell-Millars get unrivalled access. The situation that prevails in Downing Street today, Campbell giving advice to the Prime Minister and Millar attending his wife as press adviser and in other capacities,[22] is similar in most essentials to the situation surrounding Neil and Glenys Kinnock in the late 1980s.

Getting to know Cap'n Bob

The intimacy of the connection between the Kinnocks and the Campbell-Millars could not fail to attract the attention of Robert Maxwell, the chairman of Mirror Group Newspapers. Maxwell, as a former Labour MP, took a profound interest in British politics. And as proprietor of the *Daily Mirror*, he took the very reasonable view that he was a force to be reckoned with in the Labour Party. It was an opinion with which Neil Kinnock could not readily demur, but the Maxwell influence was one which he vigorously sought to resist. The extraordinary figure of Maxwell tended to inspire two powerful but opposing emotions: warmth and distrust. The two forces pitted themselves against each other in Neil Kinnock's breast. It is a tribute to his sagacity and good judgement that distrust won the day.

20. Private information.

21. As friends in North London now refer to them. The double-barrel does not reflect any newly found grandeur on the part of Campbell and Millar. It is the way that friends try and cope with finding a joint name for two people who, though they are quite clearly a well-established and permanent unit, remain unmarried.

22. Fiona Millar was appointed part-time press adviser to Cherie Blair in Downing Street immediately after the 1997 General Election.

Still, Maxwell could not be entirely ignored. His lavish hospitality could be spurned, the munificence of the proffered financial assistance viewed with the deepest suspicion, but it was an undeniable though uncomfortable fact of life that he controlled the largest Labour-supporting newspaper group in Britain. It was here that Campbell came into his own. In Kinnock's eyes, he became the acceptable face of Robert Maxwell. This was high politics of the most complex and dangerous sort. It is a testament to Campbell's subtle management that he pulled off this high-wire act without compromising his personal integrity or falling out for good with either party. This bracing period of Campbell's life, during which he volunteered to act as a rickety bridge between two adjacent mountain peaks, both of them powerfully volcanic, was to last the best part of five years.

Today Maxwell is remembered as a fraudster and a con-man. Those who had close dealings with the man are in danger of being contaminated by association. Campbell knew Maxwell as well as any present or past members of Tony Blair's government who were associated with him. Thanks to his instinct for survival, he has been damaged the least.

The demonology that today surrounds Maxwell is a severe hindrance to understanding what a magnificent, richly absurd and in some ways attractive figure he presented only a decade ago. Fleet Street today is dominated by management accountants. It lacks the extravagant, buccaneering figures who strode across the scene in the first half of the twentieth century. Maxwell was the closest modern equivalent of Lord Beaverbrook, the magnate who turned the *Daily Express* into the dominant force in British journalism until his massive legacy was squandered by negligent successors. He was never the intuitive newspaperman that Beaverbrook undoubtedly was. But both were brilliant financiers whose compulsive interest lay in the wielding of political power. They lived private lives whose complexity and lack of scruple would do justice to a Renaissance pope. They shared a fascination with journalists: it is no surprise that journalists should return the compliment.

Campbell had been a junior reporter when Maxwell, in a spectacular City coup, obtained control of the Mirror Group in the summer of 1984. It is likely that he had shared the prevailing dismay at the news of Maxwell's arrival, indeed, as we have seen, he cited his suspicion of the tycoon as a reason for joining *Today* a year later. By the time Campbell returned to the *Mirror* after recovering from his illness, in autumn 1986, the new editor, his friend Richard Stott, had moderated the worst of Maxwell's abrasive behaviour and to some extent quelled the tycoon's instinct for embarrassing self-publicity. As ever with Campbell, he made it his business to establish a personal relationship with the boss. Fellow reporters remember him accompanying Maxwell to Ethiopia during the famine on a mission of mercy to relieve the starving. Maxwell set out to the worst affected area. Upon arrival, the scenes were so shocking that the publisher broke down in tears. No one knew quite how to react until Alastair Campbell strode across to the boss. 'Maxwell was a really big man,' says one witness, 'and Alastair is a big man as well. He went up to Maxwell and put his arm round his shoulders as if he was a child. He said "Don't get upset. You are one of those people who can really make a difference."'

Only Campbell had the physical size, let alone the confidence, to approach Maxwell in that direct and personal way. It was an approach that worked. 'That is the moment,' says the witness, 'when Campbell and Maxwell really bonded.' Later, at a Mirror Group Christmas party, to which wives and families were invited, a Campbell infant was brought in a spirit of tribute into the presence of the publisher. Campbell's colleagues recollect how Maxwell held up the baby and boomed: 'This is another future *Mirror* worker here.'

Campbell's relationship with the Mirror Group chairman is another example of his easy skill at building a friendship with the individual at the peak of whatever organisation he happens to be working for at the time. With Maxwell especially, there were hazards in such a frontal approach. Maxwell was in some ways a human and generous figure. And yet he felt an instinctive need to humiliate those close to him, diminish them in stature, establish their total dependence upon him. The most notable victim of this repulsive syndrome was Peter Jay, the former British Ambassador in Washington and once hailed as the most brilliant man of his generation. Jay made the mistake of accepting the title of Maxwell's chief of staff, a grand-sounding title with salary to match. Maxwell immediately relegated him to a drudge, taking a sadistic pleasure in drawing public attention to Jay's subservient role. Campbell avoided a similar fate, always making clear to Maxwell that he was an independent power who deserved to be treated with respect. There were the inevitable rows and arguments, but Campbell invariably stood his ground. Roy Greenslade, who was editor of the *Daily Mirror* for a brief period in the dying days of the Maxwell regime, recalls one hostile encounter at the height of the crisis that brought down Margaret Thatcher. It was the night of the first ballot after Michael Heseltine's leadership challenge. As politicians mulled over the meaning of the Prime Minister's slender majority, Maxwell rang Campbell to inform him that he had an exclusive story of the highest importance. It was a story, the press baron intimated, which he would expect to see all over the front page of the following day's *Mirror*. Maxwell asserted that he had impeccable information to the effect that six Cabinet ministers were ready to resign unless Margaret Thatcher stood down with immediate effect. Maxwell was right that it was a story with colossal ramifications. Such was the subservient, fear-infected culture which Maxwell encouraged in his sprawling empire that nine out of ten Maxwell employees would instantly have done his bidding and agreed to put the story wherever the publisher wished. There was, after all, no percentage in failing to do so. If the story turned out to be wrong, then Maxwell was unlikely to return to the matter again. If, on the other hand, it turned out to be correct, then retribution on a giant scale could befall anyone who had failed to be dazzled by the brilliance of the Maxwell information.

Campbell refused to be dazzled. He bravely told his boss that he would not run with the story unless he knew the source. Maxwell could hardly believe such impudence. His roars of rage that anyone could doubt his sources of information echoed round the *Daily Mirror*'s Holborn Circus headquarters. Of course, he boomed, he would never breach a personal trust at the whim of a mere employee. But Campbell stood by his guns, and a furious Maxwell threatened to fire him. Somewhat shaken, Campbell spoke to his editor, Roy Greenslade, and Joe Haines, the *Mirror* leader-writer who carried considerable sway in the Maxwell camp. Both stood up for him.[23]

This was by no means the only occasion when Campbell defied the *Mirror* chairman. The author and journalist Andy McSmith, who worked for many years on the political desk at the *Daily Mirror*, recalls that the tycoon once imperiously summoned Campbell to join him on a trip. Campbell refused to go, citing the funeral of Sean Hughes, the little-known Labour MP for Knowsley South. 'Not a lot of *Mirror* functionaries would have dared to do that,' records McSmith. This kind of aloofness eventually earned Campbell Maxwell's respect.

All this time Campbell was growing, intangibly but rapidly, in stature. He has by nature an unmistakable personal presence. He has always possessed a valuable gift – the ability to communicate his own assessment of his

23. Ironically enough, Campbell appears to have thrown away a decent story here which had at least a strong germ of truth. The confusion may have arisen from the term 'Cabinet minister'. Kenneth Clarke and, most probably, Chris Patten were prepared to quit the Cabinet. At least half a dozen junior ministers would surely have followed suit. Greenslade tells the story in *Maxwell* (1992).

Greenslade, always an informative though never an unbiased source where Campbell is concerned, also remembers his former political editor standing up to Maxwell and threatening to quit when Maxwell demanded a leader calling for the Commander of Land Forces in Northern Ireland to replace the Ulster Secretary Tom King in the Cabinet. The story has all the hallmarks of truth (*Guardian*, 4 February 1998).

importance through non-verbal means. Westminster is full of MPs and others who, at a drop of a hat, will explain to any passing stranger why the country would grind to a halt within a matter of days if they were not around to keep the show on the road. Campbell did not, and does not, do that. He does not possess, and never has done, the faintest pomposity or self-importance. But he conveyed, even as a lowly reporter, an invisible sense that he counted for a great deal more than appeared on the surface. At Westminster, where much store is set by mysterious invocations of hidden power, this was a matter of material significance. The knowledge that he had the support and trust of the leader of the Labour Party and the chairman of the Mirror Group was disseminated with great speed.

Batting for Kinnock

When Julia Langdon stepped down as political editor of the *Daily Mirror* in the autumn of 1989, there was some surprise that Campbell was given the job. Those who did not keep their eyes wide open saw only a low-ranking Sunday political editor with no special understanding and not much track record: a tabloid journalist who had only recently become interested in politics. But there was no doubt in the mind of anybody capable of reading the signs that Campbell would get the job. Becoming political editor of the *Daily Mirror* was a formal recognition of what he was already well on the way to becoming: a man of power and substance at Westminster. Campbell, at the early age of 32, had reached the top of his profession. He had used a singularly unconventional route to do so. The cultivation of powerful men, rather than a series of hard-hitting scoops, was the key to his success. Fellow lobby correspondents have on occasion speculated that, had Campbell been a woman, he would inevitably have been accused of sleeping his way to the top.

Most young men and women making their way in the world, if they have any sense, concentrate on getting on with the job in hand. They keep their head down, steer clear of office politics, allow their achievements to speak for themselves. There are those who take the opposite approach, and set about ingratiating themselves with their superiors. This method of self-advancement is, as a general rule, pitifully transparent, even to those very people who are being wooed and flattered. Even if it works, short-term gain is the best that can be achieved. In the medium to long term office crawlers are held in derision and contempt.

There can be no question that Campbell belongs to the type of office crawler – on an epic, unprecedented, gargantuan scale. From the day he started work in Fleet Street, he made it his business to go for the very top. Intermediate levels of seniority seem to have had little or no attraction for him. Within months of going to work for the *Daily Mirror* he had become one of the closest friends of Mike Molloy, the editor and – though in private a quiet and unassuming man – a mighty figure in Fleet Street. An apparently chance encounter lay behind the association. Molloy was on holiday in the South of France. He and his family were staying in a villa near the lovely Mediterranean town of Villefranche. They were in the habit of eating out at a particular restaurant. It was, Molloy remembers, a beautiful summer's evening.

Emerging onto the street at the end of the meal Molloy heard the sound of bagpipes, as surprising a sound in the South of France then as it is today. Investigating further, he and his wife were privileged to witness the splendid figure of Campbell playing the pipes to an admiring crowd, with Fiona by his side to ensure it contributed financially to the evening's entertainment. Molloy was vastly amused by this spectacle and did not fail to offer his ten francs, muttering words to the effect that he did not realise that he paid Campbell as badly as all that. An invitation to dinner was soon forthcoming, at which event Campbell was admired almost as much as Fiona was envied by Molloy's numerous teenage daughters. The young reporter proved an amusing dinner companion. The following year Campbell and Millar were invited to join the Molloys on holiday.

. The Villefranche meeting was a happy coincidence as far as Campbell was concerned, if it really was a coincidence, something fellow reporters are inclined to doubt. It would have been an easy matter, they observe, to discover where the editor was staying and position oneself strategically for a 'chance' meeting. Most junior journalists, of course, would have tended towards an opposite course of action: found out where the editor was staying and ensured that they were nowhere in the vicinity. Among these may have been Fiona Millar. There are reports that Millar, then a *Daily Express* reporter and lacking Campbell's appetite for self-promotion, had already banned her boyfriend from busking in a nearby town where her own editor, Larry Lamb, was reputed to be staying. Like most normal people, she felt no desire to ruin her holiday by meeting the boss.

Roy Greenslade was Campbell's editor during the dying stages of the Maxwell regime. 'Alastair was never interested in employer-employee relationships. He always wanted to change the "for" to working "with". He feels he is the equal of anyone,'[24] he recalls. Greenslade's remark is fascinating. It goes a long way towards explaining the nature of the Campbell technique. His behaviour, although possessing many of the outward signs of the sycophant, has never been sycophantic. Greenslade further recalls: 'When he was political editor, he would come into my office, put his feet on my desk and tell me the splash was trivial crap.'[25] There is no reason to suppose that he took a different approach with any of his other editors, or with Neil Kinnock.

It is Campbell's readiness to tell the truth and take risks with even his most powerful patrons that marks him out as very much more than an office crawler.[26] In anyone else, his huge self-esteem would have manifested itself as an intolerable bumptiousness. But in his case, others are ready to take him at his own assessment. The most powerful in the land have always been ready to admit Alastair Campbell as one of them. And this partnership of equals is, more than anything else, what defines his relationship with Tony Blair.

There is something extremely unusual and almost disturbing about Campbell's attraction to very powerful men. It is the most noteworthy and characteristic feature of his rich and in many ways attractive personality. Most of us are complicated: Campbell manages to be even more complicated than most. His worship of power manages to coexist with a subsidiary tendency towards anarchism, though there is no doubt which is the dominant characteristic. He is interested in power only for its own sake: its incidental benefits appear to have no attraction for him. Politicians are typically driven by three separate and competing motivations: power, money and the advancement of their social position. Campbell is indifferent to money and status. This is one of the things that make him such a formidable operator. It distinguishes him sharply, for instance, from Peter Mandelson, for many years his principal rival for the ear of the Prime Minister. But Campbell is not happy within himself until his light is refracted through someone he has deemed to be an even larger figure than himself. The phenomenon is of very much more than passing significance for anyone who wants to understand the way Britain is governed as she enters the third millennium.

From the moment Campbell was appointed political editor of the *Daily Mirror* in 1989, before the Labour Conference with Neil Kinnock's heady

24. Quoted in Kevin Toolis (*Guardian Weekend*, 4 April 1998).

25. *Ibid.*

26. Campbell spoke revealingly to Kevin Toolis about his success in Fleet Street: 'I just knew I could do it. Call it arrogance, whatever. As you are promoted you confront your own myths about how great these people on a pedestal are. I was never worried that I was out of my depth' (*ibid.*).

slogan: 'Meet the Challenge, Make the Change', Campbell never had the slightest doubt what the job was all about. His predecessor Julia Langdon, though standing on the left, was journalist first and propagandist second. Campbell perceived with a Leninist clarity that his job was about advancing the interests of Neil Kinnock and the Labour Party. Journalism, in the sense that it is commonly understood, had nothing to do with it. Trevor Kavanagh, who was political editor of the *Sun* throughout Campbell's time as political editor of the *Mirror*, had to chase up a political story in his mass-market competitor on only one occasion during the four years that they were direct rivals.[27] The only scoops that Campbell got on a regular basis were his interviews with Neil Kinnock. These were always billed 'exclusive' and came round regular as clockwork.

The birth of New Labour English – and a significant death

With inner fanaticism, Alastair Campbell dedicated himself to boosting Kinnock and his allies while laying into his enemies. This process had already begun at the *Sunday Mirror*, for which Campbell continued to write his column while political editor of the *Daily Mirror*. During the late 1980s Alastair Campbell and Fiona Millar set about writing a series of hagiographies of approved members of the Kinnock team. It was a heroic project, undertaken with the same dedication and selflessness with which Beatrice and Sidney Webb set about their famous investigations into the deserving poor in the 1930s. The prose style is a strange mixture of the gushing platitudes of *Hello!* magazine and those steely tributes to heroes of the Russian working class that used to appear in *Soviet Weekly* during the Stalinist years. It would be pleasing to record that this journalistic style has since died out: but nothing could be further from the truth. Those Campbell–Millar *Sunday Mirror* profiles contained the first stirrings of what would in due course become a literary horror: New Labour English.[28] Already present in them is the stark use of words, the absence of humour, the poverty of language, the lack of interest in ideas, the sense of impatience with other points of view, the

27. A civil list leak, which was widely assumed – with no evidence – to have come from the Kinnock office.

28. New Labour English could be found in its purest form in *Progress Magazine*, the journal for party activists edited by Derek Draper. Tony Blair's *New Britain: My Vision of a Young Country* (1996) is another prime example.

bustling determination to make everything appear in the best possible light. In due course, after a number of modifications, and given a generous evangelical injection by Tony Blair, it would emerge in the form we know today. New Labour English, as it manifests itself in conference speeches, party literature, Tony Blair's annual speech to the Labour Party Conference, and in the hundreds of articles ostensibly written each year by the Prime Minister, is above all the creation of Alastair Campbell. He started it, and it spread like a disease. When this arid subject becomes, as it undoubtedly will, the subject for a PhD in the history of the English language, the aspiring doctor must not omit to pay his tribute to the source of it all: Alastair Campbell's *Sunday Mirror* column and his profiles of leading Labour figures.

Needless to say, the first profile was on Neil Kinnock. Campbell, along with his photographer Fritz von der Schulenburg, was granted privileged admittance to the Labour leader's 'detached three-bedder' in Ealing. Schulenburg produced lavish pictures of Neil Kinnock looking statesmanlike in the kitchen, and cuddling up with his wife on the sofa. Campbell complemented these with observations like: 'When it comes to cooking, the kitchen is very much Glenys-territory.'[29]

Fiona Millar visited Gordon Brown at his Edinburgh flat. There she discovered Labour's newly promoted trade spokesman and latest rising star in a state of incomparable squalor. It was clear, she informed colleagues upon her return to civilisation, that the Brown establishment had been neither cleaned nor tidied since he moved in several years before. This presented difficulties for a writer determined to present the subject in a homely and domestic light. 'Brimming with character' is the form of words Millar finally settled on to describe Brown's domestic arrangements. 'The overall impression is very much a bachelor pad.'[30]

A second problem presented itself when the moment came for photographs to be taken. Brown was wearing a dark suit, not ideal for a piece that was designed to highlight the softer side of his personality. It was indicated that it would be helpful if he changed into something more casual. Brown slipped into his bedroom and swiftly re-emerged, having changed his tie. It became clear, to the incredulity of both Millar and the photographer, that this strange, brilliant man did not possess any form of leisure wear at all or indeed any form of garment apart from his daily working suits.

29. *Sunday Mirror Magazine*, no. 2, July 1988.
30. *Ibid.*, 8 July 1990.

Campbell wrote the profile of Peter Mandelson.[31] He visited the Labour Party Director of Communications in a Herefordshire village. Some misty dream of rustic peace and tranquillity had driven him to purchase a farm worker's cottage. 'With every mile I drive from London, my mood lifts,' he told Campbell, implausibly. Mandelson still had his moustache in those days. He was photographed pruning the roses in his tiny garden, unmistakably ill-at-ease in the rural setting. The cottage itself was disposed of soon afterwards.

The Blair article was turgid. It is a testament to Campbell's growing influence and command within the Mirror Group that he was able to get it into the paper at all. It was not an interview with Blair himself, then a moderately glamorous figure who might well have been acceptable to a magazine editor short of an idea. It was a breathy account of an evening with the General Management Committee of the Sedgefield Constituency Labour Party. Campbell dutifully recorded that the 'three to one representation of the sexes was fairly accurately represented in the mixed lounge' and other such information.[32] No self-respecting journalist would have had anything to do with such a dire piece of writing, least of all in a Sunday colour supplement. What was going on here, of course, had nothing to do with journalism. Campbell was quite deliberately using his position at the *Mirror* to build alliances and strengthen his own position.

What is striking is how clinically and accurately Campbell, in the late 1980s, had identified the generation that would emerge as the dominant force in the second half of the 1990s. There was no *Sunday Mirror* interview with John Smith, John Prescott, Robin Cook, Roy Hattersley or Bryan Gould – all senior members of Neil Kinnock's Shadow Cabinet. Campbell, with his immaculately tuned antennae, understood that it was better to buy shares that were still available cheaply rather than trade in established reputations. He picked out Gordon Brown, Tony Blair and Peter Mandelson: the very three men who would build New Labour. Each was a bullseye. At this stage, like everyone else, he saw Gordon Brown as the future Prime Minister, 'with Blair a likely Chancellor'.[33]

Hagiography was not the only activity into which Campbell threw himself with enthusiasm. It was his duty to stick the boot in on behalf of Neil Kinnock, it was a task he carried out with pleasure. Sticking the boot in came naturally; it

---

31. *Ibid.*, 24 September 1989.
32. *Ibid.*, 9 April 1989. Tony Blair, unlike the bulk of *Mirror* readers, was deeply appreciative.
33. *Ibid.*, 11 September 1988.

still does today. He was always available to tear down a member of the Shadow Cabinet or an unhelpful trade union leader. Ron Todd, the leader of the mighty Transport & General Workers' Union, was one frequent target for Campbell's scorn. The TGWU, the enemy of the modernisers, infuriated Campbell. Noisy left-wing MPs like Ken Livingstone were a favourite Campbell target. Like Kinnock, he frequently found himself at odds with John Prescott, always likely to make a nuisance of himself by speaking up for the left against the modernisers. It is a measure of Campbell's prodigious ability to manage personal relationships that he remained on good terms with Prescott. Shortly after the 1992 General Election Campbell set about undermining Prescott's campaign to succeed Roy Hattersley as Deputy Leader. He itemised Prescott's many defects in an article that was almost as vicious as it was patronising. It accused Prescott of failing to come up with fresh ideas and vented claims that Labour press officers were constantly having to wade in to preserve Prescott from his own mistakes. 'He's what one critic calls "a big girl's blouse,"' concluded Campbell. 'He thinks the *Daily Mirror* is part of the conspiracy against him. The trouble with Prescott is that you're either for him or against him.' The idea of Prescott as John Smith's deputy, asserted Campbell, 'appeals to Tories no end.'

Prescott was furious. He stormed around Westminster like an enraged bull. The following week he was granted the right to reply to the charges against him. 'I can't say I like being comprehensively slagged off. Campbell says I have many talents. I wish he'd devoted more space to saying what they are.' Incredible though it sounds, Prescott's ringing riposte was ghosted for him by none other than Alastair Campbell.[34]

Attacking the Tories was the routine part of the job. The government, falling apart over Europe and convulsed with plots against Margaret Thatcher and later John Major, presented an easy target. But even in this elementary task Campbell was quick to show the strategic finesse that has been his trademark as much when Labour has been in opposition as in government. Perceiving that he and Michael Heseltine had a common objective – the eradication of Margaret Thatcher – Campbell set about forming one of the more unlikely alliances in modern political history. The flattery was overwhelming. 'He looks like a Prime Minister. He walks, talks, ducks and dives like a Prime Minister. There

---

34. Campbell's denunciation of Prescott was published in the *Daily Mirror* on 27 May 1992. Prescott's reply appeared on 2 June. I am indebted to Colin Brown, John Prescott's biographer, for pointing out that Campbell was responsible for both articles.

are times when I wonder whether Michael Heseltine, with his chauffeurs and his staff, his expensive suits and expansive speeches, doesn't think he *is* the Prime Minister,' was just a routine example.[35] Heseltine fell for it. A more solitary figure than ever after the Westland resignation,[36] he was glad of whatever support he could get. The depth of his disloyalty to the Tory Party was immense. Campbell's friendship with Neil Kinnock was no secret – though few realised quite what bosom friends the two had become. Heseltine must have been aware that by talking to Alastair Campbell he was in effect taking part in direct discussions with the Leader of the Opposition. The Campbell/Heseltine axis only ended when Heseltine's leadership challenge triggered Margaret Thatcher's removal from office in November 1990. The outcome that all three men had sought fervently to bring about, ironically enough, cost them all dear. Had Mrs Thatcher remained Prime Minister Neil Kinnock might well have won the 1992 General Election, and Heseltine, without the stigma of the assassin which destroyed his chances in 1990, might well have assumed the mantle of Tory leader.

When Michael Heseltine rejoined the government as Environment Secretary in December 1990, Campbell approached him in the Members' Lobby at the entrance to the Chamber of the House of Commons. 'Remember,' he said to the newly promoted Cabinet minister, 'We are not on the same side any more.'[37] Campbell was to rekindle the relationship a decade later when, from his new Downing Street base, he and Heseltine set in motion a pincer movement against William Hague, the beleaguered Tory leader. It was a near-identical operation to the one that had worked so well against Margaret Thatcher ten years before.[38]

Campbell used the political editorship of the *Mirror* to turn himself into a powerful player on the political scene as an instrument of Neil Kinnock. He had

35. *Sunday Mirror*, 1 April 1990. The article concluded: 'When all is said and done, Heseltine supporters will be rooting for a Kinnock victory almost as much as Kinnock.'

36. Heseltine resigned as Defence Secretary in his anger over Margaret Thatcher's refusal to help in finding a European buyer for the ailing Westland helicopter company.

37. I am indebted to David Davis MP, a friend of Campbell though not of Heseltine, for this anecdote.

38. Heseltine's campaign against William Hague has been encouraged by Downing Street. Campbell, with a grin, announced the appointment of Heseltine as chairman of a new Anglo-Chinese trading body while Tony Blair was on a trip to the Far East in the autumn of 1998. Few believed it was purely coincidental that the news was issued during Tory Conference week. A few months later the charge of disloyalty against Heseltine grew even stronger when it was learnt he had taken part in secret talks with Tony Blair before the Prime Minister's positive, mood-changing statement on the single currency. Heseltine's apparently spontaneous speech welcoming the announcement had actually been choreographed in advance with Downing Street. (See the author's front-page article, 'Heseltine and Blair in Secret Euro Plot', *Sunday Express*, 28 February 1999.)

instant access at all times to the leader's office. In return he wrote about politics the way Kinnock wanted. Andy McSmith, who worked for Campbell at this time, describes how Campbell gave in to pressure from Neil Kinnock to retract one of his stories. It concerned Peter Mandelson. McSmith reported that Mandelson had to step down from his post as Labour's Director of Communications as a result of his decision to stand for a parliamentary seat. A day or two later, the *Mirror* published a correction of the story even though there were solid grounds for believing it was true. McSmith now takes up the story: 'The original piece was under my name, the retraction was written by the *Daily Mirror*'s political editor Alastair Campbell. Generally, it is notoriously difficult to induce a tabloid newspaper to retract anything, particularly a story that would obviously stand up in court. Mandelson only achieved it by being able, once again, to call upon his relationship with Neil Kinnock.'[39]

The job created Campbell in the same way that, five years before, Peter Mandelson had been turned into a figure of substance by his appointment as Labour's Director of Communications. As *Mirror* political editor he counted for very much more than any mere member of the Shadow Cabinet. Colleagues remember that he could often be seen talking to Tony Blair in the Members' Lobby. There was no question in their minds about who had the upper hand in these conversations. Blair was merely a rising Shadow minister. Campbell by contrast was a powerful political editor, known to have the ear of Neil Kinnock and well capable of throwing his weight around at the Mirror Group. Blair's attitude was appropriately deferential, almost giving the impression that he was flattered that a man of the stature of Alastair Campbell was ready to give him the time of day.[40]

Two events brought this successful and happy period in Campbell's professional career to a conclusion. The first was the death of Robert Maxwell on 5 November 1991. The second was the General Election result of 1992 less than six months later. Campbell was devastated by the election result, but the consequences for him when the tycoon fell over the side of his yacht to his death in circumstances that remain mysterious were equally profound. The collapse of

39. This account appears in Andy McSmith, *Faces of Labour* (1997), p. 262. This book is by far the best guide to the people in the modern Labour Party. As a general rule McSmith is extremely generous about Campbell as a boss. 'If ever there was a problem you always got it straight in the face immediately. He was very direct in telling you. He might give you a bollocking, but nobody else got to hear about it.'

40. Andy McSmith, a *Mirror* political reporter at the time, says: 'I remember seeing Tony Blair talking to Alastair. It was as if Alastair Campbell was the man of weight and substance because he was the political editor of a mass market tabloid with unfettered access to the Labour Party leader whereas Blair was a recently elected member of the Shadow Cabinet' (interview with the author, April 1999).

the Maxwell empire had dramatic implications for the ownership and control of the Mirror Group: these in their turn would force Campbell, in very painful circumstances, to leave the newspaper he loved.

He had received a powerful intimation that the Mirror Group proprietor was in trouble six weeks before, at the Labour Party Conference in Brighton. Maxwell would always travel down for a day's appearance at conference. Normally he exuded bonhomie. On this occasion he looked troubled. During the course of the day he took a small number of senior *Mirror* journalists and executives individually to one side and poured his heart out to them. It is a sign of the respect and affection in which he was held by the old rogue that Campbell was one of those thus singled out.

His encounter with the desperate Maxwell came shortly before the Mirror Group proprietor entertained Neil and Glenys Kinnock to lunch. Later Campbell informed Roy Greenslade about this slightly macabre experience. He told Greenslade that Maxwell – who was far advanced in his wholesale pillage of the Mirror Group pension fund – was acting 'very oddly'. He went on: 'Just before Neil and Glenys arrived, he took me out on the balcony of the penthouse dining room. He told me, "The whole world's against me. People are out to destroy me."'[41]

The impact of Maxwell's death can hardly be over-stated. It sent Fleet Street into a frenzy of excitement which did not abate for several weeks. Whatever else there is to be said about Maxwell, there is no question that the manner of his departure from this earth was entirely in keeping with the way he conducted his affairs while he was still on it. It was also entirely in character that Alastair Campbell should have strolled onto the stage as a bit part player in the colossal drama that swept Fleet Street, Westminster and the stockmarkets on the afternoon of 5 November 1991.

Punch-up in the Commons

There are many interpretations of the now legendary fist fight which broke out that afternoon, but no question as to the essential facts. The fight was sparked when Michael White, political editor of the *Guardian*, entered the *Mirror* office

41. This account is taken from Roy Greenslade's work on Maxwell's final years (*op.cit.*, p. 271). Joe Haines told the author that he received similar treatment. He recalls that Maxwell was sitting on a parapet leaning back towards the sea. Haines feared that he might fall off. Maxwell told Haines: 'I'm going to need your loyalty over the next few months.' Haines replied: 'I've always been loyal to the *Mirror*.' Maxwell replied: 'I don't mean the *Mirror*. I mean a personal loyalty.'

in the House of Commons Press Gallery very shortly after news of the publisher's watery demise had broken over the newswires.[42] He wished to share a joke with the *Mirror* political editor. According to most witnesses and subsequent reports, White said: 'Cap'n Bob, bob, bob, bob . . .' There is an alternative account, also based on eye-witness testimony, that White was singing: 'We're bobbing along.'[43] Either way, Campbell did not think it funny. White, taking the view that his joke would be more amusing a second time round, returned a few minutes later. His reception was no warmer than before, only on this occasion he was warned that violent retribution would certainly follow if he did not make himself scarce. White did indeed withdraw at this point, only to reappear within a short space of time. Campbell struck him. White struck back. A fracas ensued.

Both Campbell and White are over six feet tall. But White, whose foreign suits and fastidious but slightly fleshy features cause him closely to resemble the worldly communist mayor of a provincial French town, is the less muscular and well-built of the two. Ian Aitken, then an eminent and revered *Guardian* columnist, found himself closest to the centre of affairs. As best he could, he endeavoured to interpose himself between the two warring political editors, muttering as he did so: 'Come, gentlemen, come.' Neither took the slightest notice of him, and all Aitken got for his efforts was a bloodstained shirtfront. 'I felt rather ridiculous,' he later recalled, 'standing there in the tiny *Mirror* office with these fists flying over my head.'

In due course, the two journalists were separated. There was no conclusive winner, though some claim White sustained a cut nose. Sympathy for the two contestants was broadly divided along class lines. Tabloid men stuck with Campbell, while correspondents from the broadsheets instinctively favoured White. Later, the pair received an angry letter from the Sergeant-at-Arms, warning of the repercussions if they ever again came to blows within the confines of the Palace of Westminster.

Campbell's motives for striking White have never been established. His detractors, eager to link him as closely as possible to the memory of Robert Maxwell, suggest that he was driven by the wish to defend the reputation of the dead tycoon, whose criminal activities had not at that stage been revealed to the world. His allies, on the other hand, led by his friend Roy Greenslade, insist that loyalty to Robert Maxwell had little or nothing to do with Campbell's

42. The following account is based on the author's interviews with several witnesses as well as Michael White.

43. Shaun Woodward, then Director of Communications at Conservative Central Office, now Tory MP for Witney, insists that this was what White sang.

behaviour. In February 1998, Greenslade wrote an article in the *Guardian* which was aimed at clearing Campbell's reputation from all kinds of slights and innuendoes.[44] In it he introduced a new element into the drama which unfolded in the *Mirror* office on the afternoon of Robert Maxwell's disappearance, suggesting that personal venom between Campbell and White was the spark. 'Too much has been read into the famous punch-up with the *Guardian*'s Michael White on the day of Robert Maxwell's death,' wrote Greenslade. 'It was a silly spat that had more to do with Alastair's and Michael's own relationship than a display of misguided loyalty to Captain Bob.'

Greenslade is close to Campbell, and his views are always informed and worthy of respect. It is perfectly possible that White and Campbell did not get on. Enmities between journalists – particularly left-wing journalists – are commonplace. It is easy to imagine that White found Campbell's writing simplistic and resented his apparently effortless access to the highest Labour circles. Campbell, for his part, probably regarded White as long-winded. Furthermore, he worked for the *Guardian*, a newspaper Campbell has always held in disdain. Nevertheless, the Greenslade claim that some kind of personal vendetta lay behind the fight has the hallmarks of special pleading.

All the signs are that White was offering quite enough provocation as it was. Here the testimony of another eye-witness, Ian Hernon, is invaluable on a number of counts. Hernon, then political editor for the Central Press, is a journalist of the old school. The proud son of a professional footballer, he has come up the hard way. Hernon had seen it all before. He is a far more renowned drinker and pugilist even than Campbell was himself when at the very height of his powers in the 1980s. For excitable political journalists, a public fist fight between two members of their profession was a matter of some moment. Not for Hernon. As he remarked later, the Campbell/White fracas would never have passed muster on a Friday night in certain Glasgow pubs of his acquaintance.

So Hernon was able to be dispassionate. His assessment of the situation has one further merit. He owes nothing to Campbell himself. Nearly a decade later Campbell was accused of attempting to have Hernon thrown out of the parliamentary lobby.[45] Hernon has less reason than any other man alive to do the Prime Minister's Press Secretary a favour.

The first important fact that Hernon points out, and which others have missed, is that the door to the *Mirror* room was shut when Hernon appeared.

44. *Guardian*, 4 February 1998.
45. See chapter 11, p. 182.

That is highly unusual, possibly unprecedented. The tiny *Mirror* room, which holds five or six journalists, is just one of a honeycomb of small rooms off the Press Gallery corridor known as the Burmah Road. Embarking on the trek down the Burmah Road, it is the first you come to on the left, opposite the lobby notice-board. It is a hospitable place, and frequently a centre for the exchange of civilised gossip enabling *Mirror* men to become acquainted with the latest lobby buzz.

Any lobby correspondent as experienced as Michael White would know for sure that a closed door was a sign that the occupant did not want to be disturbed. Nor is it surprising that on that of all afternoons Campbell would have wanted to deter visitors by sporting his oak. As speculation about the fate of Robert Maxwell mounted he would have needed to make dozens of highly sensitive calls. He needed to discover for himself what had happened. The Kinnock office was badgering him for information. There were stories to be written, tributes to be arranged. As Hernon puts it: 'Campbell was sitting with his left-hand side facing the door talking to the newsdesk. He was behaving like a professional. During the course of a very fraught ten minutes Michael White kept coming in making jokes. Alastair snapped but didn't immediately punch him. He warned him first. The idea that Alastair hit Michael because he was outraged that jokes were being made against his great leader is ludicrous.'

All this suggests that Michael White richly deserved to be thumped, and that Campbell was acting within his rights when he hit him. There is still compelling evidence, however, that Campbell was moved and upset by Maxwell's disappearance. Two witnesses testify to this. Ian Aitken, whose view of events was closest of all to the action, insists that he 'was quite distressed.'[46] So does the Tory MP Shaun Woodward.

Woodward, then the Conservative Party Director of Communications, was passing the *Mirror* room when the fight occurred. Woodward is clearly open to the charge of bias. But those who know him best would probably acquit him. There are politicians who make things up for base political advantage. And there are politicians who do not. Woodward – and scores of Labour MPs would endorse this – belongs in the latter category. 'Alastair was in tears,' said Woodward. 'And to be fair to Michael White, he didn't realise that. He was not sobbing, but he was in tears.'

Alastair Campbell is an emotional man. It would be disturbing if he were not moved by Robert Maxwell's death. Maxwell had been his boss for seven years.

---

46. Aitken to this day feels that Campbell over-reacted.

He was a man he sometimes spoke to on a daily basis. His career had flourished under Maxwell. He knew his family. Campbell had nothing to reproach himself with about his dealings with the old rogue. He maintained a steady independence from his employer, though always sensing that the publisher was not quite sixteen annas to the rupee. Campbell's apologist Roy Greenslade insists that Campbell felt no 'misguided loyalty' to Maxwell. But there was nothing misguided about the loyalty he quite properly felt to the old man when he died, and which he expressed in a respectful article in the following day's *Mirror*. 'He was a big man with a big heart – helping sick employees in need and backing charities,' he wrote.[47] A short time later, when the world learnt with fascinated horror of the crimes that Maxwell had committed, Campbell was not among those who dashed into print to condemn his former boss. This may in part have been because he had no need to distance himself since he had nothing to reproach himself for. And partly, perhaps, because he still felt a lingering fondness for the monster.[48]

47. *Daily Mirror*, 6 November 1991.

48. Long after Maxwell's death Campbell was quoted in the *Sunday Times* (5 May 1996) as saying: 'Very few of us on the *Mirror* didn't realise that there were things to worry about him but even now there are an awful lot of people who sit around saying what a laugh it was.'

Chapter Six

'OH, SOD OFF PRIME MINISTER, I'M TRYING TO DO MY EXPENSES'

The piece of lettuce who passes for Prime Minister.
Alastair Campbell on John Major, Today, *9 May 1994*

The death of Maxwell and Neil Kinnock's departure to the fringes of the political stage after the 1992 General Election deprived Campbell of two great patrons who had driven his career forward for seven years. He never reached anything like the same intimacy with John Smith as he did with Neil Kinnock. Smith, unlike his predecessor Neil Kinnock or his successor Tony Blair, never saw the point of journalists. He did not share the media's sense of their own importance. He failed to see the need to – as he would have seen it – waste his time with Campbell or, for that matter, any other reporter.[1] There was nothing personal about this. Smith always spoke warmly of Campbell in a way he emphatically did not about, for instance, Peter Mandelson. When it came to the media, he was simply a very old-fashioned politician, a throwback to the days of Attlee and Churchill.

John Smith's most dangerous critic

It was not long before Alastair Campbell emerged as one of the new Labour leader's most articulate, powerful and dangerous critics. This was partly because he found it hard to shake off the legacy of Kinnock. Neil Kinnock has always been an exemplary former leader of his party, often in deeply trying circumstances. This is far from an easy role to play well, as successive former Tory leaders have demonstrated. But Kinnock has played it to perfection. It was hard for his closest allies, however, to display similar fortitude. They resented Smith's obvious belief that he would become the next Labour Prime Minister on the basis that he was not Kinnock – and nothing else. And, more

---

1. His press adviser Hilary Coffman used to nag away at Smith to see more of Campbell.

urgently, they believed that Smith was squandering Neil Kinnock's modernising legacy.

All great revolutionary movements need their period of tribulation, suffering and exile. For the handful of men who dreamt up New Labour, John Smith's leadership was that period. It cannot be said that they spent their time of martyrdom in any physical discomfort. They plotted – and there was a great deal of plotting – over well-stocked North London dinner tables and in elegant villas in the South of France. It was – but only to the uncurious eye – a good time in the life of the soon-to-be New Labour leader Tony Blair. He was proving to be a formidable Shadow Home Secretary and talented performer on the Labour front bench, his star gradually rising at the expense of his closest friend and deadliest rival Gordon Brown. And yet, when alone with his friends, he fretted. He feared that ponderous, plodding, complacent John Smith could throw it all away and let the Tories back again. He saw himself as condemned to an arid life of perpetual opposition. In his darkest moments, he spoke of chucking it all in and returning to the bar.[2]

This mood of despair bordering on prostration is well conjured up by Philip Gould, now political consultant to Tony Blair but then one of the 'beautiful people' so roundly condemned by John Prescott in the wake of the 1992 defeat. The frustration of the John Smith years seeped out of Gould who, having played a role in President Clinton's 1992 election campaign, felt a messianic urge to teach the lessons of that famous victory to the British Labour Party. He saw no signs that John Smith was ready to learn them.

The biggest sufferer of all was Peter Mandelson. He had been elected Member of Parliament for Hartlepool in the 1992 General Election. But that was no compensation at all for the fact that John Smith promptly thrust him into the outer darkness. He did not appreciate Mandelson and had no place for his skills. Internal exile did not suit Mandelson, who yearns for the centre of power as desperately as a fish yearns for water.

Campbell threw in his lot with these men. He became the strongest public voice of disaffection with what they saw as John Smith's slow-moving and lazy leadership. In the aftermath of election defeat the Labour Party was convulsed by one of its great internal debates: this one was about the lessons of 1992. The left said that Kinnock lost because he abandoned Labour's natural working-class base. The modernisers claimed that he failed because he did not abandon it enough. There was no question as to which side of the barricades Alastair

2. Private information.

Campbell stood on. In article after article he made the case for radical change. Less than a year into the Smith leadership, Campbell was already at it. Taking advantage of a rare invitation by the *Sunday Telegraph* to write a column, Campbell turned on the Smith leadership. 'I see the real divide as between "frantics" and "long-gamers"' he wrote.

The long-gamers all believe Labour has time on its side. There is no point, they say, in wasting energies and risking the Tory theft of ideas, in a period that will be forgotten by the next election. But what makes the frantics frantic is that the party does not know what it is for, other than to oppose the Government in parliament. There is little sense of the party finding itself a wider role.[3]

Campbell had no hesitation in naming John Smith as the leader of the despised 'long-gamers'. He cited as accomplices Smith's deputy leader Margaret Beckett, Robin Cook, John Prescott, Jack Cunningham and Frank Dobson. Campbell had very much more difficulty in identifying his frantics, coming up with just Tony Blair, Gordon Brown and Jack Straw as well as 'several lesser known shadow cabinet members.'

Campbell banged away at Smith's leadership right up to his death in May 1994. Less than a fortnight before the Labour leader died, he was at it again in the *Spectator*: 'Labour are so used to enjoying the Tories' troubles that they have stopped thinking about their own,' he thundered. 'If the current line is held to the election, the ducking and diving of Labour will become as big a turn-off as the deceit and dissembling of Conservative ministers.'[4]

There is no question that Tony Blair, Peter Mandelson and Philip Gould were egging Campbell on from the sidelines. According to Tony Blair's biographer Jon Sopel, the Blair faction steered interested parties towards Campbell's *Spectator* article for an illuminating insight into the melancholy state of affairs that prevailed under their lacklustre leader. The modernisers were going nowhere under John Smith.

And nor was Campbell. He was caught up in the wreckage of the Maxwell empire and being swept away. Shortly after the election he was approached to lead a management buyout of the *Daily Mirror* in its rudderless post-Maxwell state.[5] He showed no interest. The arrival of David Montgomery, the former editor of the *News of the World*, as chief executive of the Mirror Group in

3. *Sunday Telegraph*, 7 February 1993.

4. *Spectator*, 30 April 1994.

5. By the Conservative MP David Davis. Davis, a former main board director of Tate & Lyle, has powerful City connections. There is no question the offer was genuine.

October 1992 sealed his fate. Montgomery was put there by the banks after a cleverly executed boardroom coup, and he set about doing their bidding with a cold-hearted relish that *Mirror* journalists found inexplicable. Even today the passions aroused by Montgomery's arrival remain at boiling point. The Ulsterman – who has since been himself deposed in another coup, though not before the *Mirror* share price had trebled – remembers discovering 'a conspiracy of indulgence. While Maxwell ripped off the company, he found it convenient to indulge the journalists.'

There is truth to the Montgomery claim. Maxwell, with his low peasant cunning, had found it a simple matter to destroy the print-workers' unions. He had found it easier still to outwit the accountants whose job it supposedly was to make sure that the books were straight. But he had taken a profound pleasure in retaining the Mirror Group's reputation for ensuring that its journalists lived like lords. The big cars, the expensive suits and the lavish expense accounts continued as before. Only the best would do for the *Mirror*. In the lobby Campbell was known by envious fellow journalists as 'Club-Class Campbell'. On overseas trips he travelled – like all *Mirror* men – in extreme comfort while fellow reporters on other papers sweated it out economy-class.

High Noon at the *Mirror*

Joe Haines, Group political editor, was the first to go. Richard Stott resigned as *Mirror* editor soon afterwards. He fled to become editor of *Today* newspaper, and soon his paper became a sanctuary for disenchanted *Mirror* journalists. It was not long until, for the third time, it fell to Stott to lend a helping hand in Campbell's career.

David Montgomery's decision to get rid of Campbell still looks strange. Campbell was by now a star, his presence a selling point for any newspaper. He was, by any standards, a highly desirable property. Montgomery did not think so. Perhaps he saw him as irretrievably associated with the Stott regime. Even now, he professes himself unimpressed by the *Mirror*'s political coverage during the Kinnock period. 'Politically the *Mirror* had no originality,' says the Ulsterman. 'It had no new tunes. It was flogging a dead horse. Its journalism of the pre-Smith era was going nowhere. It was strident, repetitive and boring.' Montgomery made Campbell's departure inevitable by bringing in an outsider to fill the vacated slot of Group political editor. The figure he alighted upon was David Seymour, a political writer on *Today* newspaper. This was a clear snub to Campbell. He did not take the news well when it was broken to him in early 1993 by David Banks, the latest editor to emerge at the troubled newspaper.[6]

Banks is a generously proportioned man. At a conservative estimate he weighs eighteen stone. It is as well that he does. Shortly after Campbell went into his office, the sounds of screaming, shouting and abuse started to emerge, and then there came a crash – a chair being thrown across the room. It later emerged that the chair had been thrown not by Campbell but by Banks. His subsequent explanation for this act of random violence was that Campbell was ranting, raving and completely out of control; hurling a chair somehow seemed, in the circumstances, the natural thing to do. In due course the tall and usually authoritative figure of Campbell emerged, white-faced. One witness says that he looked 'desolate and totally abject'. He crossed the editorial floor and entered the office of Amanda Platell, the managing editor.

It is ironic that the final rites for Campbell's long occupancy at the *Mirror* were carried out by Platell. A dark, beautiful, passionate Australian, Platell is quite capable, when occasion demands, of behaving like a character from the most lurid novel imaginable about Fleet Street. She has, indeed, made a thinly veiled fictional appearance in several, as well as writing one or two herself. This occasion did not so demand. It was her role to be sensible, pragmatic, sympathetic and maternal. Campbell came into her office and sat on the comfortable sofa provided only in the offices of the most powerful *Mirror* executives. According to one witness to the scene, who viewed events from the ante-room outside Platell's office, Campbell looked a 'broken and crumpled' figure. The former political editor of the *Mirror* was deeply affected by the course events had taken. In the words of one observer, he was 'tearful but not crying'. He informed Platell: 'This is the worst day of my life.'

Then they got down to business. Platell and Campbell understood one another. They played out their allotted roles to perfection. It became clear very quickly that money was the issue for Campbell. Technically, the *Mirror* believed that there was no case that the appointment of David Seymour amounted to constructive dismissal. Campbell's responsibilities remained the same. His position was not affected one jot. On the other hand the *Mirror* understood Campbell's disappointment. 'Alastair told me,' Platell later told friends, 'that I treated him with such dignity that he felt that under the circumstances it could

6. Actually Campbell had been alerted in advance to his impending fate by his friend Richard Stott, whom Seymour soon told of the *Mirror* approach.

not have been handled better.' At the end of the conversation Campbell rose to leave. Before doing so, he turned to Platell and told her: 'Having spoken to you I can walk out of here with my head held high.' It was a greatly restored Alastair Campbell who stepped purposefully out of the *Mirror* building for the last time. Though in truth, it was not Amanda Platell alone who had made all the difference. The promise of a severance payment worth approximately £100,000 had also greatly helped.

Six years later, in the spring of 1999, Amanda Platell was hired as the Conservative Party Head of Media. The first time she attended Prime Minister's Questions Campbell smiled at her across the chamber, and gave her a quiet wave of welcome. It is also typical of Campbell that he never allowed past personal antagonism to cloud his relationship with David Montgomery after he went to work as Tony Blair's press spokesman.[7]

Stott to the rescue for the third time

Three times Richard Stott has intervened to help Alastair Campbell out of a tight spot. He secured him his first job in Fleet Street. He brought him back to the *Daily Mirror* after his nervous breakdown. And now as editor of *Today*, days after Campbell left the *Mirror*, he offered him the post of Assistant Editor (Politics) vacated by David Seymour, whose move to the *Mirror* had just brought about Campbell's departure.

At least Campbell was among friends at *Today*. It was to be his only stint on a Murdoch-owned paper – the Australian tycoon had acquired *Today* when Eddie Shah's vision came to grief – during his fourteen years as a journalist. Richard Stott was giving a dazzling demonstration of how an irreverent left-wing tabloid paper ought to be run. Even so, Campbell's presence at his old stamping ground had a curious feel to it. He resembled a well-heeled traveller living in bed-and-breakfast accommodation while seeking somewhere permanent to stay.

Campbell's column cannot have taken up much of his time. His tone was now more trenchant, assured and savage than in the old days at the *Mirror*.[8] The

7. Campbell, for instance, made an advance call to Montgomery to inform him that the *Sun* was coming out for Labour on the eve of the 1997 General Election campaign (interview with the author, May 1999).

8. An invaluable characterisation of its contents appeared in Francis Wheen's *Guardian* column on 17 February 1999. Wheen focuses on the remarks Campbell may later have had most cause to regret. He is most informative on the crashing contempt that Campbell clearly felt for the monarchy. See also *Private Eye*, February 1999.

attacks on John Major were venomous. The Conservative Prime Minister was by this stage a universal target, but no one struck home more regularly or with greater brutality than Alastair Campbell. Even today, Major cannot mention Campbell without a shudder.[9] The relationship between the two is curious. It started on an encouraging note. Campbell was swift to spot Major as a rising force when he joined the Cabinet after the 1987 election, ranking him alongside Tony Blair and Gordon Brown as one of six 'names to conjure with' in his famous article of September 1988. So determined was Campbell to attach himself to the Major bandwagon that he was the only Tory politician granted his own *Sunday Mirror* profile.[10] When John Major finally secured the Tory leadership upon the downfall of Thatcher in 1990, lobby journalists remember an astonishing scene: the *Mirror* political editor thrust his way through the mêlée surrounding Major in the Commons, put his arms round his neck and embraced him vigorously. This typical Campbell gesture could have been taken as an act of either gross impertinence or warm affection. The new Prime Minister – famously tactile himself – responded in kind.

That moment represented the high-point in the relationship between the two men. Some psychological insight – or perhaps merely the savage instinct of the playground bully – subsequently enabled Campbell to sniff out the Prime Minister's vulnerable points in a way that others could not. He refused to give John Major any of the respect that a Prime Minister is accustomed to expect. The abuse which found its way into print was vicious enough. On one occasion Campbell called Major 'the piece of lettuce who passes for Prime Minister';[11] on another 'simply a second-rate, shallow, lying little toad of a man.'[12] This kind of language, from a respected political columnist, was unusually strong but capable of being brushed aside as an established part of the game. What was unusual, and shocking, was the abuse that Campbell would dole out to John Major in person. Within a very short time he had made it perfectly plain that he regarded the Prime Minister as a ridiculous figure of no consequence.

Lobby correspondents all know the Prime Minister of the day well. They meet him about the House of Commons, sometimes at formal lobby meetings, and most of all on overseas trips. On long-haul flights and at receptions in foreign embassies the Prime Minister allows lobby men to gather round and he

9. Private information.
10. Sadly, such is the inadequacy of the *Mirror* library that I have been unable to track down this item.
11. *Today*, 9 May 1994.
12. *Ibid.*, 30 May 1994.

or she will often talk freely on the issues of the day. It was at these events that Campbell would make his contempt so clear. He would shout derisive remarks in the hearing of John Major. On one of John Major's earliest trips abroad, on the Downing Street VC10, the Prime Minister wandered back to the press seats. He was full of ebullience, eager to talk. Campbell glared at him: 'Oh, sod off Prime Minister,' he said. 'I'm trying to do my expenses.'[13]

Campbell's cleverest jibe of all, because it preyed so precisely on John Major's own social insecurities, was his observation that the Prime Minister tucked his shirt inside his underpants. He claims to have noticed this phenomenon on Major's first major overseas trip to Washington at Christmas 1990, but did not bring it to the attention of colleagues until the following month, when lobby journalists flew out with John Major to the Gulf.[14] Major's underpants soon became an urban myth, and were adopted as a Major trademark by the *Guardian* cartoonist Steve Bell.

On overseas journeys with the Prime Minister the British press corps have always borne a close resemblance to a collection of clever sixth-formers accompanying a teacher on a school trip. There is a healthy conflict between the teacher's wish for his pupils to do what he thinks is interesting and the pupils' own strong desire to go off and do their own thing. Campbell took this tension one stage further. He ridiculed and humiliated the teacher, destroying his authority by turning him into a figure of fun. After a while, the rest of the lobby caught on and began to treat John Major in the same way. In due course this attitude fanned outwards to embrace fashionable opinion in London, and thence to the rest of the country. But there is a strong case to be made that it all started with Alastair Campbell and the underpants. The conversion of the Tory Prime

13. Campbell recalls this remark in his column in *Today* on 17 February 1994. 'I realised the moment the words had formed in my mouth that it was wrong to speak in this way, but it was too late. Familiarity had bred contempt.'

14. Campbell claims credit for the observation, but we only have his word to go on. At the time he did not write up the underpants story himself, explaining later that he was 'only 90 per cent sure of the accuracy of the claim'. Once he passed it on to colleagues, if he did so, it spread quickly. Ian Aitken of the *Guardian* is often given the credit for using it first in print; the *Mail on Sunday* also has claims. Aitken insists that his own informant was not Campbell but another source, whom he does not feel at liberty to identify. When he wrote his story he had no idea of Campbell's role. Campbell first boasted in public about his insight in his *Sunday Mirror* column on 17 March 1991. He explained: 'Somewhere over the Atlantic, a jacketless Mr Major left his comfy quarters at the back of the plane to join the press for an hour or two. At one point I was standing behind him as he bent down to talk to someone. I noticed three layers of clothing – his trousers, followed by what looked like the elasticated top of a pair of underpants, followed by his pale blue shirt closest to his skin.' Though no independent corroboration of Campbell's assertion that he originated the John Major underpants sage has emerged, there seems every reason to take him at his word. Campbell had no reason to lie about the episode, and it is entirely in character.

Minister into a ludicrous, comic-cuts figure was probably the greatest of all the services that Campbell has done for Labour.

After John Major, the biggest target of Campbell's *Today* column was the royal family. The move from the *Mirror* seems to have released him as a writer. He felt able to tackle a broader range of subjects, and in a more rancorous way. Much has been made of the close relationship Campbell later forged with the Palace after moving to Downing Street. That is true: there is a very strong argument to be made that Alastair Campbell, with the assistance of Peter Mandelson, saved the monarchy from destruction with their timely advice in the wake of Princess Diana's death in the late summer of 1997. The Palace remains grateful, and properly so, for the guidance that Campbell offered. It was of the highest calibre.[15]

But there is no mistaking, either, the screaming derision and contempt that Campbell felt for the royal family before the constitutional proprieties of Downing Street bore down heavily upon him. The early 1990s represented the nadir of royal fortunes. The Palace was forced to endure the divorce of the Prince and Princess of Wales, the Windsor fire, the absurdity of Sarah Ferguson and much else besides. Kicking the royals was a national pastime as much as kicking John Major. Campbell was even more unpleasant than most. 'There are many reasons for the decline in royal esteem,' he announced in May 1993. 'One is that royals are thick.' He labelled Prince Philip 'insensitive and stupid'[16] and Prince Charles 'an overprivileged twit'.[17] Princess Diana – later to be converted into the People's Princess – was 'vacuous, shallow, silly and egomaniacal'[18] while her brother, Earl Spencer, was a 'hypocritical upper-class little pillock.'[19] As Campbell stated in his *Today* column in February 1994, 'I have never gone for the notion that the royal family represents all that is right in this country. They represent to me much that is wrong in this country, notably its class system, obsession with titles, dressing up and patronage and the arrogance of unelected power.'[20]

15. Author's conversation with Palace officials.
16. *Today*, 10 May 1993.
17. *Ibid.*, 9 May 1994.
18. Quoted in *Private Eye*, February 1999. Francis Wheen was the first to highlight the prodigious disgust Alastair Campbell expressed for individual members of the royal family, as well as for the institution itself. His important *Eye* article contains a generous selection of the most offensive attacks. Only the Queen herself seems to have remained exempt from Campbell's withering contempt.
19. *Ibid.*
20. *Today*, 24 February 1994.

Campbell's own core political beliefs are not sophisticated, but they are strongly felt. They still embrace some of the angry rancour of his student days at Cambridge towards the young army officers and Old Etonians who set the social tone for the university. He has never expressed that emotion quite as eloquently as he did when attacking Prince Charles in his *Today* column on 9 May 1994. In an extraordinary outburst he described Britain's future king as 'someone who cannot hold his marriage together, does not see his own kids from day to day, delegates their upbringing to nannies and private school spankers, went to a Spanking Academy himself, needed the power of patronage to get into university, apparently wants to send his own sons to Eton, *the* Spanking Academy, whose advisers all come from similar establishments and are similarly ill-suited to speak about the real world, and who courts his mistress with lavatorial suggestions.'[21] Here speaks the real Campbell, the angry, disaffected Alastair Campbell who mulled over his many grievances at the Late Night Bar at Gonville and Caius College. That side of Campbell, for worldly and pragmatic reasons, has mainly been kept hidden since. Something about the heady, destructive national mood of the mid-1990s, fuelled by the witty, lucid anarchism of Richard Stott's *Today* newspaper, let it loose in the last months before John Smith's death propelled Campbell towards government.

It is interesting to speculate what would have happened to Campbell if John Smith had not died when he did. In 1994 his career was drifting. He was established as a minor celebrity of sorts. The fisticuffs in the lobby with Michael White had begun the process of building a wider Campbell profile.[22] The flurry of publicity that surrounded his departure from the *Mirror* increased it still further. Alastair Campbell was in any case an extremely accomplished media performer. His rugged good looks worked well on television and he had a pleasant speaking voice. Best of all, from the point of view of television and radio producers, he was always available and would jump through any hoop. He hosted one late-night television show at the height of John Major's back to basics crisis from a bed, having failed to persuade any number of Tory MPs to share it with him.

There is a nether world out there where politics and the media meet, and a living of sorts to be made out of a portfolio of chat-shows, occasional columns

21. *Ibid.*, 9 May 1994.
22. At the time he told colleagues that it was 'a very good short-term career move.' Sir John Junor, the legendary ex-editor of the *Sunday Express*, commended Campbell's action highly in his *Mail on Sunday* column.

and paper-reviews. It is inhabited by sepulchral figures like David Mellor and the Labour MP Austin Mitchell. Campbell was heading in that direction in the months before John Smith died. He was out of sympathy with the Labour leadership, his friends were in exile, and he himself was slowly drifting away from mainstream politics. He was spending his life reviewing newspapers very early in the morning and appearing on chat shows very late at night. It must sometimes have seemed to him that there was barely time to get home and shave between the two activities.[23]

But the television makeup girls loved him to bits. They found him madly attractive and voted him 'most popular newspaper reviewer'. They discovered he had a taste for Toblerone bars, and to this day present him with them at party conferences.

23. In March 1999, at a Fabian Society conference, Campbell launched an attack on the *Today* programme paper-review, which he described as 'a vehicle for getting in stories not worth reporting in their own right' (*Broadcasting Politics*, Fabian Special 42, March 1999). Coming from such an inveterate paper-reviewer, this remark must have contained an element of self-hatred.

Chapter Seven

THE RISE OF THE MEDIA CLASS

*Of course we want to use the media, but the media will be our tools, our servants;
we are no longer content to let them be our persecutors.*
  Peter Mandelson

Today newspaper found it hard to get hold of Alastair Campbell on the morning
of John Smith's death on 12 May 1994. The reason was entirely characteristic:
he was reviewing the newspapers on BBC television.[1] Campbell never suffered
the agonising conflict of loyalties that afflicted his friend Peter Mandelson as
this saddest of days unfolded.[2] From the start he felt a complete conviction that
Tony Blair would and should become Labour leader.

Campbell threw himself into the Blair campaign. He had known the future
Prime Minister since 1985, and been heavily involved in advising him on how
to handle the press since 1989 if not before.[3] The connection grew closer still
after the 1992 election, when Campbell emerged as the leading Fleet Street
voice speaking up for the New Labour modernisers. The relationship was so
close that Tony Blair's biographer refers to Campbell in 1993 as Blair's 'proto-
press-secretary'.[4]

Well before the spring of 1994, Alastair Campbell and Fiona Millar had
concluded that Blair and not Gordon Brown would succeed John Smith. In the
summer of 1993, the Campbell-Millars shared a holiday villa in Majorca with
Philip Gould and his wife Gail Rebuck. Peter Mandelson joined them. It was a
conspiratorial group and the three exiles devoted much time and effort to
rubbishing Smith. In between lamenting the inadequacies of the – in their
opinion – ponderous Leader of the Opposition, they speculated about the
future. Campbell and Gould expressed their view that Blair was the coming

1. See for example Donald Macintyre, *Mandelson*, p. 251.
2. See *ibid.*, pp. 251–71 for the most authoritative account of Mandelson's dilemma; and the present
author (*Sunday Express*, 17 January 1999) on how Mandelson poured his heart out to a near-stranger
hours after John Smith's death.
3. According to Tony Blair's biographer John Rentoul, p. 445, Alastair Campbell was heavily
involved in advising Blair on how to handle the trade unions when the future Labour leader was Shadow
Employment Secretary.
4. *Ibid.*, p. 333.

man: they could hardly believe it when Peter Mandelson stood up for Gordon Brown.[5] This was the holiday on which Mandelson made the momentous decision to shave off his moustache, providing a rare scoop for Campbell in his *Today* column upon his return to Britain.

Alignments in the post-Smith era

To all intents and purposes Campbell had an official role in the Blair leadership campaign. He appeared on *Newsnight* on the very evening of John Smith's death to proclaim Tony Blair the inevitable winner of the forthcoming leadership contest. This utterance, made with stone-cold conviction and total moral certainty, horrified Peter Mandelson, who promptly rang Campbell to berate him. Campbell was unmoved.[6] He went on to write Blair's glossy campaign leaflet, given the ineffable title of *Principle, Purpose, Power*. He plotted merrily away on behalf of Tony Blair, leaving no stone unturned in an attempt to bury all of Blair's opponents and Gordon Brown in particular. This vigorous activity was noted by the Brown camp with dismay but not surprise. Paul Routledge, Brown's far from dispassionate biographer, records with disapproval that in the days immediately following John Smith's death, Campbell was 'briefing heavily and continuously against Brown.'[7] Routledge contrasts Campbell's unsportsmanlike behaviour with Brown's reverential attitude towards Marquess of Queensberry rules. 'Brown,' Routledge wearily records, 'was reluctant to begin even the softest press campaign against Blair.'

It is one of those enduring minor mysteries that at this point Brown never really held a grudge against Alastair Campbell, in spite of his leading role in extinguishing whatever faint hopes he might have had of becoming party leader. Against Peter Mandelson, who did his utmost to keep these hopes alive,[8]

5. An account of this summer holiday appears in Donald Macintyre, *op.cit.* It reveals the existence of a holiday video of Gould and Campbell 'ribbing Mandelson about his fixation with Brown as a future leader'. This information was presumably placed there by Mandelson's allies in an effort to mend fences with Gordon Brown and absolve him of charges of betrayal from the Brown camp.

6. Macintyre, p. 256. Campbell was not, however, the first journalist to finger Blair as the inevitable winner. Andy McSmith, Campbell's former colleague from *Mirror* days, did so on the BBC *Six O'Clock News*. There may be earlier examples still.

7. Routledge, *Gordon Brown: The Biography* (paperback, 1998), p. 206. As a committed Brownite Routledge's version of events cannot be taken on trust, but it is corroborated by a great mass of independent testimony. It is supported by Donald Macintyre, who records (*op.cit.*, p. 257) that Mandelson intervened on behalf of Brown to ask Campbell to desist.

8. It is one of the many achievements of Macintyre's masterful biography of Peter Mandelson that it establishes this important point irrefutably.

he has ever since nurtured a deadly resentment. Brown never reckoned Campbell as an ally, taking him from the very first as a member of the fraternity of North London media folk who – in Brown's considered opinion – conspired to deprive the Labour Party of its rightful leader.[9] For their part Alastair Campbell and Fiona Millar took the view from very early on that Brown was too personally idiosyncratic ever to become a plausible or satisfactory candidate for Labour Prime Minister.[10]

This mutual coolness has never stopped the two men doing business for the very good reason that they have the highest respect for each other's talents. The case of Peter Mandelson, whose central role in the Blair leadership campaign was kept secret at the time, is something entirely different. Gordon Brown's sense of betrayal, even though unjustified by facts, goes very deep: far beyond words. It operates upon a more complicated level than mere reason.

At the end of the campaign, the question arose whether to offer Campbell the position of press spokesman. In retrospect the choice looks obvious: not at the time. Nobody questioned Campbell's abilities, his loyalty or his immense personal charisma. But there was his past to consider. It was only eight years since he had emerged from hospital after suffering a breakdown: there was no guarantee that the same thing might not happen again. It was absolutely certain that all the old stories of the pornography and the boozing would come out.[11]

Tony Blair looked to Peter Mandelson for advice about Campbell. There is some evidence that Mandelson did not weigh in as generously on behalf of his old friend as he might have done. Mandelson had his own position as Blair's private media counsellor to protect. He knew Campbell's vast ability, but also the way he did business: direct with the boss. It is possible that Mandelson might have preferred a figure he could control more easily than Campbell. Five years before, he had supported Julie Hall for the position of Neil Kinnock's press spokeswoman, which was never the happiest of appointments. Among her many qualities one stood out: she was never likely to threaten Mandelson in any way.

The evidence suggests that Mandelson did his best to steer Blair quietly away from Campbell. There were a number of powerful candidates. Philip

9. Private information.

10. Private information.

11. They did. Campbell told Kevin Toolis in 1998 that 'When I took the job I said to Tony that the pornography, the drinking, the nervous breakdown would all be out within a week. I was wrong – the porn was headlines in two days' (*Guardian Weekend*, 4 April 1998). See 'Saucy Secrets of Blair's New Boy', *News of the World*, 11 September 1994.

Bassett, then industrial editor of *The Times* but recruited to Downing Street in 1997, fancied his chances.[12] Colin Byrne, the former Labour Party press officer, was cited as a contender. Certainly, Mandelson urged the case for others, including Andy Grice, then political correspondent of the *Sunday Times*. Derek Draper, Peter Mandelson's former assistant, admits that Mandelson 'made the case for Grice at one stage. And Alastair would know that.'

A further complication was introduced by Neil Kinnock, who was a summer guest of the Campbell-Millars in the South of France that year. Kinnock argued passionately that Campbell would be mad to take the job. He said, with considerable truth, that it would ruin his family life. It was a view which Fiona Millar strongly supported. In order to avert this impending calamity, Kinnock offered his friend the job of *chef de cabinet* in his new Commissioner's office in Brussels. It is probable that some report of these discussions filtered through to Tony Blair because the newly elected Labour leader suddenly turned up in the Campbell-Millar holiday home near Avignon as well. So for a few heady days in August Campbell found himself the object of a tug of love between the past and present leaders of the Labour Party.[13]

But Campbell never really had a choice. There is a strong sense in which he had been preparing for his latest attachment all his life. Even his period as press relations man for Robin Fenner, certainly his time at the *Daily Mirror*, above all his years of devotion to Neil Kinnock, had all been useful schooling for this particular post. Campbell had always sought to be the instrument of a very powerful man. Now the ultimate opportunity had come his way. Two years later he said that what eventually decided him was imagining two post-General-Election situations. 'Two things came back to me the whole time,' he said. 'The first was that we lost the election and I was there thinking I could have made a difference. And the other was that we had won and I could have been a part of it.'[14]

12. Philip Bassett, now a senior member of the Downing Street Strategic Communications Unit, is viewed by Whitehall insiders as a likely successor to Campbell if he were to step down as Press Secretary.

13. See the illuminating account given in Jon Sopel, *Tony Blair: The Moderniser* (1995), p. 239; also Philip Gould, *The Unfinished Revolution* (1998), p. 214. Gould quotes Campbell as follows: 'Fiona was basically hostile, she felt it was too much. Neil was totally hostile and he was there on holiday for part of the time and was saying it will completely ruin your life. It will ruin your family's life, it will ruin your health. Life as you know it is over. Forget it, don't do it. And then Tony appeared, stayed for a few days and we talked about all sorts of things, but in the end it was me thinking, you can't really say no to this...'.

14. Quoted in Gould, p. 214. See also the interview with Helena de Bertodano, *Sunday Telegraph*, 19 March 1995.

The New Labour *coup d'état*

Alastair Campbell's appointment as press spokesman for Tony Blair was announced in September 1994, during the TUC conference at Blackpool. The inner core of New Labour was now complete. It comprised – and continues to comprise – just five men. They are: Tony Blair himself, Gordon Brown, Philip Gould, Peter Mandelson and Alastair Campbell. No one else really mattered apart from these five. And this remains the case today despite the partial estrangement of Gordon Brown and Peter Mandelson's resignation from the Cabinet. It is a sign of the endurance of this tight-knit group that even after his resignation, Mandelson has remained almost as potent a presence as when he was a Cabinet minister. These five had been the modernisers who fretted and strained under John Smith's leadership. Now they were let loose. They could do what they wanted. Nothing stood in their way. They had secured control of the Labour movement and over the coming two years they would use that dominance to create a new political party and an entirely fresh political force in Britain. The importance of this development cannot be overestimated. Bitter jealousies, enmities and hatreds divided them as individuals – indeed these were so poisonous that Peter Mandelson and Gordon Brown were not to exchange more than three or four consecutive words for the following two years. But more powerful by far were the factors that bound them together: a profound contempt for the traditional structures of the Labour Party and existing institutions of British government, a lethal understanding of raw political power and how it can be achieved and then exercised in the modern British state; above all, an awesome will to win.

They included some of the most fascinating men that British politics has thrown up this century. No individual as exotic as Peter Mandelson has blossomed quite so close to the heart of power since George Villiers, Duke of Buckingham, strutted his stuff at the court of James I four hundred years ago. Alastair Campbell was an extraordinary individual: he was soon to turn into an entirely novel constitutional phenomenon. Gordon Brown, brooding and complex, his brilliant political mind quite unable to come to terms with everyday human life, was already a massive figure on the political stage. Philip Gould, the author of the first sacred text of the New Labour movement,[15] was the least known of the five. But

15. Significantly titled *The Unfinished Revolution* (1998). The book by Peter Mandelson and Roger Liddle published before the General Election was called *The Blair Revolution* (1996). Revolution is a favourite word among the Blairites, and with good reason.

for Blair and the others he was a talismanic figure, always at the forefront of the modernising mission.[16] Tony Blair was the only one of them who seemed normal but that of course was a delusion: he was the most extraordinary of all.

In the summer of 1994 these five men carried out a *coup d'état* of breathtaking brilliance and simplicity: the election of Tony Blair as leader meant that they seized control of the Labour Party. It is too easy to take for granted the magnitude of the accomplishment. Labour is a great political party with many hundreds of thousands of members. But with the will, the genius and the luck of the Spaniard Pizarro conquering the Inca empire against massive odds, they won the battle and have since consolidated their power. Their hold, however, remains fragile: they are still outnumbered, and were circumstances to change, they would be vulnerable to surprise attack.

Looking back with hindsight it is possible to see that the primary architect of this extraordinary feat was Peter Mandelson. This flawed politician of high talent possessed the narrow, desiccated frame of the true revolutionary – a Robespierre or a Trotsky. Mandelson had been there since the beginning. On his route to power he had endured two heart-rending defeats, in 1987 and 1992, as well as those wilderness years under John Smith until it all came good for him with the leadership election of 1994. He was not to enjoy the fruits of power for long. It was the more solidly built, square-framed, practical politicians – Blair, Campbell and Brown – who survived to reap the rewards of the revolution that Mandelson had worked so hard to bring about, and whose nature perhaps he understood best of all.

16. Philip Gould, the son of a teacher, was brought up in the suburbs of Woking, in Surrey. He failed his 11-plus and left school at the age of 16 with one O-level in geography. Showing great perseverance, he overcame this drawback to take a Master's degree in political theory at the London School of Economics. There he was taught by Michael Oakeshott, the influential Tory philosopher.

In America Gould would be called a 'political consultant'. Much of his job involves conducting focus groups on behalf of Tony Blair. He was one of the 'beautiful people' blasted by John Prescott after the 1992 General Election. This was a misleading description. His suits were shabby, his hair was out of control and he carried vital Labour Party documents around in a plastic bag. (On 17 March 1997, the day John Major called the last election, Gould left the New Labour campaign plan outside the Burger King restaurant at Euston Station. It was retrieved by party officials without mishap.)

Gould was with the Clinton campaign at Little Rock in 1992, noting how the Presidential candidate reinvented the Democratic Party to appeal to middle America. He brought back Clinton's techniques and ideas to Britain. At the heart of his political philosophy is the belief that the Labour Party of the 1980s abandoned 'ordinary people with suburban dreams', a phrase used in the very moving opening chapter to *The Unfinished Revolution*, pp. 1–17. Though in every way entirely different from that formidable politician, Gould is in a sense Tony Blair's Norman Tebbit. Both men took that vital but too easily neglected constituency – the lower middle class – seriously. Gould's mission has always been to reclaim these people for Labour. In May 1997 that is what happened.

Mandelson's and New Labour's genius was to grasp that the key to power in modern Britain was the media. Revolutionaries in the past have focused on the obvious symbols of state – the armed forces, the prisons, government buildings and the Royal Palaces – and used the mob as their instrument of destruction. Mandelson realised that today the media mattered far more than all these put together. Two hundred years ago the French revolutionaries stormed the Bastille. In 1994 and since, the insurrectionaries of New Labour have taken as their target the BBC, ITV, the newspaper editors, the broadcasters and the parliamentary lobby. They were all there for the picking. The newspapers have never been a negligible, and are sometimes a potent, force in politics. In the 1990s the print media allied with broadcasting combined to turn into a devastating power in the land: they suddenly achieved critical mass.

There have been many attempts to define New Labour. Before the last election Tony Blair made an inept and half-hearted attempt to place a 'stakeholding economy' at the heart of his political philosophy. That swiftly foundered. Since the election the notion of a 'third way' in modern politics has been promoted by New Labour thinkers. This idea has more plausibility, but even less popular force, than its defunct predecessor. 'Third way' discourse has a tendency to oscillate between the deeply banal and the profoundly obscure. It is very much more accurate to define New Labour by its relationship with the media: it was the first ever Media Class opposition. In due course it became established as the first ever Media Class government with Tony Blair installed in No. 10 Downing Street as the first ever Media Class Prime Minister.

Campbell's own input into the formulation of these ideas was strictly perfunctory. His role in their projection, however, was characteristic. Tony Blair launched the 'stakeholding' theme with a speech to local businessmen in Singapore in January 1996. It came too late to suit British broadcasters. Campbell therefore arranged for Blair to extract the relevant passages from the body of the text and place them at the very start of the speech. 'The guests were utterly bewildered,' recalls one British member of the audience.

The rise of the Media Class

The rise in the status of journalism in all its manifestations has been one of the most striking developments of our time. Very little more than a generation ago, journalism was a dishonourable and poorly esteemed profession. Now talented journalists have become fêted celebrities. They wield immense social, economic and political power which the Media Class has gathered unto itself at the expense of the great institutions of the state, the monarchy and the church.

Nowhere is the elevation of the humble jobbing journalist more apparent than in political reporting. In the immediate post-war epoch, right up to the election of Harold Wilson as Prime Minister in 1964, the attitude of political reporters to the House of Commons and to politicians was profoundly deferential. It was practically unheard of for parliamentary correspondents – the title Political Editor and the grandeur that implies did not develop till the late 1960s[17] – to have lunch with a Cabinet minister. Indeed, one of the primary requirements of the lobby man was to arrange, though not to attend, lunches on behalf of his proprietor. Gerald Herlihy, the political correspondent of the *Graphic*, was for a number of years in effect the social secretary to his proprietor's wife, Lady Kemsley.[18]

Political reporters were divided between 'parliamentary' correspondents and 'political' correspondents. It was the function of the former to report, partly in the flamboyant manner of a theatre critic, the events of the previous day in the Commons chamber. These articles were given abundant space. Parliamentary correspondents were considered very much more important than political correspondents, whose membership of the lobby enabled them to share some of the privileges of Members of Parliament. These lobby men would add a few lines to the account of the previous day's parliamentary drama, modestly drawing attention to items of particular significance.[19] This division of power within the profession indicates how political reporters accepted Parliament on its own terms. Politicians were judged very much in the way they wanted to be judged.

Prime Ministers in the post-war period did not deal with political reporters at all, and very rarely even with newspaper editors. They maintained a warm relationship with the great press proprietors, whom they met at society functions and country houses. When Churchill suffered a stroke in June 1953 the illness was never reported. This serious disruption in the life of a serving Prime Minister was one of the biggest stories the press had had to cope with since the war. Yet it was covered up with ease. Downing Street merely indicated to the great proprietors – Beaverbrook, Bracken and Camrose – that it would be

17. It was a way of getting round statutory pay restraints.

18. I am indebted to Ivor Owen for this information.

19. The low status accorded lobby men is indicated by the fact that the parliamentary lobby is deemed worthy of just two out of more than 1100 pages in Stephen Koss's *The Rise and Fall of the Political Press in Britain* (1981).

inconvenient if this distressing illness got out, and it never did.[20] Eventually it was Churchill himself, restored and at the despatch box of the Commons, who chose to reveal that he had had a stroke:[21] a tribute to the then inviolate power of Parliament.

Churchill, during his second term as Prime Minister, held reporters in such low esteem that he refused to let them in through the front door of Downing Street when they turned up for their diet of daily official announcements. He banned them from the building and insisted that they use a room in the Cabinet Office further up Whitehall instead. When he reluctantly handed over power in April 1955, his successor Anthony Eden attempted to ingratiate himself with the press by rescinding the ban. But the feudal spirit remained. Harold Evans, who served as Press Secretary to both Harold Macmillan and Sir Alec Douglas-Home, adopted the demeanour and approach of a superior gentleman's gentleman. Downing Street briefings were conducted in the spirit of the butler at a great country estate addressing the domestic staff. Nobody thought this was odd or offensive.[22] Lord Poole, chairman of the Tory Party under Macmillan, once pronounced on the subject of lobby correspondents at a Chatham House discussion. They were very decent fellows, he opined, but not quite the sort of people one would invite into one's own home.[23]

The parliamentary reporter needed two qualities: an outstanding shorthand note and the ability to keep his head down. Very few of them had been to university: they had come up the hard way, starting with local papers in the provinces. Anthony Howard, who later became editor of the *New Statesman*, entered the lobby as a reporter for *Reynolds News* in 1958. He recollects that there were two other graduates in the Press Gallery: Bernard Levin of the

20. Only the *Liverpool Daily Post* broke ranks. Once again I am indebted to Ivor Owen, a member of the Press Gallery at the time, for this information. Churchill's biographer, Martin Gilbert, records his aide's recollections of writing by hand to Beaverbrook, Bracken and Camrose and sending the letters to London by despatch rider: 'All three immediately came to Chartwell and paced the lawn in earnest conversation. They achieved the all but incredible, and in peacetime probably unique, success of gagging Fleet Street, something they would have done for nobody but Churchill.' (*Winston S. Churchill*, vol. 8, *Never Despair: 1945–65*, 1988).

21. Ivor Owen remembers this moment vividly.

22. See the essay by Peter Riddell in Jean Seaton's collection of essays *Politics and the Media: Harlots and Prerogatives at the Turn of the Millennium* (1998) for an invaluable and highly informative analysis of the relationship between the Westminster-based media and politics. Harold Evans in due course received a knighthood for his pains.

23. I am grateful to Anthony Howard, very much the sort of lobby correspondent who does get invited into private houses, for this anecdote.

Spectator and T. F. Lindsay, the sketchwriter for the *Daily Telegraph*. 'Lindsay practically fell round my neck. He greeted me like a long lost soul,' records Howard. When Harold Wilson entered No. 12 Downing Street (the house which serves as the Whips' Hall, the large back room of which is sometimes used for Prime Ministerial press conferences) to give his first lobby briefing the day he became Prime Minister in 1964, the room stood to attention as he walked in.[24] That sort of behaviour is inconceivable today. Perhaps the change reflects no more than the impoverishment of modern manners and the collapse of deference. But the collapse of deference is synonymous with and part of the story of the rise of the Media Class.

It was Wilson who first gave parliamentary reporters some kind of self-respect. He regarded them as important people. He called them by their Christian names. He read their work and was able to contrast their individual styles and modes of operation. He was at ease with them socially and they with him. He would invite the more important members of the lobby fraternity down to Chequers. He awarded knighthoods to two working political journalists, Francis Boyd of the *Guardian* and Harry Boyne of the *Telegraph*. He took them with him on overseas trips, and frequently made himself available to brief the lobby in person. On such occasions the sign would go up on the lobby notice-board: 'Sunrise Red at 4 p.m.' This obliged the Tories to respond in kind. Their leader Edward Heath, in the curious Masonic terminology then favoured by lobby men, was known as 'Celestial Blue'.[25]

Wilson was the first Prime Minister to grasp the rising importance of the press. Alan Watkins, the political columnist of the *Independent on Sunday*, is today an elder statesman of the Press Gallery. In the early 1960s he wrote the Crossbencher column for the *Sunday Express*. Throughout the two years before the 1964 General Election he would see Wilson once a week, on Fridays. The Leader of the Opposition would take endless trouble to furnish him with political gossip for his column. 'Like Senator Joe McCarthy, he knew the deadlines,' recalls Watkins. On one occasion, Watkins recalls ringing the Labour Party to check some minor detail about defence policy. He was surprised to receive a call back from the Leader of the Opposition himself.

---

24. Recalls Ivor Owen, who was there.

25. I am grateful to Jack Warden, then of the *Daily Express*, for this information. 'Red Mantle' was the code for Leader of the House Richard Crossman and 'Blue Mantle' the code for his Tory shadow. Warden says that Crossman was magnificently indiscreet at these briefings and candid about Cabinet rifts, often willing to volunteer information. But the lobby journalists made surprisingly little use of the information thus offered.

'Even I was surprised,' states Watkins, 'that Harold Wilson was taking an interest in what I might be writing.'

But it all went horribly wrong with Wilson. After a short space of time political reporters started to conclude that they had been taken for a ride. Devaluation of the pound in the autumn of 1967 perhaps sealed things. Thereafter the easy friendliness of the early days was replaced by bitter enmity and mutual contempt. But Wilson's fascination with the press continued. Only this time it was malevolent. He would plot and intrigue against individual reporters. David Wood, political correspondent of *The Times*, was an early case. The Prime Minister went to extreme and demeaning lengths to prevail upon the editor and proprietors of *The Times* to dismiss Wood. William Rees-Mogg, then *Times* editor, responded to these endeavours in the only way possible: by promoting David Wood to the rank of political editor. Another subject of Wilson's obsession was Nora Beloff, the *Observer* journalist who was first to draw attention to the powerful and to this day highly mysterious influence exercised by Marcia Williams on the Prime Minister. Wilson summoned David Astor, the owner and editor of the *Observer*, to see him in his office at the Commons. When Astor arrived, Wilson produced bulky files of Beloff's newspaper cuttings, heavily annotated and underlined. After rambling on like a man obsessed on the subject of the sinister influences at work upon Beloff, the Prime Minister then announced: 'Of course, I know all about the people she sees. In fact our people keep an eye on her to see just what she is up to.' Names, offices and meetings were provided for Astor's inspection. When checked back with Beloff later they proved accurate in all respects. Astor presumed that Labour Party trusties rather than MI5 officers were behind the surveillance, though the matter has never been satisfactorily explained.[26]

Late at night Harold Wilson would sit up with his tiny coterie of advisers, among them Gerald Kaufman and Marcia Williams, sifting through the first editions. They would assess likely sources for stories, always alert for signs of conspiracies being hatched against the Prime Minister. Any item that proved particularly difficult would result in a call from George Wigg, the Paymaster-General, to the editor or the correspondent concerned. A generation later, Tony

26. This account is drawn from the eye-popping chapter on Harold Wilson's relations with the political press in James Margach's absorbing book *The Abuse of Power* (1978). See also a more measured account of Harold Wilson's relations with the lobby in Ben Pimlott's biography of the former Prime Minister. Pimlott says of Nora Beloff: 'read today, her regular column appears innocuous enough, distinguished from rivals in other papers mainly by its relative ignorance of what was going on and of the issues that mattered' (*Harold Wilson*, paperback edition, 1993, p. 448).

Blair's New Labour would take an even greater interest in the press. For the most part, however, the assessment and analysis were devolved to party officials rather than carried out by the Party Leader himself.

Harold Wilson was the first Prime Minister to understand the importance of 'spin-doctoring'. The expression was not current in his day; 'Public Relations Officer' was the expression used then. The word 'spin-doctor', which conveys the greater degree of menace, subterfuge and mystique in the modern PRO's job, came later. It originated in the United States and is said to have derived from baseball. According to Dr Emma Lenz of the *Oxford English Dictionary*, the first recorded use of the term was by Saul Bellow in his 1977 Jefferson Lectures. The *Collins English Dictionary* (1999 edition) defines 'spin-doctor' as 'a person who provides a favourable slant to an item of news, potentially unpopular policy etcetera, especially on behalf of a political personality or party.' The word was not taken up in Britain until the early 1990s, when it was indelibly associated with the rise to public prominence of Peter Mandelson and his school of New Labour media experts.[27]

Wilson's catastrophic error was to try and carry out the task of spin-doctoring himself rather than delegate it to others. His first Press Secretary, Sir Trevor Lloyd-Hughes, was too scrupulous to fulfil the demands of the job. By the time that Joe Haines, an experienced press gallery hand with a fine political brain, was brought to bear in 1969, the problem had got out of control. Haines was condemned to fight a defensive war. It was often conducted with marvellous tactical astuteness but the chance to seize and then control the agenda, which was to be grasped with such brutal skill and strategic finesse by his successor Alastair Campbell twenty-five years later, had been well and truly cast away by the time Haines arrived on the scene.

The Media Class began to sense an intimation of its own future power during the Wilson premiership, but it did not emerge as a fully-fledged force on the national stage until the 1980s. Margaret Thatcher was a vital part of the story. The Media Class was her closest ally as she smashed down national institutions and challenged traditional sources of authority. She was often embattled and isolated within Parliament and even her own Tory Party, and the close alliances she formed with press proprietors, and through them with the political editors, became a key source of her power. The political press was no longer content, as it had been in the 1950s and the first half of the 1960s, to be a passive and neutral player in national debate. In the 1980s it developed with staggering

---

27. See the useful section on the derivation of the term in Stephen Bayley, *Labour Camp* (1998).

speed into a brilliant, potent and deeply destructive force in its own right. For a long time that force was harnessed to Margaret Thatcher and the Tory Party. Some observers lazily considered that the alliance would last for ever.

There was much that was new about the press of the 1980s. Though nobody was yet fully aware of it, the balance of power between reporter and reported had switched. The reporter now met his subject on equal terms. In some areas – financial reporting is an example – the old deference held. But in politics it first collapsed, then went into reverse. The Media Class became an élite at Westminster. It suddenly became the case that journalists, now for the most part graduates, were cleverer, more self-assured, far better paid and very much more influential than most of the people they were writing about. The brightest and the best were going into the media, by contrast it seemed the dunderheads who went into politics. The cold cult of exposure made the problem worse. Brilliant men and women who felt drawn to public life steered clear for fear that some private vice or past misdemeanour would come to light: some of them became journalists and joined the Media Class instead.

Parliamentary correspondents – the old breed of gallery reporters who ruled the roost up to the 1960s – went into rapid, terminal decline. Their shortcoming was that they reported politics straight. Political correspondents – whose training was to put a slant on the news rather than merely report – had become the dominant force. Newsdesks and editors made it plain that they wanted stories with a sharp, polemical edge. Lobby men used their privileges to trawl the corridors of the Commons in search of rifts and scandal. Neither was in short supply.

Television was the decisive force behind the rise of the Media Class. All democratic politicians can have only one overwhelming preoccupation: the voter. There are 30 million of them out there but no one really knows what these mysterious creatures want or why they behave the way they do. Numerous experts claim special insights of one sort or another. There is no final way of telling whether they are right or whether they are talking gibberish. A previous generation of statesmen at least had the advantage of dealing with the voter direct. Open-air meetings, the verbatim publication of political speeches in newspapers, door-to-door canvassing: all gave that opportunity. Television took most of that away. The last generation of great political orators went out with Aneurin Bevan in the 1950s – Neil Kinnock, a natural orator of genius, was born a generation too late. Newspapers abandoned the practice of handing over precious space to unprocessed political discourse not much later. With the rise of television politicians were handed over, trussed and bound, into the hands of the Media Class.

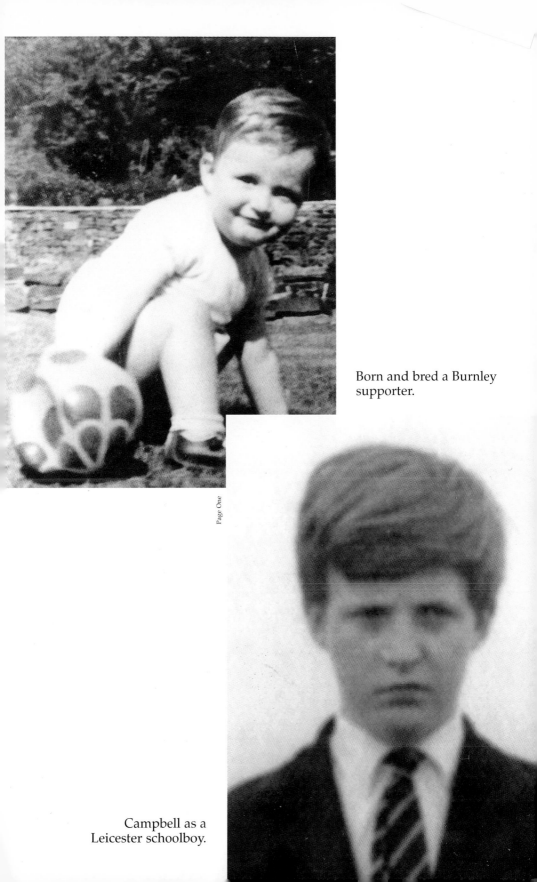

Born and bred a Burnley supporter.

Campbell as a Leicester schoolboy.

Gonville and Caius College ~ Freshmen ~ 1975

Tieless in Cambridge:
Campbell as a
Gonville and Caius
freshman, 1975.

Busking with
bagpipes

Above left: Robin Fenner, the Conservative councillor who gave Campbell his first spin-doctoring opportunity.

Above right: Robert Millar, 1981. He gave Campbell a privileged introduction to Labour politics.

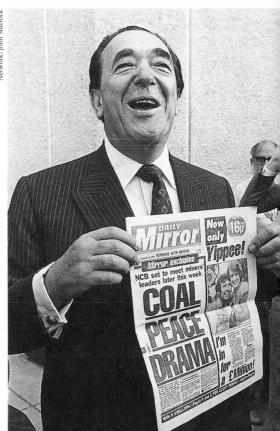

Robert Maxwell: an irresistible influence.

Above left: Campbell lays down the law to Neil and Glenys Kinnock, 1987.

Above right: Daily Mirror reporter interviews Isseyas Afeworki, General Secretary of the Eritrean People's Liberation Front, 1988.

Campbell with the Mirror establishment, *Sunday Mirror* Editor Eve Pollard and Royal Correspondent James Whitaker, 1990.

Fiona Millar with eldest son Rory, 1989.

On the campaign trail, April 1996. Blair meets Clinton; Campbell tries to duck out of shot.

Watching the boss's back.

Alastair Campbell, Peter Mandelson and David Hill, General Election Campaign 1997.

Power Women: Pauline Prescott, Cherie Blair and Fiona Millar.

Gordon Brown and Charlie Whelan: the more formidable opposition.

A rare shot of Alastair Campbell smiling. General Election Campaign, 1997.

From then on, politicians could set their own agenda only with the greatest difficulty, and only on the terms set by the Media Class. Media Class values had to apply. The media have no morality in the sense that the word is traditionally understood. But they prefer the short-term to the long-term, sentimentality to compassion, simplicity to complexity, the dramatic to the mundane, confrontation to the sensible compromise. They can destroy with a pitiless and awesome brutality. But they can rarely create anything new, original and good. They yearn for the stark contrast between hero and villain. It is hard to imagine any environment for political decision-making that could be more damaging and unhelpful. By the 1980s, however, the Media Class had established itself as the most powerful force in British national life, comparable in a number of ways to the over-mighty trade unions in the 1970s.[28]

For nearly a decade Margaret Thatcher rode the monster. The Media Class was not her natural ally, though it appeared to be so at the time. Large sections of the Media Class, above all the liberal élites which congregated in the broadsheets and the BBC, were always ranged against her. But they were unable to challenge the dominance she achieved through her alliance with the proprietors of United Newspapers, Associated Newspapers and above all News International. They gave an agenda to their editors, which was put into brilliant effect by two newspaper geniuses in particular: Kelvin MacKenzie of the *Sun* and David English at the *Daily Mail*. Their journalism was so well-focused and brilliant that its influence was impossible to resist, even by those who detested it most. And Margaret Thatcher's extraordinary personality fitted like a glove with the screaming Media Class demand for heroics, for confrontation and for drama. The eventual downfall of Thatcher, however, created an entirely new state of affairs and in due course unleashed the Media Class in a new direction. Under the bland and weak new Conservative Prime Minister John Major, the Media Class finally came of age. It threw off the Tory agenda and set about creating one of its own. It turned on the Conservative Party with an unspeakable ferocity and tore it apart.

It is impossible to understand Alastair Campbell, Tony Blair or New Labour without grasping all of the above. Campbell's earliest and most formative political experience was as a member of the tiny team of Neil Kinnock loyalists. He suffered at first hand as the Tory political editors ripped the man he

28. I am indebted to Hywel Williams, with whom I have spent many hours discussing the nature and impact of the Media Class. See Williams' account of the collapse of the last Tory government, *Guilty Men* (1998), pp. 14–20.

loved to shreds and destroyed his chance of ever becoming Prime Minister. Nowadays Neil Kinnock, a warm and decent human being, blames his own personality defects for his failure to win in 1992.[29] He need not be so hard on himself. The tabloid campaign to destroy Kinnock was the Media Class at its most brilliant, effective and repellent. Certainly Kinnock had weaknesses: they were magnified out of all proportion. Today William Hague, the Conservative Party leader, is a victim of the identical process of slaughter, carried out in many cases by the very same reporters. Campbell was a senior member of the Kinnock court in both the 1987 and 1992 General Elections. The experience scarred him for life, and this goes far to explain the strange bunkered isolation that persists inside Downing Street today: former members of Neil Kinnock's court are like dogs which have been brutalised by a cruel owner as puppies. They are never happy with outsiders, only at ease within a tiny circle of trusted intimates.

But Campbell, with his cool, urbane and powerful intelligence, made certain that he learnt all the lessons going from the obliteration of Kinnock, and when the Tories fell into difficulties in the first half of the 1990s he was ready to apply them. First of all he did so, to vicious effect, as a journalist. No one else spotted Major's weaknesses so quickly or exploited them so clinically. This painfully acquired knowledge is what made him such a perfect choice to become press spokesman for Tony Blair.

It was immediately apparent to Campbell, just as it was to Tony Blair, that there was an extraordinary opportunity opening up for the Labour Party in 1994. The two men discussed it in great depth that summer as they talked about the task ahead at the Campbell villa in the hills above Avignon. The chance was there to claim the Media Class – for more than a decade the insuperable obstacle that lay between the Labour Party and government – for themselves. It was a chance that the vilified and despised Neil Kinnock would never have been able to seize. It was a chance that John Smith, with his old-fashioned attitudes and rather admirable imperviousness to the North London media establishment, would never have wanted to grasp. But it was a chance that was tailor-made for Tony Blair, the new media-friendly leader of the Labour Opposition.

The best that Neil Kinnock had ever been able to look for was to neutralise the awesome hostility of the British media – and that in itself was a forlorn enough hope. With Alastair Campbell to help him, Blair would pursue a far

29. Nicholas Watt, *Guardian*, 17 June 1999.

more audacious objective and seek to turn the domestic media into allies and friends. Campbell's view, which he expressed again and again with considerable force, was that the tabloid press, in the past such an enemy of Labour, held the key. Campbell made it a condition of his job that every possible means should be exerted to bring the *Sun* aboard. Not that the Labour leader, whose own views already lay in that direction, needed any convincing.

Tony Blair raised one other matter with Alastair Campbell in those fleeting days in August. After swearing his new Press Secretary to secrecy, he informed him of the plan to abolish the Labour commitment to wholesale nationalisation in Clause 4 of the party constitution. It was a move that at once appealed to Campbell. Not so much because he was a New Labour moderniser who wanted this venerable and cherished antique moved out of Labour's front parlour: what Campbell liked about it was the strategic genius of the move. It would enable Blair to hit the ground running as Labour leader, make a symbolic statement of who he was and what he was about. 'What appealed to me,' Campbell said later, 'was the sheer boldness of it and the fact that this was someone who wasn't going to mess about.'[30]

Nevertheless, for a man of his sophistication, Campbell got off to a surprisingly poor start as Tony Blair's press spokesman. He loves being at the centre of attention – this characteristic should not be underestimated in Campbell though it is a vice he has since learnt to keep better hidden. He revelled in all the press interest he now attracted.

He gave too many television interviews. For several weeks he harboured the illusion that it would be possible to maintain his broadcasting career while acting as spin-doctor to Tony Blair. It was quite clear to everybody else that the job of press spokesman was to work quietly behind the scenes. Campbell thought that it could be combined with the role of high-profile public spokesman. He felt hurt and slighted when some of the breakfast television programmes that had used his services as a paper-reviewer dropped him for reasons of political impartiality. When the BBC political correspondent Nicholas Jones suggested that there was a contradiction in maintaining both roles, Campbell expressed outrage.[31] He was soon to find out the justice of Jones' remark the hard way. Campbell went on the *Frost Show* to review the papers, a practice he was reluctant to abandon. In a moment of unfathomable ineptitude he allowed himself to be drawn into a discussion of Labour Party

30. See Gould, p. 215.
31. See Nicholas Jones, *Soundbites and Spin Doctors* (1996), p. 163.

plans to renationalise the railways. His remarks managed both to contradict the position that had been publicly stated by Tony Blair earlier in the week as well as confuse the position that John Prescott was to set out later that day. Shortly afterwards Tony Blair introduced his press spokesman to a newspaper executive with the following words: 'This is Alastair Campbell. He gets more publicity than I do.'[32] This casual remark was delivered as a joke: it was actually a pointed public warning to Campbell to keep his head down. He eventually had the good sense to take it.

Sorting out Peter Mandelson

Labour's media operation at the first Party Conference in 1994, Campbell's first in harness, often came close to shambolic. This was not entirely his fault, for he had not yet severed his link to *Today* newspaper. But he must be held mainly to blame. Journalists working in Blackpool that year quickly discovered that there were no less than three separate spin-doctoring operations going on at the same time. There was the official Labour media team, led by the popular, competent and reliable David Hill, Director of Communications since the 1992 election. There was Campbell, who was briefing erratically on behalf of Tony Blair, but was not yet fully in control of his own operation. Unseen, but nevertheless omnipresent, there was also Peter Mandelson. This led to numerous clashes as one set of spin-doctors countermanded the other and vice versa. An especially vicious row exploded over briefing for Tony Blair's speech, but there were a number of other examples.

The collision between the Tony Blair operation and the Labour Party briefing machine was easy enough to solve. But Peter Mandelson was always going to be a central problem for Alastair Campbell. The two men had been close friends for the best part of a decade by the autumn of 1994; it was with Mandelson that Campbell forged one of his earliest political friendships. As with all relationships which involve Mandelson, this one was difficult, complex, and punctuated by long, frosty periods. Dealing with Peter Mandelson is not at all like doing business with a regulation member of the human race. At times the charm can be overwhelming. But the ordinary rules of human discourse do not apply. The smallest dispute or upset can be enough to send him into a sulk for months. He remains, however, one of the most fascinating of all British politicians, a national asset who should be treasured as such. Campbell was spared none of

32. See Joe Haines, 'Commentary', *Daily Mail*, 30 March 1998.

the contradictions. Indeed, knowing him better than most, he and Fiona Millar, who, according to friends, at times found Mandelson especially irksome and came to associate him with profound disruptions of ordinary family life, had more than most to put up with.

At times the relationship could be very warm indeed. In October 1990, when Mandelson stepped down as Director of Communications for the Labour Party, Campbell fixed him a column in the *Sunday People* newspaper, then edited by his old saviour Richard Stott. Not content with merely setting up the column, Campbell then actually wrote it. According to Westminster legend, Mandelson would trudge up to Campbell's Gospel Oak home on Wednesday evenings to take dictation.[33] On occasion the support was more personal still. Shortly before the 1987 General Election campaign the *News of the World* ran a story on Mandelson's complex private life. The friend he turned to for support at this time of intense distress was Alastair Campbell, and he spent the Saturday night before the story broke with Campbell and Millar.[34] Nor was it all one way: Peter Mandelson was one of the very first to get in touch when Campbell suffered his breakdown.

At other times, however, distance bordered on hostility. The Campbell/ Mandelson relationship was embarking on one of its problematic stages in the autumn of 1994. This was, of course, inevitable from the moment that Campbell accepted the job of press spokesman. There were two distinct problems here. The first was that Mandelson, with very considerable justice, regarded himself as an expert on the media. He felt that he had a lot to offer. Furthermore, he was attached to the press. There was no way that Campbell was ever going to halt the flow of informed briefing from the MP for Hartlepool to selected journalists. All he could do was stem the tide, and try and make sure that he alone was seen as the official voice of the Opposition Leader.

Campbell's solution was striking enough, and typically robust. First of all he took advice. Finding himself on one of his breakfast television shows with Sir Bernard Ingham, Margaret Thatcher's legendary Press Secretary, he took the old-timer aside afterwards and asked what course of action he would recommend. Ingham's reply was as laconic as it was brutal: 'Slit his throat.'[35]

33. This legend has been exaggerated. Derek Draper, Mandelson's assistant at the time, recalls long agonising evenings where the prospective MP for Hartlepool would sweat the column out on his own, without external assistance of any kind, reluctant to humiliate himself by bothering Campbell on the matter.

34. This is one of many illuminating nuggets of information to be discovered in Donald Macintyre's biography (p. 143).

35. Nicholas Jones, *Soundbites and Spin Doctors*, p. 170.

The opportunity to take offensive action came the day after Tony Blair's conference speech. An over-excited *Times* report credited Mandelson with the authorship of important sections. Campbell chose to take umbrage, professing to believe that the item in question had been placed there by Mandelson himself.[36] He responded in his *Today* column the following day: 'Having been a close friend of his since the days before he started wearing cufflinks, I have none of the traditional hang-ups about Peter, and fully intend on becoming Blair's Press Secretary to exploit his expertise, which in some areas is second to none. Speech-writing, however, is not one of them, but such is his ubiquitous appeal that *The Times* yesterday suggested he had helped write Blair's speech. I know from the days when Peter was a *People* columnist that writing was never his strong point, and that he had to look to his friends to help him out. Know what I mean?'[37]

To place such an item in a newspaper was a bold strategy. It was a public pronouncement by Campbell that he would be no pushover, and a demonstration that he was in no way afraid of Mandelson. All that was wise, and even commendable. But it also drew attention, in the most public way conceivable, to the tensions and rivalries within the court of Tony Blair. That was unprofessional, the kind of mistake that Campbell would never have tolerated in others.

This minor skirmish was merely a symptom of a much more visceral conflict between Mandelson and Campbell, who, whether they liked it or not, were on the way to becoming direct personal rivals. They now found themselves in the position of two powerful courtiers competing for the attention of the monarch. In 1994 there was no question who was the senior of the two. Peter Mandelson was the more powerful, in terms of age, ability, experience and above all his mesmeric hold over Tony Blair. Campbell seems – with some difficulty – to have been partly ready to accept this secondary role in the autumn of 1994.

But he really had no choice. He had yet to prove himself. He was not yet the dominating figure he was to become. That autumn Campbell accompanied Tony and Cherie Blair to the annual *Tribune* dinner. Half-way through, the Labour Leader's consort realised that she had forgotten something in her bag. Campbell was despatched to retrieve the item from the car.[38] It was a very public demonstration of his subordinate status and, as such, inconceivable only two or three years later. In January 1995 Jonathan Powell, a career diplomat

---

36. An entirely reasonable assumption though in this case, friends of Mandelson insist, wholly false.
37. *Today*, 6 October 1994.
38. I am indebted to Mark Seddon, the *Tribune* editor who hosted the event, for this telling anecdote.

from the Washington embassy, was appointed Tony Blair's chief of staff. He was understood by members of the inner team to be senior to Campbell. Today Alastair Campbell is accurately perceived as the Prime Minister's closest and most valued adviser, and is routinely called the 'real Deputy Prime Minister'. That was nowhere near the case when he first went to work for Tony Blair in 1994.

Chapter Eight

'THE MOST BRILLIANT ELECTION CAMPAIGN IN HISTORY'

At least no one can say we peaked too early.
John Major, during the General Election campaign, 1997

It would be wrong to make too much of Campbell's errors of judgement and somewhat inferior status during those early days. His contribution was immense from the start. He had an entirely clear-sighted and ruthless vision of where Tony Blair was heading; he threw himself into the revolutionary changes which the new leader immediately began to impose. It was perhaps Campbell more than anyone else who can take the credit for the brilliant and bold decision to change the name of the Labour Party. While Blair, Mandelson and even Philip Gould dithered when confronted with this momentous development, Campbell calmly and without hesitation pressed for change. It was Campbell who came up with the 'New Labour, New Britain' slogan for the 1994 Labour Party Conference. At first it was rejected by the others as too stark, too confrontational and too dangerous. Campbell argued them round. Nobody today would dispute that he was absolutely right. It was an excellent example of his rare political talent: the gift for the simple, telling phrase and the determination to make sure it works. Later Gould, who had himself a strong claim to authorship, generously acknowledged that 'it was Campbell who turned the term "New Labour" into an entirely new identity for the party.'[1] The process has since been taken even further. Party membership cards are now in the name of New Labour, and are no longer red but orange.

His contribution in pushing through the plan to ditch Clause 4 was almost as important. In this case Campbell had no claim to originating the idea, but played a central role in its execution. This was the more difficult part. Had the operation gone wrong, Tony Blair's leadership of the Labour Party might have foundered before it had properly begun. The key problem was securing the whole-hearted assent of John Prescott, Tony Blair's deputy – and put there as the voice of the unions and the Labour left. Dealing with John Prescott at the

1. See the revealing account in Philip Gould, *The Unfinished Revolution*, p. 219.

best of times is very much like handling a piece of high explosive. Dealing with Prescott over the plan to drop the cherished commitment to wholesale nationalisation was like handling a nuclear bomb. It is a tribute to the implicit trust that Tony Blair already felt in Alastair Campbell that he handed over this life and death negotiation to his press spokesman. It is a tribute to Campbell's immense professionalism and formidable diplomatic skills that he justified his leader's trust completely: the nuclear bomb, despite a few sweaty moments, never went off.[2]

Campbell has one great advantage: almost everybody likes him. Men warm to his blokeish, casual manner. He gives every appearance, though this is misleading in any number of respects, of being a regular guy. When he signed up to Tony Blair's inner circle in 1994 he was entering a seething world of bitterness, resentment, passion and blind hatred. Brown was consumed with an overwhelming resentment against Blair and not even talking to Mandelson. Brown's relations with another powerful Labour politician, Robin Cook, were worst of all. Mandelson was shortly to fall out with Gould, whose relations with Brown were never easy. Blair's relationship with Mandelson, who once flounced out of a meeting with the party leader and Shadow Chancellor, was complex beyond belief, though not as complex as Mandelson's relations with Brown.[3] And so forth. And yet Campbell navigated his way through it all. He refused to be drawn in. He maintained satisfactory relations with all parties. By standing aside from the frenzied emotional turmoil which surrounded the Labour leader he steadily acquired extra authority for himself.

All things to all men

It was not merely the Blair circle with which Campbell coped in such a level-headed fashion. He was a popular figure with MPs from all sides of the party. Being Scottish helped. Bernard Shaw once remarked that the moment an

---

2. See the fascinating version in Colin Brown's reliable and warm-hearted biography of the Labour deputy leader, *Fighting Talk*, pp. 254–5. See also Gould, p. 221. Campbell told Gould: 'There was no way we could have done it without John Prescott – not just John reluctantly agreeing, but John actually giving his blessing to it. The night before I was up practically all night, up and down the stairs to John's room, and going through it. In the end it was John who said: if you are going to do this, you have got to say it, you can't bugger about.'

3. Donald Macintyre's biography of Peter Mandelson is the indispensable guide to this problematic and alarming area. Though he wisely shrinks from exhaustive or impertinent analysis, he provides the raw materials for a profound psychological study of the emotional drama at the heart of the Blair government.

Englishman opens his mouth he is either despised by one half of the population or resented by the other. This was not the fate of Campbell. He comes from outside the English class system. His voice is a curious but attractive cocktail of northern vowels, a Scottish lilt and much else besides. He has the ability to make anyone who has dealings with him feel that he is a blood-brother. With dour old Labour types Campbell was able to produce his support for Burnley Football Club and lashing of red-blooded sentiment on the subject of grammar-school education, redistribution of wealth and so forth. He left them feeling that he was one of them. With a sharp-suited New Labour type, Campbell was able to provide an acceptable North London address, impeccable modernising credentials and an awesome set of connections. He was very good with Tories too. Conservative MPs like Alan Clark and Michael Heseltine loved Alastair Campbell. His self-assurance, cynicism, arrogance, instinctive grasp of the nature of power and clear sense that he had been born to rule convinced them against the evidence of their own eyes that he had been educated at Eton. Clark liked Campbell so much that he invited him and his family to his family home, Saltwood Castle. He once, in a moment of impulsive generosity, offered him one of his collection of vintage cars as a gift.[4] Campbell, always immune to temptation in financial matters, had the good sense to refuse. Later, after the 1997 General Election, the two men continued to talk at least once a week,[5] and Clark was to become an important informal link between No. 10 Downing Street and certain Tory Party factions. It was a connection that gave Alan Clark great pleasure but was understandably viewed with grave suspicion by the Conservative Party leadership.

Alastair Campbell's protean personality took in all of these, but most grievously deceived were old-fashioned Labour types. His success in massaging the warm-hearted and instinctive Labour soul – that section of the party which, unlike its brain, remained impervious to Tony Blair – is another tribute to his extraordinary gifts. He knows little and feels less of the magnificent history of the Labour Party. His father was a member of his local Conservative club. His first political involvement was as the press relations adviser to a Conservative Party councillor. Campbell came to Labour late in life and then as a journalist, never as an activist. He has no serious links with the trade union movement. Every action he has ever taken and every word he has ever written has been on the side of the Labour modernisers, first Kinnock and then Blair. And yet there

4. Private information.
5. Or so Clark intimated to friendly Tory MPs.

is no question that the Labour Party regards him more or less as one of its own whereas Peter Mandelson and Philip Gould are objects of hatred and suspicion.

This is partly because Mandelson and Gould are more courageous than Campbell. Mandelson had the guts to stand up in public and fight for the difficult changes that had to be made by New Labour: his unpopularity is an enduring and most admirable characteristic of this complicated and tortured man. The same can be said of Gould, who has often born the brunt of attack from the left, but never of Campbell. He has played a more cunning, calculating and double-edged game. This subtlety has helped the modernisers. It enabled him to act as the bridge between Blair and Prescott over Clause 4. He could play the part of Tony Blair's ambassador to the Labour Party in a way that Peter Mandelson could never dream of.

The paradox is that Campbell, for all his red-blooded general political opinions, is the biggest moderniser of the lot when it comes to changing the Labour Party. It is the absence of deep personal Labour roots, the relative ignorance of the party's history, the lack of interest in or knowledge of the party's guiding ideas, that help make him the force he is. Peter Mandelson and Philip Gould are modernisers but they were born and bred in the Labour Party, it is part of their innermost being. That is why even they recoiled for a time from the final irrevocable step towards New Labour: for them it felt like an act of parricide. When they created New Labour they destroyed some important part of themselves. This was not so with Alastair Campbell: he was simply making a neutral, calculated political decision. It was the same for Tony Blair. The fact that neither Blair nor Campbell has ever really been fully part of the Labour movement in its traditional sense is one of the things they have in common.

The Harriet Harman Affair

Human nature can harbour many contradictions. Campbell's breast could contain both a clinical indifference to the old Labour Party and a passionate commitment to some of old Labour's most bloody-minded notions.[6] Most New Labour compromises or adaptations – for instance the commitment to the

6. Only a few weeks before John Smith's death, in April 1994, Campbell stood in for Simon Heffer, then political columnist of the *Spectator*. The article he wrote is the nearest thing he has produced to a personal political manifesto, and it is curious to contrast it to what Tony Blair has actually achieved in office. It called for a 'more interventionist approach to the economy', higher taxes and more spending on the health service and education.

market economy or not to raise taxes – he either swallowed or warmly embraced. But neither he nor Fiona Millar would budge on comprehensive education. They took the ultramontane stance. In their book it was not merely sufficient to send one's child to a state school. It must also be non-selective and, for good measure, the nearest. This was what the Campbell-Millars did with their own children, and they expected no less of anybody else.

An early victim of this ferocity were some near neighbours in Gospel Oak, North London where they lived. There is no need to mention the name of this unlucky couple who, as many parents do, removed their child from the state system and put him into a private school. Up to that moment the two families had been close, in and out of each other's homes, embarking on joint projects in the way families do who have young children in common. From that day forth they were distinctly cool.

The Campbell-Millars can be accused of intolerance but never of hypocrisy. There have been better schools than the Gospel Oak Primary School in the Labour-run borough of Camden. But the Campbell-Millars did not respond, as many middle-class parents would have done, by taking their children away. Instead Fiona became a school governor and threw herself into the life of the school. When a government report[7] exposed the institution's many shortcomings, the Campbell-Millars stormed into action. They took the lead in a campaign that in due course forced out the headmaster. One of the most violent denunciations of the hapless head came from Campbell as he addressed a special meeting of more than a hundred parents called to discuss the school's future.

Both Alastair Campbell and Fiona Millar emerge with flying colours from this episode. It shows two things. First – and everybody who knows them at all well testifies to this – they are magnificent parents, desperately concerned that their children should be brought up in what they consider the right way. Campbell was extraordinarily busy in the early months of 1995. There are plenty of ambitious men who would never have taken the time off work to involve themselves with the problems of their children's school, with all the tedious detail and little tasks that involves.

Second, they have strong beliefs and principles which they are ready to put into practice. The unswerving rectitude of their approach is awesome. But the

7. Ironically, the devastating report from an independent team of school inspectors that sparked such a strong reaction from the Campbell-Millars was a triumph for Tory education reforms. Labour fought hard to keep school inspection under local authority control. This episode was well covered in the *Daily Mail*, 26 January 1995, p. 14 and 7 February 1995, p. 15.

stern moral approach to the situation of friends who have wrestled, perhaps just as honestly as they did, with the central dilemma facing middle-class parents in an inner city is undeniable. And it was about to claim another victim. It was the great misfortune of Harriet Harman that she raised her head at the very moment when Alastair Campbell's socialist convictions reared up, like Marshall Pétain at the Battle of Verdun, and proclaimed: '*Ils ne passeront pas.*'

For the best part of a decade Harriet Harman was one of Campbell's golden girls. He missed no opportunity to build up the career of this clever and well-connected ornament of Neil Kinnock's Labour Party. The modernisers wanted her for themselves: on television her fetching good looks, headmistress manner and upper-middle-class accent conveyed precisely the image they wanted. With the arrival of Tony Blair Harriet Harman's future appeared even more assured than ever. That was until Alastair Campbell flattened it.

Ms Harman, the daughter of a Harley Street doctor and niece of the Countess of Longford, is in many ways an old-fashioned figure. She was impelled into politics by the least sordid of all motives: an overwhelming desire to change the world for the better. Scorning the expectation of her class, she chose not to marry a stockbroker and live a life of horsy banality in the home counties. She threw herself instead into the turbulent left-wing politics of the 1970s, became a civil rights activist, and in due course married an affable trade union official named Jack Dromey. She presented him with three children: it was the education of these youngsters that first sounded the death-knell for Harman's promising front-bench career.

The Dromeys lived in a South London inner city borough whose impressive level of burglary, car theft and violent crime was not matched by high standards in its schools. There was no critical mass of local middle-class parents to put pressure on the local teachers as there was in Campbell's more salubrious North London suburb. It is hard not to feel sympathetic with Harman in her predicament. The eldest child was despatched across borough boundaries to the Oratory School in West London, a trailblazer for the Blairs' eldest son Euan. Even this minor infringement produced abuse from Alastair Campbell who, when Cherie and Tony Blair followed suit, blamed Harman for setting this unsavoury precedent. But the real storm only hit when Jack Dromey and Harriet Harman made the agonising decision to send their next son to St Olave's, a grammar school in Orpington. Harman knew it was a provocative act: almost the entire Labour Party was opposed to selection at the age of eleven. She told Tony Blair all about it several months before the story broke. One of the major problems was that Blair, knowing the inevitable reaction from his strong-minded assistant, did not dare to inform Campbell.[8] All through the winter of 1995–6 it remained Harriet Harman and Tony Blair's little secret until, in the third week of January 1996, it was unearthed by Joe Murphy, the political editor of the *Mail on Sunday*.

Murphy, one of Westminster's most meticulous and thorough reporters, received a tip that Harman was sending her son to a local grammar school. He obtained a map of her area of South London, and a list of likely schools. After three or four calls he struck lucky: St Olave's confirmed that a young Harman was indeed on the list. Unluckily for Murphy, the school then alerted the Labour Party: the game was up.

The Harman story was an early test for Tony Blair's already renowned press machine. It failed comprehensively. The story could not have been worse handled and the fault was all Campbell's. His first reaction was devious. He decided to squash Murphy. Having learnt about the story on Friday, Campbell promptly denied the *Mail on Sunday* their cherished and well-deserved scoop by handing it over to friendly journalists.[9] The *Daily Mirror* and the *Independent* were party to this tawdry act of petty larceny.[10] Their half-hearted attempt to portray Harman's actions in a friendly light failed completely. Within hours, the Labour Party was ablaze.

Campbell's behaviour at this juncture was self-indulgent. Most of the Labour Party, the press and even the Shadow Cabinet were baying for Harman's blood. Only Tony Blair, Peter Mandelson and a very few others wanted to save her. It was one of the biggest tests that Tony Blair's leadership of the Labour Party has ever faced. There was no question at all what course of action Campbell was obliged to take. It was his duty to fling himself, every muscle straining, into the breach. Two issues were at stake that long week in January 1996 when the future of Harriet Harman hung in the balance. The first was selective education. The second, and by far the more important, was the continued authority of Tony

8. Private information.

9. This decision raises an interesting issue. Joe Murphy, now political editor of the *Sunday Telegraph*, says: 'What it all illustrated was who owns information these days. It used to be the case that when a journalist found something out it belonged to him or her. Now the party machines feel that any information about themselves is their own property and they can give it to friendly papers or do what they like with it.' This is a dangerous and worrying development. The knowledge that checking out a story is tantamount to handing it over to the opposition can deter reporters from confirming stories in the proper way.

10. Somehow, through channels that remain mysterious, the *Daily Mail* obtained the story as well. It certainly did not receive it from Labour. The *Daily Mail* has traditionally taken a special pleasure in stitching up its Sunday stablemate.

Blair and the entire modernising project. But Campbell went into a sulk. There are even reports that he downed tools and took himself off home. What is certain is that he was culpably absent on parade.

As a result of Campbell's extraordinary behaviour, the Harman situation went from bad to worse. The Labour machine stalled. Ten days later, in a memo to Tony Blair and Gordon Brown, Philip Gould wrote: 'There are a lot of lessons to be learnt from last week, but the most immediate was that once again, under real pressure, our message crumpled and we failed to retaliate effectively.' Gould suggested the defence that could and should have been used: 'As a parent Harriet Harman is making the best of a bad system; in government she will make sure all children get the best. What Britain needs is more politicians who face the real dilemmas of everyday life, because they are best able to change the lives of everyday people.'[11]

It was an obvious defence. For a fully functioning Alastair Campbell, deploying it would have been child's play. In the end it was Peter Mandelson – showing yet again what a brave politician he is – who went in to bat on Harman's behalf. It was enough to save the day, but not before great damage had been done. Harriet Harman had been marked out. The assassins, waved on by Alastair Campbell, would come back to get her.

Looking back on that week, Campbell's disloyalty was striking. It would have been unforgivable enough from a senior member of the Shadow Cabinet. But Campbell was not an elected politician, he was an appointed apparatchik. And yet he chose to follow a principle of his own rather than spring to the defence of his boss. It was a sackable offence, one that he was to repeat when Blair later sent his son Euan to the Oratory. Yet no one in the Blair inner circle thought that Campbell's behaviour was odd. It goes to show his compelling ability to get others to accept him on his own terms.

Wooing the Media Class

It is a clear indication of the needs and imperatives of New Labour that Tony Blair's two closest advisers, before and after the General Election, Peter Mandelson and Alastair Campbell, were trained in the media. When they were not fighting like ferrets in a sack – and they were professional enough and had enough shared past to avoid open conflict for much of the time – their complementary qualities made them a perfect fit. Mandelson was stronger on strategy,

11. Quoted in Gould, p. 274.

Campbell on execution. Mandelson had the more probing, subtle mind while Campbell was more brutal and direct. Mandelson's genius lay above all with television and broadcasters, while – at first at any rate – Campbell really understood only print journalism. Both of them were fully paid-up members of the Media Class.

Mandelson's training was in broadcasting. He was part of that talented generation which passed through London Weekend Television in the early 1980s, then fanned out into national politics and the commanding heights of the British media. It includes Greg Dyke, appointed Director-General of the BBC in June 1999; Sir Christopher Bland, chairman of the BBC Governors; Barry Cox, treasurer of the Tony Blair campaign team in 1994; Michael Wills, now a junior minister; and – incongruously – Bruce Anderson, future biographer of John Major and now political columnist of the *Spectator*, to name a few.

Mandelson has a brilliant feel for how broadcasting works, which explains why he was so effective for so long as Labour's Director of Communications. There is a widespread view that there was something sinister about the immense influence he undeniably exercised in broadcasting circles for many years. This view is false. Mandelson had a knowledgeable and precise grasp of the values, pacing, judgements and deadlines of news stories. It was this professionalism and insight, far more than illegitimate influence, which gave him such sway with BBC reporters. They would have been mad not to want to listen to what Mandelson had to say. The same applied to their bosses.[12]

Campbell offered the same Rolls Royce service on the press side. He was able to play the rhythms of the daily news cycle as on a violin. He knew the needs and weaknesses of every lobby journalist and was always as happy to meet the one as he was to prey upon the other. The herd instinct of the lobby, with its cruel, pitiless mob mentality, was home territory for Campbell.

Between them, with superb professionalism and endless, loving attention to detail, these two and others put into effect the new electoral technology which New Labour had imported from the United States: the giant media war-room, the 24-hour monitoring of television, radio and press outlets, a rabid rebuttal service, a savage clampdown on MPs and Shadow ministers who spoke out of turn. The move of Labour's headquarters from John Smith House in South

12. John Sergeant, veteran political correspondent of the BBC, records: 'Mandelson really got under the skin of junior BBC correspondents. They were more interested in his feedback than their bosses'. The point is that his comments were brilliant and to the point. He actually knew the business. He would say: "You should have used x rather than y" and you knew he was right. He would have made a bloody good TV news producer.' Conversation with the author, May 1999.

London to a new office in Millbank Tower in October 1995 was the symbol of this profound change in methodology which followed Tony Blair's arrival. A few souls wanted to bring the name John Smith across the river as well, in tribute to the recently deceased leader. They were swiftly silenced. Smith, who would have hated Millbank and everything it represented, was rapidly becoming a non-person.

A team of 150 staff was swiftly assembled, growing to nearly twice that as the General Election itself approached. Mandelson and David Hill, the Labour Director of Communications and a reassuring relic from the old regime, set up shop. The benefit of hindsight does not make it any simpler to understand how the Millbank campaigning machine operated. Indeed, it only serves to complicate matters. The formal Labour Party hierarchy, which had been so dominant under previous Labour leaders, took a back seat and the process was driven forward by New Labour modernisers, above all Gordon Brown and Peter Mandelson. These two were still not on speaking terms and the atmosphere was occasionally wrecked by arguments and disputes over petty matters of precedence. Campbell, thanks to his particular responsibility to Tony Blair, was able to steer clear of much of this. Until the election campaign itself got underway, he did not even have his own office in the building. On the irregular occasions that he put in an appearance, he made use of a desk outside the office Peter Mandelson used in his capacity as Chairman of the Labour General Election Planning Committee.

Nothing like Millbank had ever been seen in British politics before. It was American both in inspiration and in its structural preference for process rather than substance. The process was awesome. Campbell poured scorn on these foreign influences coming from Washington at first: but he swiftly changed his opinion when he saw their uses.

New Labour introduced a new concept into British electoral history: the permanent campaign. Until the arrival of Tony Blair, election campaigns started the day that the Prime Minister went to see the Queen to hand over the seals of office and ended approximately three and half weeks later when the British people went to the polls to vote. In between times, the winning party was allowed to get on with government. New Labour, with Media Class connivance, abolished that agreeable mode of life. The General Election campaign of spring 1997 had actually begun almost three years before, practically the moment that Tony Blair became Leader of the Opposition.

Labour's ferocious internal discipline was the key to its success. In stark contrast to the Conservative Party, then at the height of a period of crazed self-laceration over Europe, Labour MPs were prevailed upon to limit their public utterances to the bland platitudes imposed upon them by the party machine. Those handfuls who found this discipline unbearable were harassed like dissidents in a totalitarian state. One radio producer remembers Clare Short, in the Shadow Cabinet only on sufferance and always regarded by the Labour machine as a liability, showing some spirit and militancy on air. It was shortly after she had made a public attack against 'people who live in the dark', widely regarded as a reference to Campbell and Mandelson. Within seconds of taking off her headphones, she was being bleeped with a request to ring Millbank Tower urgently. She turned down further interview requests. Austin Mitchell, an unruly Labour back-bencher, compared Tony Blair to a North Korean dictator, an analogy which contained a certain amount of resonance. Instantly he was contacted by Millbank and told not to conduct any more media interviews.

When stories went in a direction Millbank did not like, punitive action was swift. High-profile rows, like the one sparked by the peremptory letter from Alastair Campbell to the BBC Director-General John Birt in 1996 demanding that Tony Blair's conference speech should lead the BBC News, were relatively rare.[13] Day-to-day bullying at a lower level, however, was routine. Tim Allan, Campbell's deputy in the Labour Press Office, was especially awkward to deal with. On one occasion Michael Brunson, political editor of ITN, had to intervene to separate him and a furious producer. Hilary Coffman, a veteran press officer and in private life a modest and becoming person, became renowned at the BBC for a highly aggressive manner. Campbell, uncharacteristically, stayed clear of this hand-to-hand fighting with broadcasters. But he thoroughly approved of his subordinates' tactics. He cheered them on and gave them useful tips about how to make themselves even more unpleasant.

What gave Labour complaints an edge was that they were inevitably well-researched and sensibly focused. The vigilance was extraordinary. Roger Mosey, then the editor of Radio Four's *Today* programme, recalls: 'If you had a line that Labour didn't like on the 6.30 a.m. bulletin you got called instantly. Often Labour complaints had some substance. That was their cleverness. If there was a glimmer of an inaccuracy they were onto you.'

---

13. Campbell was alarmed that the BBC would choose to lead on the result of the O. J. Simpson court case instead. The BBC indignantly protested that news judgements were a matter for them alone. Nevertheless, they put Blair rather than Simpson at the top of the 6 p.m. bulletin. The best guide to the sordid battleground where politicians meet the media is to be found in the works of BBC political correspondent Nicholas Jones. His recent trilogy – *Soundbites and Spin Doctors* (1996), *Campaign 1997* (1997) and *Sultans of Spin* (1999) – is full of priceless information. The great point about the indefatigable Jones is that, unlike so many of his trade, he cannot be bought.

Tory Central Office, once spoken of in hushed tones as an awesome machine, now full of anxious and baffled men, was well aware that something was going on. But it could not comprehend exactly what. Eventually, after much deliberation and many meetings, it produced a secret weapon: a junior back-bench MP called Alan Duncan. Tory Central Office temporarily suffered from the delusion, which was fully shared by Mr Duncan, that he was the Conservative Party's answer to Peter Mandelson. The two spin-doctors shared a fondness for expensive, hand-made suits and a certain prissiness of manner, but in all other respects Duncan's attempts to emulate Mandelson only highlighted the general Tory hopelessness. 'There was the time when Duncan was appointed spin-doctor to the *Today* programme,' remembers one senior BBC figure. 'For a few days he would ring up at midnight and ask what was going on. The Tories just never understood what it was all about. From time to time Duncan would get angry and threaten to report us. He just didn't have any credibility.'

One of the impediments that prevented Duncan from being a satisfactory spin-doctor was the fact that he wasn't nearly as nasty as he looked. However hard the broadcasters hit the Tories, they never bore grudges. The legendary Sir Bernard Ingham, whose influence on the young Alastair Campbell can hardly be overstated, had understood the value of denying access. Programmes that irked Margaret Thatcher suddenly found that no senior minister would go on to be interviewed. It was a brave producer who was prepared to live in such a lonely state for ever. The risk of non-cooperation did not exist as far as John Major's Tory Party were concerned. Sportingly, like dogs returning to a brutal master in the full and certain knowledge that they were going to be thrashed, they kept coming back for more. Campbell and Mandelson never made that sort of mistake. They controlled who appeared where, and made the fullest possible use of that control. Any programme that questioned the glowing public image of Tony Blair and his Shadow Cabinet found itself ostracised. This was the fate of *World at One*, the influential lunchtime news programme. To the outrage, bafflement and blind fury of Labour spin-doctors, it asked hard and probing questions and refused to be put off. The high-profile interviews went to friendlier and more helpful programmes.

The importance of not being Mandelson

Daily political journalists need above all else high-calibre, intelligent and well-informed briefing from someone who has total access to his boss. That Campbell could deliver to the daily lobby. He did not trust journalists, or even like them much, and made no pretence that he did. But he provided a professional service.

He learnt a great deal from Peter Mandelson, in particular about how to handle the broadcast media, but also steered clear of his mistakes. Mandelson's method of doing business with the press was to single out a tiny number of favourites. He had half a dozen trusted souls with whom he would share almost everything: Andrew Grice of the *Sunday Times*, Donald Macintyre of the *Independent*, Patrick Wintour of the *Guardian*, the columnist Robert Harris, perhaps Lance Price of the BBC. Before the 1992 election Mandelson, Macintyre and Harris would gather together late in the parliamentary week in one of the many bars that are to be found deep in the bowels of the House of Commons. Intruders were not made to feel at all welcome if they sought to join their select little group. Throughout the pre-1997 period the Members' lobby of the Commons would be treated to an unchanging ritual at 4 p.m. on Thursday afternoons. Andrew Grice would be hanging casually about the lobby. Then Peter Mandelson would stroll in purposefully. Grice would walk up to him in a deferential manner. Mandelson would glare at him, as if he had never seen him before in his life. A few words would be exchanged. The two men would then walk off together presumably to confect Grice's story in the *Sunday Times* for the weekend. This ceased only when Mandelson was promoted to the Cabinet in the summer of 1998.

All of Mandelson's contacts came good at the moment he needed them, when his career hit the rocks six months later. The rallying round over the affair of the undeclared loan from Geoffrey Robinson loan was splendid to behold, a credit to the loyalty and good feeling of all involved. The trouble as far as Mandelson was concerned came not from the half-dozen journalists that he and his devoted and precocious adviser Benjamin Wegg-Prosser[14] had sedulously cultivated. It came from the scores who had been scorned, neglected, abused and left out in the cold.

Campbell did not make the Mandelsonian error of cultivating a White Commonwealth. He treated all of the lobby with the same amiable contempt. Even those he conspicuously liked, such as Tony Bevins of the *Independent*, appeared to derive no special benefits from the association, while those for whom he appeared to feel a particular dislike, like George Jones of the *Daily*

---

14. Wegg-Prosser's admiration of Alastair Campbell is so extreme that once, chancing to find himself in possession of one of Campbell's ties, he is said to have carried it about him all evening, examining it happily from time to time. I am indebted to Tom Baldwin of *The Times* for this anecdote.

Telegraph, seemed to suffer no special penalties. Campbell rapidly acquired, as Mandelson already possessed, a reputation for bullying journalists when events failed to go his own way. Some reporters minded about this and thought it was unfair. Others found bruising encounters with Labour Party spin-doctors bracing, adding greatly to their enjoyment of the day. One thing everybody could agree upon, however. Abuse from Mandelson was somehow vicious and nasty, hissed out as if he meant it, and inevitably followed by a long period of unpleasantness. Campbell's bollockings, though more cogently expressed and often accompanied by the implied threat of physical violence, were less personal and far less long-lasting. They came and went within the hour, like a summer thunderstorm. They were good clean fun, always greatly improved if the victim retaliated in kind. Indeed, Campbell is one of those dominant males who feels fully at ease only with someone with whom he has entered into bruising public combat. Many theories sprang up in the parliamentary lobby to account for the difference in approach between the two men. The one that gained widest currency was simply that Mandelson was the nastier piece of work. The more generous and perceptive view came from Mandelson's supporters: they are sure that he made the mistake of thinking of journalists as friends, as people who genuinely liked him. When they let him down – in other words did their job – he felt in some way personally betrayed. Campbell, by contrast, never had any illusions about the profession. He thought of his former colleagues as fallen men and expected them to let him down. When they did so, he therefore felt none of the special rancour that overcame Peter Mandelson. That is one reason why, by the admittedly extremely low traditional standards of Labour press spokesmen, Alastair Campbell was moderately even-handed in his dealings with political journalists. It was yet another example of his good sense and sound judgement. He made just one, very important, exception. He made plain from the very outset that he would do whatever he could to make life easy and comfortable for the *Sun* newspaper, Rupert Murdoch's mass market tabloid.

News International

The twentieth century, like a football match, has been a game of two halves. The first half embraced the rise of communism and two world wars and was overshadowed by the emergence of figures of world historical importance such as Stalin, Hitler, Churchill and Gandhi. It was the more interesting but perilous half.

It is obvious that the most potent figure of the latter half of the century has been not the great statesman but the international businessman. Of these the most interesting and important – at any rate in the Western hemisphere – has been Rupert Murdoch who, as a young Oxford graduate in the 1950s, spotted the vast potential of the media business.

News Corp, with its massive portfolio of international interests – in Britain it owns *The Times*, the *Sunday Times*, the *Sun*, *News of the World* and Sky TV – has turned him into one of the most powerful men in the world. National politicians, even one as successful as Tony Blair, are permitted only a few years at the top, and just one country to play with. A man like Murdoch spans the decades and the continents: he possesses far more clout than each transient generation of passing politicians.

For the past two decades all British politicians have faced one central question: how to deal with Rupert Murdoch. For those who have handled him effectively and well, like Margaret Thatcher, the rewards have been immense. For those who got it wrong, like Neil Kinnock, the effect has been catastrophic. Blair and Campbell, with their killer noses for power, were wide awake to this. They were equally clear about the answer. They were willing to prostrate themselves to bring Murdoch across to New Labour. It was Campbell's fixed conviction – one fully shared by Tony Blair – that the support of Rupert Murdoch's mass-market *Sun* was a necessary, and possibly a sufficient, precondition for Labour victory at the General Election.[15]

Never has a newspaper group been courted as News International in the months following Tony Blair's election to the leadership of the Labour Party. For the Labour Party this was in some ways Blair's most shocking policy-change: it had collectively refused to speak to the Murdoch press since News International, in a union-busting move, shifted its centre of operations to

15. The belief that 'It's the *Sun* wot won it' (*Sun*, 11 April 1992) was put about in the aftermath of the 1992 election by a number of interested parties. First to make the claim was the *Sun* itself, on the Saturday after polling day. Neil Kinnock helped give the idea credence when, on 13 April, he announced that he was stepping down as Labour leader. Kinnock blamed the Conservative press for bringing about the result. Alistair McAlpine, Tory Party Treasurer under Margaret Thatcher, was another early proponent of the view that Tory editors had won the election, setting out his views in the *Sunday Telegraph* on the weekend after polling day. Neither Kinnock's nor McAlpine's analysis was disinterested. Kinnock, a hurt and baffled man in the aftermath of 9 April 1992, felt an instinctive need to blame outside factors for his defeat. McAlpine was eager to deprive Chris Patten, Tory chairman during the campaign, of as much of the credit as he could. The evidence that the *Sun* played a decisive role is mixed. But that is not important. The important thing is that the next generation of Labour politicians came to believe that it had.

Wapping in the East End of London in the mid-1980s.[16] The relationship had been marked by the bitterest hostility and recrimination, made worse when the *Sun* claimed the credit for the defeat of Kinnock in the 1992 General Election.

This courtship operated at a number of levels. First Rupert Murdoch himself was wooed like a beautiful woman. When he came to town, Blair and his lieutenants would drop anything to have dinner with him. After Blair's annual Party Conference speech, the Labour leader's first priority was to speak to Murdoch. He would allay his concerns on some issues, highlight political movement in others: always courteous, deferential and eager to learn Murdoch's own opinion. One of Tony Blair's most priceless gifts has always been the ability to impress older men and bring them over to his way of thinking. This process of intensive cultivation reached its crowning moment in the summer of 1995 when the Labour leader flew half-way across the world to address a meeting of News International executives on Hayman Island, just off the Queensland coast. Blair's decision to embark on this 25,000-mile round trip, made at the prompting of Campbell,[17] was an extraordinary act of fealty. The Political Class was paying homage to the Media Class.

Only President Clinton counted for more with Blair in those three years of opposition: and even that is debatable. Murdoch's needs and wishes became New Labour's needs and wishes. One of Tony Blair's first acts in office was to inform his MPs to pay 'more attention to the tabloids'. He meant the *Sun*. Relations became warmer still when Les Hinton was appointed executive chairman of News International in the winter of 1994–5. Hinton had been in the United States during the Wapping dispute a decade before, so brought none of the baggage from that time.[18] He invited a succession of Shadow ministers down to Murdoch's hideous East London headquarters, which Blair often visited himself. It was noticed with approval that whenever New Labour

16. There were occasional meetings, conducted with the same furtive secrecy as encounters between hostile powers in wartime. Shortly before the 1992 election Charles Clarke, Neil Kinnock's chief of staff, met the editor, Kelvin MacKenzie, and senior executives of the *Sun*. Clarke did not venture to tell the Labour leader about it until after the meeting had taken place. John Smith, urged on by his Director of Communications David Hill, was pondering the painful process of rapprochement before he died.

17. See Macintyre, p. 326 for Campbell's role.

18. Les Hinton is one of the very few people who has lunched Alastair Campbell. Being teetotal, Campbell normally scorns invitations to lunch, though he will invite visitors into his Downing Street office around 1 p.m. They are instructed to bring sandwiches with them. Lunch with Campbell, being a rarity, has therefore become a prized opportunity, something to boast about. Accepting lunch with Hinton was therefore one of Campbell's ways of indicating that he placed an especially high value on their relationship.

politicians arrived, they were conspicuously well-briefed on all issues close to Rupert Murdoch's heart.

News International had three practical worries on its own account, all of which Tony Blair acted quickly to address. He promised that Labour in government would not undo the Thatcher union reforms. He produced satisfactory assurances that no privacy laws or statutory controls on the press would be introduced. And he gave every impression that Labour in government would not prove awkward over two issues vital to Murdoch: competition and cross-media ownership. The 1992 Labour manifesto had pledged draconian measures to curb the powerful foreign-owned press: these were watered down to become practically meaningless by 1997. Tony Blair himself has always insisted that no deals of any kind, either explicit or implicit, have ever been struck with the Murdoch empire.

The warmth of the rapprochement between News International and New Labour was increased by the incompetence of the Tory high command. The Major government was doing its unavailing best to push the 1996 Broadcasting Bill through the Commons. This piece of legislation was a matter of acute anxiety as far as News International was concerned. New Labour was eager to provide Murdoch with every imaginable assistance – Labour MPs were encouraged to team up with Tory right-wingers to defeat the government in committee – whereas the Conservatives had become so blind to the realities of power that they were oblivious to Murdoch's concerns.

At one stage it became a matter of overriding importance to Rupert Murdoch whether or not News International should or should not be denominated a foreign company. It was quite impossible to get either Stephen Dorrell or Virginia Bottomley, the last two Heritage Secretaries in John Major's dying administration, to focus on the issue. Meetings were offered at official level. After months of negotiation the government agreed to a meeting between Michael Heseltine and Rupert Murdoch so that the News International boss could express his concerns.[19] It was Murdoch's first encounter with a Tory minister for many months. The meeting took ages to sort out, and it was never followed up. Soon afterwards the relationship between the Tories and News International, which by then had seen the writing on the wall for the government, broke down completely. By well before the 1997 election it had become a question of when, rather than if, the *Sun* came out for Labour.

19. Heseltine was apparently chosen for the task on the bizarre grounds that he owned Haymarket Publications, a magazine company, and so might understand something about publishing.

Campbell devoted almost as much attention to cultivating News International journalists as News International management. Tony Blair's first article for a Murdoch-supporting paper came as early as August 1994. It was a half-page column in the *News of the World*. Though Campbell had not yet taken over as Press Secretary, it bore the marks of his handiwork.[20] It was the first of scores of articles by Tony Blair that were to appear in Murdoch papers over the coming years. Few were seen,[21] let alone written, by their ostensible author. This was where Campbell's hard-won tabloid expertise came in handy. When English football fans rioted late at night in Dublin, there was a page 6 piece in the *Sun* the following morning. It expressed the Leader of the Opposition's considered opinion that 'a game we love is once more condemned by a group of idiots who shame our country.'[22] This required very fast footwork – a late-night negotiation with the *Sun* newsdesk followed by the swift turnaround of the copy which would appear under the Blair byline. It was Campbell at his most productive and efficient. Other papers woke up to the ease with which Blair articles could be obtained. Soon the Leader of the Opposition became the most prolific journalist in Fleet Street by far. Most weeks would see the publication of half a dozen Blair articles at least, sometimes rising to twenty or more. It was not long before the burden of writing his comment pieces became too great for Campbell alone, and he was forced to farm out the work to junior members of the press office. After the General Election the task of writing Prime Ministerial articles was delegated to a special Downing Street office, the Strategic Communications Unit. Composed partly of ex-journalists and partly of civil servants, this industrious group has been known to fashion more than a hundred exclusive pieces by Tony Blair in a single week.[23] In due course the market suffered from saturation. Articles by the Prime Minister turned into a shop-soiled commodity and comment editors would greet them with a groan. Downing Street eventually woke up to this and steps were taken to curb production.

But Tony Blair articles, even when they were still in fashion, were the least of the many services provided by Alastair Campbell to the *Sun*. It was swiftly

20. *News of the World*, 28 August 1994. The piece came just weeks after Murdoch himself made his first public gesture towards the new Labour leader. In an interview with *Der Spiegel* on 8 August he pointed out that his newspapers had assisted Harold Wilson when he was in power. Murdoch said: 'Only last year we helped the Labour government in Canberra. I could even imagine myself supporting the British Labour leader, Tony Blair.'

21. Either before or after publication. Private information.

22. The *Sun*, 16 February 1995.

23. Taking the provincial press into account.

noticed by correspondents from other papers that *Sun* journalists were the only ones spared Campbell's routine barbarism and scorn. When they asked questions, he listened politely and with an expression of lively interest, which contrasted with the sneer of contempt he held in reserve for ordinary jobbing hacks. He made a point of praising what he viewed as the *Sun's* responsible reporting, contrasting it with the alleged recklessness and bad taste of the BBC and the *Guardian*.[24] He developed the warmest of relationships with the paper's editor, Stuart Higgins.[25] On one occasion Higgins and his most senior colleagues were invited to Blair's Islington home. The Leader of the Opposition was effusively hospitable. The same could not be said of his wife Cherie, once alleged to have banned the *Sun* from her home. She was nowhere to be seen, and Blair was obliged to make the coffee. Wherever possible New Labour would hand the *Sun* exclusives, a habit that soon began to annoy *Mirror* journalists. The *Mirror* had traditionally regarded itself as the only tabloid Labour paper and was understandably proud that it had stuck with the party through the dog days of opposition. Now it found itself left out in the cold. As Campbell accurately surmised, there was nowhere else to go, at least not till after the election. The deep feelings of resentment and betrayal at Campbell's old paper were never stronger than in the days following the extraordinary *Mirror* budget scoop in November 1996.

On the eve of budget day *Mirror* editor Piers Morgan found himself in uncomfortable possession of one of the greatest newspaper exclusives of all time. He received a dossier of documents containing the contents of the following day's budget. Kenneth Clarke's final effort to win back the voters for the Tory Party had fallen into his lap. It was the first time that budget secrecy had ever been breached on such a scale. To the astonishment of Fleet Street, Morgan played safe and decided not to publish his scoop, preferring to make a great show of virtue instead by handing it back to Downing Street.

But rather than sit on the budget leak entirely, he gave some hints about its contents to the Labour Party in order, so he thought, to help Gordon Brown savage Kenneth Clarke during the budget debate. But the following morning's

24. See Nicholas Jones, *Soundbites and Spindoctors*, p. 167. Jones is highly revealing on the Murdoch relationship. See also two remarkable articles in the Murdoch-owned *Today* during Campbell's first Labour Press Conference as Tony Blair's press officer on 7 and 10 October 1994.

25. Alastair Campbell and Stuart Higgins were old sparring partners. Fifteen years before the *Daily Mirror* had sent Campbell down to a West Country village which had agreed to conduct the experiment of not watching television for a week. Campbell's job was to record the effect. Higgins was despatched by the *Sun* to ruin Campbell's story and persuade the villagers to turn their sets back on. Campbell rarely speaks, however, to Higgins' successor, David Yelland, who is wooed instead by Anji Hunter.

Sun, to Piers Morgan's surprise and dismay, confidently and accurately predicted each and every newsworthy budget item – Clarke's decision to cut income tax, raise car tax, lower corporation tax, the lot. At the time the story went round that a *Mirror* journalist, infuriated by the pusillanimity of Morgan, was responsible for passing over the information. That is indeed one possible solution to the mystery. But there are some senior figures at the *Mirror* who refuse to be dissuaded from the highly improbable notion that Labour handed over their famous scoop lock, stock and barrel to the *Sun*.

The General Election, 1997

Well before the General Election on 1 May 1997 it had become obvious to most political journalists that Labour was en route to an historic victory, very likely of landslide proportions. They made their dispositions accordingly. Looking back, it is an amazing tribute to the hold of the Tory press machine that so many papers felt capable of endorsing John Major and his broken-backed Tories. Among Sunday papers two out of the four broadsheets – the *Sunday Times* and *Sunday Telegraph* – stuck with the Conservatives. Both the middle market tabloids – the *Express* and the *Mail on Sunday* – stayed firm. But at the bottom end of the market the Murdoch-owned *News of the World* made the switch from Tory to Labour.

The daily market was more fluid. The *Daily Telegraph* gave a despairing endorsement for John Major, but *The Times* felt unable to do so. Instead it sat on the fence. In a move which did nothing for its reputation for sound judgement, it counselled its readers to vote not for the Tory candidate, nor the Labour one, but for the most anti-European candidate. The middle market was unchanged. Both the *Express* and the *Mail* urged the virtues of John Major upon their readers. The *Sun*, however, produced its endorsement for Labour the day Major called the General Election.

At the 1992 General Election approximately 70 per cent of the newspaper market, judged by the number of readers, was Tory. In 1997 that figure was more or less reversed. Alastair Campbell had done his bit in opposition. Now it was time for government.

Chapter Nine

DOWNING STREET

In order to ensure the effective presentation of Government policy, all major interviews and media appearances, both print and broadcast, should be agreed with the No.10 Press Office before any commitments are entered into. The policy content of all major speeches, press releases, and new policy initiatives should be cleared in good time with the No. 10 Private Office [. . .] Each department should keep a record of media contacts by both Ministers and Officials.

Ministerial Code: A Code of Conduct and Guidance on Procedures for Ministers (Cabinet Office, July 1997)

Many sympathetic observers thought that Campbell would never last as Tony Blair's Downing Street Press Secretary. They took the view that he was simply too interesting to do the job well. There is all the difference in the world between doing the job in opposition and doing it in government. Opposition calls for opportunism, flair, brilliance, cheek: all qualities that Campbell was known to possess in abundance. Government calls for discretion, meticulous judgement, sobriety of approach, self-effacement. Nobody yet knew whether Campbell was capable of acquiring any of these qualities, but some of the evidence suggested that they were foreign to his nature. The job of a Press Secretary is to promote the interests of the Prime Minister, and keep himself well in the background. This too seemed an unlikely feat for him.

The doubters were proved wrong. Far from turning out a disaster, he turned out to be an inspirational choice. Before entering Downing Street, Campbell had already earned the respect, though not the universal affection, of the press. Afterwards, he very quickly converted himself into a figure of huge and commanding authority in Whitehall. Officials soon came to value his massive capacity for hard work, the calibre of his decision-making and the fact that he so clearly spoke for the Prime Minister. They rubbed their eyes at the contrast with the dithering and indecision of the final stage of the Major epoch.

In due course, his sway and influence ran further still. He is viewed with reverence in Buckingham Palace and even the White House. International institutions like NATO and the European Commission have felt the full force of his personality. Alastair Campbell has emerged since the 1997 General Election as one of the prodigious figures of our time. Before going on to explore exactly how this came about, it is necessary to pause a moment and explore the nature of the appointment which he took up on 2 May 1997.

The post of Downing Street Press Secretary

The post of Press Secretary was invented by Ramsay MacDonald upon taking power after the 1929 General Election.[1] The incoming Labour Prime Minister, bruised by his fleeting experience of power five years earlier, felt that he needed professional advice about how to cope with an overwhelmingly hostile Tory press. He chose a Foreign Office official named George Steward. Over the following eleven years, Steward developed the basics of the job more or less as it exists now. The Press Secretary briefs lobby journalists twice a day. The first briefing takes place at 11 a.m. in 10 Downing Street and a second at 4 p.m. in the lobby briefing room in the Commons. The Press Secretary has an office in Downing Street.[2] He travels with the Prime Minister on overseas trips and is constantly available to give guidance to accredited political journalists. A good Press Secretary has always been a source of huge strength to the incumbent at Downing Street. Successive Prime Ministers have discovered that an effective Press Secretary can play a vital role in imposing their own version of events on Whitehall. That is a function, as successive Prime Ministers have also discovered, that can easily be abused.

John Major was too scrupulous a man to go along this road. He might have been better off if he had. Three Press Secretaries served him during his six-year term of office. Being John Major's Press Secretary was rather like being captain of the England cricket team: held up to ridicule and derision, batting on a losing wicket, doomed. Given the traumatic circumstances, all three of the men who devoted themselves to serving Major managed well. More surprisingly still, they all flourished afterwards. Gus O'Donnell, always popular with the press, has been picked out by Gordon Brown as a high-flyer and is regarded as a future Permanent Secretary at the Treasury. His successor, Sir Christopher Meyer, skilfully navigated through the horror and carnage of the Major years. He resembled a man in an immaculately cut suit making his way across a muddy and death-strewn battlefield, only to emerge both spotless and unscathed at the other end. How he pulled the feat off no one will ever be able to guess. Sir Christopher now serves as British Ambassador in Washington, that most prized of all Foreign Office appointments. The third and final occupant of

---

1. See the useful chapter on the history of the job in Robert Harris's *Good and Faithful Servant* (1990, chapter 5). See also the invaluable Memorandum submitted by Colin Seymour-Ure, Professor of Government at the University of Kent, to the Select Committee on Public Administration (29 July 1988).

2. Campbell's large room is on the ground floor, with a window looking out onto Downing Street. It is the bow-fronted window to the left of the policeman guarding the front door.

the post, Jonathan Haslam, later found a billet in the City. All three were career officials, whose final loyalty always lay with the Civil Service rather than with John Major. Strict Civil Service rules governed what they could and could not do on the Prime Minster's behalf. Tony Blair decided, long before he entered Downing Street, that this was a handicap that should never be imposed on Alastair Campbell.

Only two Press Secretaries in living memory bear comparison with Campbell. They are, firstly, Joe Haines, who acted as press adviser and hatchet man to Harold Wilson, and secondly, Sir Bernard Ingham, who performed the identical function for Margaret Thatcher for the full eleven years of her famous premiership. Technically, Joe Haines was a Downing Street civil servant. In fact, the niceties of the job did not interest him. Like Campbell, he was a former lobby journalist and Labour partisan who believed that his only function was to serve and protect the Prime Minister. He did his best to convert the Downing Street press office into a political weapon for Harold Wilson: his first action on returning as Press Secretary after the Labour victory in the 1974 General Election was to sack half the Downing Street press staff.[3] He used his position to become far more than a press officer. He advised on policy, wrote Wilson's speeches, was heavily drawn into ministerial appointments and even helped compose Honours Lists. Haines was a forerunner to Alastair Campbell in two ways. He showed how the job could be used explicitly to foster political ends. More striking still, he showed that the title itself could be used as a cover for anything at all if the possessor put his mind to it and that was what the Prime Minister wanted. Harold Wilson told Haines in his conspiratorial way: 'I'll call you Press Secretary because it sounds good and it helps conceal what you really do.'[4]

Joe Haines has played a large part in Campbell's life. After the Wilson years, he ended up on the *Mirror*: it was Haines who, somewhat reluctantly, gave Campbell his first job as a lobby man. When Campbell went to work in Downing Street, Haines sent him some advice: 'The Press Secretary is not there to help the press. He is there to help the Prime Minister.'[5]

But the biggest trailblazer for Campbell was not Haines. It was Sir Bernard Ingham, Margaret Thatcher's Press Secretary. Periodically, from his well-earned retirement, Sir Bernard takes a fierce relish in issuing thunderous denun-

3. 'The office was overstaffed with unpolitical people,' remembers Haines today. 'I sacked five on the first day, out of eleven.' After the act had been carried out, Wilson's Principal Private Secretary, Robert Armstrong, came round to complain. But it was too late.
4. Author's interview with Joe Haines, 23 February 1999, Tonbridge.
5. *Ibid.*

ciations of his successor for misusing the powers of his office.[6] Since Sir Bernard was not whiter than white himself in this respect, these are typically greeted with widespread hilarity round Whitehall. But Sir Bernard was a magnificent figure in his day, the only Press Secretary before Alastair Campbell to have attracted a book in his own right. This work, by the journalist Robert Harris, sets out in compelling detail how Ingham used the lobby system to cut the ground from under the feet of ministers who had fallen out of favour.[7] Francis Pym, one of Margaret Thatcher's Foreign Secretaries and John Biffen, Leader of the House, were two who got the Ingham treatment.

For Campbell's first formative five years in the lobby, until the ejection of Margaret Thatcher in 1990, Sir Bernard was the Prime Minister's Press Secretary. The two men got along well. Campbell is one of the few journalists whose name is mentioned with approval in Ingham's autobiography. They had a great deal in common. Both were outsiders. Sir Bernard's birthplace, Hebden Bridge, of which he made much, presenting it as an island of virtue and good sense in a corrupt and hostile world, stood at one of the outlying reaches of Donald Campbell's veterinary practice.[8] One minor consequence of this was that both men were Burnley FC fans, though Campbell's support was doubtless the more intense.

There is no question that Campbell studied Ingham with fascination, noting how the Yorkshireman used the powers of his office to deadly effect. At one stage Campbell even set about writing a novel, with Sir Bernard as the central character. He was 50,000 words into the text when one day Fiona Millar pressed the wrong key and the document was obliterated.[9]

Campbell would not have been possible without Ingham in the same way that Sir Joshua Reynolds would not have been possible without his teacher Thomas Hudson. The young Reynolds learnt all there was to be gained from the honest artisan style of the West Country portraitist, then moved on and synthesised his influence into something altogether more accomplished, cosmopolitan and profound.

6. See, for example, 'If I were Alastair Campbell I'd Shoot Myself', *Mail on Sunday*, 8 November 1998.

7. See Harris, *op.cit.*

8. It is a mystery why Sir Bernard, having devoted so much effort to praising Hebden Bridge, has chosen to spend his retirement in Purley, Surrey. Sir John Junor, the great *Sunday Express* editor, was a similar case. Few of Junor's columns failed to mention his native Auchtermuchty in glowing terms, but the thought of abandoning the comforts of the English home counties and actually going to live there never seems to have occurred to Sir John.

9. See *The Times*, Diary, 10 September 1994.

In short, Sir Bernard showed the way for Campbell, just as Margaret Thatcher showed the way for Tony Blair. Campbell shares Sir Bernard's appreciation of the tabloid press. Both men have been fond of levelling the charge of triviality, distortion and fabrication at the press in general. Both have made a point of exempting the *Sun* – conventionally held to be more guilty of these three practices than any other Fleet Street paper – from these grave criticisms. Both men have bullied and blustered their way through lobby briefings. Neither has bothered to conceal his dislike of journalists, though the trait is more pronounced in Campbell. Both have been utterly loyal, but it is probably fair to say that Ingham's loyalty was to his mistress alone. Campbell's goes beyond Tony Blair: he is deep at the heart of the New Labour project. Campbell has never used lobby briefings as a way of cutting the ground from ministers in the way that Ingham used them to destroy Francis Pym and John Biffen. On the other hand, Ingham, unlike Campbell, was rarely seriously accused by lobby men of distorting the truth.

There is one other, most important, difference between the two men. Ingham was an accident, Campbell is deliberate. When Margaret Thatcher became Prime Minister in 1979, the last thing on her mind was the appointment of her new Press Secretary. The appointment ranked so far down her list of priorities that she delegated the task to someone else. Sir Bernard was appointed on the basis of a ten-second interview. Had it lasted any longer, it is possible that he would not have got the job, for she would have discovered that in 1965 he stood as a Labour Party candidate for Leeds City Council. More probably she would not have minded. In the opinion of Margaret Thatcher back in 1979, the post of Press Secretary was as unpolitical as it was unimportant. This was partly because she thought of civil servants as neutral. But it was mainly because, twenty years ago, the rise of the Media Class and the central problem it posed for government was not yet evident to senior politicians.

She very quickly discovered her mistake. By the end of her eleven-year term, Bernard Ingham and Charles Powell, her Private Secretary, were two of her most trusted and powerful advisers. When Tony Blair entered Downing Street seven years later, he was under no illusions whatever about the importance of his Press Secretary. He knew that the media today have the power to destroy, and to create, a Prime Minister or a party leader. For Blair, the identity of his Press Secretary was a matter of the highest importance. Sir Bernard Ingham came to carry great weight under Margaret Thatcher. But Alastair Campbell was to carry ten times more under Tony Blair. With Campbell, indeed, the job entered another dimension.

On arriving in office he was immediately handed a massive new power that no previous Downing Street Press Secretary had ever possessed. All previous occupants of the job had been civil servants. This meant that they were servants of the state, prevented by strict Civil Service rules from getting involved in party politics. Sir Bernard Ingham, for instance, had to take a three-week holiday during General Election campaigns. Tony Blair was determined to find a way around this for Campbell.

The obvious solution was to make Campbell a 'Special Adviser', one of the shadowy group of figures who are allowed into Whitehall to give ministers political advice. But this solution created a new problem: these Special Advisers, under Civil Service rules of impartiality, are never permitted to hold executive powers: they can be observers only.

Following long discussions with senior civil servants before the election, Campbell and Blair boldly cut the Gordian knot: they made Campbell both a civil servant and a Special Adviser. The solution gave him the freedom to throw himself into politics, as well as the power to order civil servants around. It was unconstitutional, and it required a change in the law to allow it to happen. A meeting of the Privy Council was called within forty-eight hours of the election, and special Orders in Council were issued giving Alastair Campbell sweeping new powers and freedoms of a kind that no Press Secretary has ever enjoyed before.[10] It was a sign of how deeply serious New Labour was about government.

In the evolutionary scale at Whitehall, Sir Bernard Ingham was Neanderthal Man, while Campbell was *Homo sapiens*. Campbell is the twenty-first Press Secretary to occupy the post since George Steward seventy years before. It can accurately be said that under him the job came of age. John Biffen, the recipient of the worst of Ingham's bile and poison, once remarked that his tormentor was the sewer but not the sewage. Campbell, to adapt that unpleasing metaphor, is both the sewer and the sewage.

Campbell and Blair

Anyone who observes Alastair Campbell together with the Prime Minister instantly gets the message. The two men are on terms of complete equality. Often, indeed, Campbell has the upper hand. He will go into a room where

10. Three of these new hybrid posts were created. Besides Campbell's, the second was filled by Jonathan Powell, the No. 10 Chief of Staff. The third has been left vacant.

Tony Blair is talking to businessmen or party officials and stroll up to the Prime Minister with elaborate casualness. 'Come on, we're off,' Campbell will say and Tony Blair will spring to attention. Campbell does not hesitate to slap Blair down crudely in meetings. Once, in front of Stuart Higgins, editor of the *Sun*, he contradicted Tony Blair three times on a sensitive issue of party policy. There was no formality about it, no courtesy, no deference: merely a brusque finality. This dismissive style was converted into straight abuse when Cherie and Tony Blair made the decision to send their son Euan to the Oratory School. Campbell shouted and swore at Tony Blair. He is reported to have been 'white-faced with anger'.[11] Before the election, Mike Maloney, a *Mirror* photographer, went round to the Blairs' Islington home to take some portrait shots. Campbell was there to mind the event, but was called to the phone. When he returned he discovered that the *Mirror* man had prevailed upon Tony and Cherie Blair to rub their noses together, Eskimo-fashion. Campbell went mad. 'You prat!' he stormed at Blair. 'What are you doing? Maloney is the original baby-faced assassin.'[12]

Political reporters get a privileged view of the intimate Campbell/Blair relationship. Sometimes, at receptions, they can be seen giggling together like a pair of schoolboys. They have acquired each other's mannerisms. If you watch the pair together closely, you can sometimes see the identical look of exasperation appear on each of their faces at the same moment. 'They do it independently, without looking at one another. They spend so much time in each other's company that they know exactly what the other is thinking automatically,' says one close friend of both men.

On trips abroad, when Blair and Campbell come back to the press pack to talk, there is never any question that Campbell is the dominant partner. This has been so from the very first. Not long after Blair became party leader, he went on a trip to Paris. The press came with him, eager to monitor the new Labour leader in action. They travelled on Eurostar and halfway through the three-hour journey Blair and Campbell went to the bar area to meet the travelling lobby journalists. It was striking how the Leader of the Opposition batted all hard questions in the direction of his press officer, not even making a pretence of answering them himself.

This syndrome has become so pronounced that the Prime Minister and his Press Secretary now ham up the relationship. On a Prime Ministerial trip to

11. Private information.

12. See the *Sunday Telegraph*, 6 April 1997. To his shame, Maloney was prevailed upon to hand the pictures over.

Washington in the spring of 1999, Campbell was briefing journalists in the cavernous jumbo jet which had been provided by British Airways. The plane was empty, apart from the small group of officials travelling with Tony Blair and the score or so of journalists. Take-off had been quite frightening: the plane was so underweight that it seemed to project itself vertically upwards after leaving the runway at Heathrow. Not long into the flight, Alastair Campbell arrived to brief journalists: they gathered round to hear what he was saying. Ten minutes later the Prime Minister himself arrived to join them. No one moved to greet him, as all ears were strained to take in what Campbell was saying. Tony Blair stood alone, an isolated figure in the empty plane. Then he quipped: 'Don't mind me: I'm just the Press Secretary.'[13]

Broadcasters get an even more astonishing insight into Tony Blair's outright dependency upon his press adviser. One famous journalist, who has inter- viewed the Prime Minister on a number of occasions, says: 'It is quite uncanny. You are interviewing two people. Alastair will sit on the other side of the table, writing notes and handing them across. Blair gets incredibly nervous on these occasions. If the Prime Minister shows signs of getting lost Campbell is quite capable of stepping in and giving him the line.' Joy Johnson, who worked with Campbell in the Labour media team before the election, describes Campbell's awesome influence thus: 'When you heard Bernard Ingham speaking, you heard Margaret Thatcher and when you heard Margaret Thatcher speaking you heard Margaret Thatcher. When you hear Tony Blair, very often you hear Alastair Campbell.'

For television interviews, Campbell makes sure that he becomes an invisible third participant in the event. He is skilled at placing himself within the inter- viewer's line of vision and making signs such as tapping his watch. As one well-known broadcaster puts it, 'It's very hard to tell who's the boss. When they are together it's impossible to say.' Campbell's role is so dominant that some broadcasters cannot resist mocking it. Once, Campbell and Blair were sitting in the BBC 'green room', the reception area where studio guests wait to go on air. John Humphrys, the *Today* programme and *On the Record* presenter, went into the room to greet the pair. He deliberately walked straight past the Prime Minister and held out his hand with a 'Good of you to come, Alastair'. Then he turned round and, in mock surprise, greeted Tony Blair, who by then was looking somewhat perplexed.[14]

---

13. The author is grateful to lobby journalists on the trip for this anecdote.
14. Private information.

Campbell appears in control from start to finish. After one visit to the television studios, Blair lingered behind, chatting to a couple of journalists. Suddenly the door opened with a flurry. It was Campbell. 'Come on, Tony,' he shouted. 'We're off. Get a fucking move on.'

There have been some extraordinary relationships at the heart of Downing Street, but none as extraordinary as this one. It answers the deepest need in each man's character. As Tony Blair's biographers have shown, the Prime Minister has always sought out gurus to guide him through life's intractable complexities. At different times that role has been played by Peter Thomson, the priest he met at Oxford, by Derry Irvine, his head of chambers, by Gordon Brown and by Peter Mandelson. All these figures are still on the scene and all have a significant role to play in maintaining the mental and spiritual equilibrium of the Prime Minister. But the person he relies on most today, his rock of strength in Downing Street, is Campbell. And Campbell, too, has got what he has searched for all through his life. He has always wanted a relationship of privileged intimacy with the most powerful member of whatever organisation he has joined. Now he has the ultimate: he is on intimate terms with the man who is running the country.

And Campbell does a superb job. He gives first-class advice. He is always by the Prime Minister's side. On overseas trips, long after Tony Blair has fallen asleep, Campbell is still awake beside him, dealing with calls, preparing the following day's business, making sure they are not caught unawares. When asked once how he does it, he replied: 'I don't drink and I don't smoke.' His judgement is never clouded by that half-bottle of wine over lunch. He never wakes up bleary, hungover, unable to cope. He wakes up ready for action and wide-awake for the problems of the coming day.

Campbell vs. Blair's ministers

The following episode demonstrates with total clarity the enormous power that Campbell now wields even over the most powerful members of the Blair government. It took place in the early spring of 1999. Alastair Campbell and the Prime Minister made the long trip up to Glasgow. At least, that was how the forty-five minute flight seemed to them. To them, the dour Old Labour stronghold of Scotland's largest city has always seemed further away than Washington or Rome.

Blair, accompanied by Campbell, attended a local function. As they came out, the Scottish Office minister Helen Liddell went up to greet Campbell. She knew him well. Liddell was one of the rising stars of the government, the local minister, and on her home territory. She was confident and in command. What happened next can best be described by Bill Greig, the highly respected political editor of the *Scottish Daily Express*, who was there and witnessed it all. 'Helen bounced in front of Alastair with a cheery greeting. Ali walked straight on. He didn't even slow down his stride for a single second. He just said "See ya" as he went by, not looking in her direction. It was a cold and calculated snub. You could see her being left clumsy and uncomfortable. She crumpled up. She was obviously hurt. You could see her thinking: that's not just Alastair. That's what the Prime Minister thinks of me too.' A few months later, Liddell was moved out of her job at the Scottish Office. This unpleasant story demonstrates why Campbell can become an object of fear among ministers.

Campbell enjoys equality with the Prime Minister. But other ministers, with the exception of the Chancellor of the Exchequer and, debatably, the Deputy Prime Minister and the Foreign Secretary, defer to him. They may make no announcement without first clearing it through Campbell's Downing Street office. Before making any public utterance, on any subject of importance, it is ensured both that they are aware of the Downing Street line and that they follow it. Every day, around lunchtime, all Whitehall departments are faxed a transcript of the lobby briefing given by Campbell at No. 10 earlier in the day. This, in the words of one senior official, 'is sacrosanct. It is taken with the utmost seriousness by ministers. It gives them their line for the day.' When Campbell speaks at meetings, ministers strain to listen. As one middle-ranking minister says of Alastair Campbell: 'When we meet him, we are in the role of client. He is in the role of boss.'

Campbell's role as the formal link between the government and newspaper editors gives him a frightening hold over ministers when their private lives enter the public domain. Nothing illustrates this more graphically than the sad circumstances surrounding Foreign Secretary Robin Cook's separation from his wife Margaret. According to the best available account,[15] Campbell gave Cook what amounted to an ultimatum. He told him that 'clarity in news management' would prevent the story from getting out of hand. Cook took this to mean that he must rapidly choose between his wife and his mistress. Campbell played a similarly prominent role in the resignation of Welsh Secretary Ron Davies in the autumn of 1998. 'Alastair is always present at the fall of a Cabinet minister,' notes one old Whitehall hand.

15. John Kampfner, *Robin Cook* (1998).

One indication of the altered relationship between ministers and the Downing Street Press Secretary is the 4.30 p.m. briefing given to political journalists by the Leader of the House of Commons on Thursday afternoons. This event is a long-standing lobby practice. The Leader of the Commons will attend the afternoon briefing, technically at the invitation of the lobby itself, in order to inform reporters about the week that lies ahead in Parliament. His or her briefing almost always follows immediately after the regular afternoon briefing from the Press Secretary. When that has wound up, the floor is passed to the visiting Cabinet minister. The Press Secretary will, however, remain present. The attitude of Press Secretaries before Campbell was one of deference and respect. It is noticeable that this is no longer the case. When the current Leader of the House, Margaret Beckett, briefs the lobby, Campbell holds the floor as well. In fact, he will often have briefed Mrs Beckett ahead of these meetings. An example is the lobby briefing held on 22 July 1999, the day of the Eddisbury by-election. Colin Brown, lobby chairman, threw open the floor to Mrs Beckett, who had to leave early. In fact, however, Campbell fielded all questions, even though some of them – in particular those relating to mooted government plans to legislate against fox-hunting – fell directly within her remit. There was absolutely no question that Campbell, not Beckett, was the dominant figure.

The most noteworthy example of Campbell's contemptuous attitude towards ministers came within a year of the General Election. It caused a row at the time and played a role in the decision by the Select Committee on Public Administration to launch an investigation into what he does. It is not surprising that it did so. This was the affair of the Harriet Harman and Frank Field memos.

Alastair Campbell's defenders make much of the fact that Campbell has never been proved to brief against ministers in the style of Sir Bernard Ingham. His abstinence in this respect is held up as a virtue, proof that he does not abuse the powers of his office in the way his renowned predecessor is alleged to have done. It is a fair point: he has never been known to undermine ministers in open lobby briefing, though what is sometimes said in private one-to-one conversation with senior and trusted lobby correspondents may be another matter. But the memos that Campbell sent to Social Security Secretary Harriet Harman on 15 January and 26 February 1998 had precisely the same effect. These missives were despatched at a time when there was talk of leaks from Harman's department. She was ordered, along with her junior minister Frank Field, to clear all press briefings with Downing Street. The memos could not have been more scathing and dismissive. They were faxed to Harman's office, and circulated around her department and ministerial colleagues, exactly as Campbell knew they would be.

What was so striking about the affair was that Campbell, an unelected official, should have felt able to write to a Cabinet minister in such terms. Harman later complained to the Prime Minister about the Campbell memos. Blair just shrugged his shoulders and said: 'That's Alastair.' From the moment the memos were sent, Harriet Harman was swinging in the wind and waiting to be cut down, just as John Biffen or Francis Pym were after being savaged by Bernard Ingham. The episode shows, in the most blatant fashion, that power in the Blair administration lies in a tiny coterie around the Prime Minister and not with Cabinet ministers, let alone elected MPs. This is no accident. This is how New Labour in government was always meant to be. Nor did the Prime Minister and Alastair Campbell ever make the slightest secret of their intention. On 10 March 1997, just days before John Major called the General Election, Tony Blair addressed the Newspaper Society. He said that people must be clear 'that we will run from the centre and govern from the centre'.

New Labour in power

Few Prime Ministers have thought so carefully about how they would govern as did Tony Blair before he entered Downing Street. Few Prime Ministers have had the time. John Major was suddenly propelled into a situation he never anticipated. Harold Wilson was given just months to prepare for the 1964 election after Hugh Gaitskell's death the previous year. Jim Callaghan was too busy clinging to office. Sir Alec Douglas-Home and Harold Macmillan, as true Tories, both regarded thinking about the matter as an unprofitable and faintly disreputable activity.

Only one other post-war Prime Minister brooded about government as much as Tony Blair and that was Margaret Thatcher. She had four years to do so, between being elected leader of the Tory Party in 1975 and becoming Prime Minister in 1979. In the intervening period, she thought about policy, while Blair, in his three years of opposition, thought about process. She thought about what; Blair thought about how. She thought about content, while Blair contemplated form. It was Blair's brilliant perception that, in a country with few real grievances, a large part of politics is about presentation and the articulation of mood. Thatcher changed Britain profoundly. But she left the British state much as it was. Blair's principal legacy will be the imposition of the most revolutionary set of changes in how Britain is governed since the Glorious Revolution of 1688. He also – and this is a curious thing – wants to change the kind of people we are. Tony Blair and those close to him think that the British people are too grim, pessimistic, drab and sour – in a word, too British. They want to turn Britain into a different country and the British into a different people, with a new set of institutions and a different morality.[16] It is all very ambitious, very complicated, very strange, and, in its way, admirable.

New Labour is hostile to tradition, class, existing institutions, history. This hostility is based on three things: ignorance, hope and, ironically enough, New Labour's own tormented past. New Labour had a gruesome birth, out of the corpse of the Labour Party of Keir Hardie, Aneurin Bevan, Clement Attlee and John Smith. The ghosts linger on, and still from time to time their rattling chains must surely disturb the slumbers of Tony Blair. New Labour established itself by turning on its past, on the once omnipotent National Executive Committee, the trade unions, the Clause 4 commitment to the nationalisation of the means of production, the singing of the Red Flag at the end of the Labour Conference every autumn. Most of all, of course, it has grown to vigorous life thanks to an act of pure parricide: the murder of the Labour Party, with – as we have seen – Alastair Campbell playing the part of first assassin. New Labour wishes that the Labour Party had never existed. It thinks, much more strongly than the Tories, that Labour was all a terrible mistake. Philip Gould, in his important work *The Unfinished Revolution* (1998), explains this hypothesis at considerable length. 'In establishing itself as a socialist party immutably linked to trade unionism, Labour broke with Liberalism and cut itself off from the other great radical movement in British politics,' mourns Gould. 'The separation of Labourism and Liberalism stopped dead the possibility of building one united progressive party, similar to the broader coalitions in the United States and Scandinavia.'[17] Gould and Blair blame the Labour Party for making the twentieth century a Tory century.

In opposition, Tony Blair turned upon the venerable institutions of the Labour Party. In government, he has turned on the venerable institutions of the British state – the House of Lords, the representation of the hereditary peerage. Members of the Wilson Cabinet did business together at Brooks and spent weekends at grand country houses. With the splendiferous exception of Peter Mandelson – who in his pomp was sometimes styled Tony Blair's

16. For instance, see Tony Blair's speech to the Labour Party Conference, Brighton, 3 October 1995, where he called for a 'new spirit in the nation', or the ideas set out in Mark Leonard's pamphlet for the Blairite think-tank Demos, *Britain. Reviewing our Identity* (1997).

17. Gould, p. 27.

'ambassador to the upper classes' – the new government has no time for that sort of thing.

Clubland and the House of Lords were obvious targets – easier to hit than a low pheasant flying into the wind. But it soon became apparent that the peaceful revolution Tony Blair had in mind went very much further. It became clear that he had no appetite for the institutions of constitutional democracy which have sustained British government for the last three hundred years. His contempt for the House of Commons, for its irritating insistence on discussion and debate, for the way that it demeaned the authority of the Prime Minister by opening him up to criticism and public question, was immediately obvious. Luckily, thanks to Labour's landslide majority, the new government has not needed to worry too much about the Commons. The Prime Minister goes there as rarely as possible. His voting record is the lowest, by far, of any Prime Minister since the office took modern form in the early eighteenth century. Blair attends just five per cent, or one in twenty, of all votes held in the Commons.[18] Even Thatcher, in all her pomp, voted six times as often as Blair. Public announcements of importance are made, first, in the television studios and the newspapers and second, very much as an afterthought, in the Commons chamber. This flagrant flouting of traditional practice sends the Speaker, Betty Boothroyd, into paroxysms of fury and despair. She regularly rebukes ministers for neglecting the Commons chamber. They, in turn, could not care less, either about the neglect of Parliament or about Ms Boothroyd's fury. Intermittently, New Labour makes half-hearted attempts to destabilise the Speaker, but they have not yet succeeded, mainly because in their view she does not matter enough to put too much effort into getting rid of her. They think of her as a minor nuisance, no more than that. Indeed, it is a sign of the degradation of the Commons under New Labour that the office of Chief Whip, which until 1997 was one of the most feared and powerful in both Labour and Tory governments, has degenerated into a middle-ranking post of no especial importance. It has entirely lost the very substantial mystique that it used to possess. Not one of the tiny clique of advisers huddled around Tony Blair is a parliamentarian. This is in striking contrast to that of Margaret Thatcher, who was also accused of neglecting the Commons. Her close coterie included a number of 'House of Commons men', of whom Ian Gow was the most notable. One very senior

18. After a year of power, the Prime Minister had voted in 12 out of 233 divisions, or approximately 5 per cent. John Major's average was 30 per cent. Even when Margaret Thatcher had her huge 1980s majority, she always averaged 30 per cent.

official close to Downing Street says: 'Basically, in No. 10 Downing Street there is a complete contempt for Parliament and that attitude permeates the whole government.'[19]

Most telling of all is the complete eclipse of the Cabinet system. Books of constitutional theory still occasionally make the preposterous claim that the Cabinet is the fountain of British government, with the Prime Minister merely the first among a collection of equals who assemble at Downing Street every Thursday morning in the splendid Cabinet Room. In reality, Cabinet government has been in decline for decades, and the autocratic rule of Margaret Thatcher nearly dealt it the *coup de grâce*. There were some stirrings of life after Thatcher, a reflection of the feebleness of the Major premiership, but they have been completely eclipsed under Tony Blair. He frequently does not attend, and when he does, the show rarely lasts more than forty-five minutes. It remains the case that matters of importance are discussed, but both the quantity and the quality of the discussion about these important matters are negligible.[20] A sign of the tributary status to which Cabinet has been condemned is the fact that Alastair Campbell now sits in on its meetings, the first time that a Press Secretary has been permitted to do so as a matter of course.[21] Decisions are made elsewhere. The impoverishment of the Cabinet is an outward symbol of the way power has been taken out of the hands of elected ministers of the crown, and pulled towards the Downing Street machine. Once the glory of the British system of government, the Cabinet has been converted into a formal and ornamental part of the British constitution. It has suffered the fate of the Privy Council, which fell into disuse three hundred years ago but maintains a shadowy and inconsequential existence to this day.

The power that has drained from Parliament, from ministers, from the Cabinet and other traditional institutions of state has had to go somewhere. It has been amassed instead, in part, by the Media Class which has gained in power and authority at the expense, chiefly, of Parliament. But the greater part has been seized by Tony Blair at Downing Street. It is fair to say that, before he arrived in power, political power in Britain had the configuration of a mountain range. No. 10 Downing Street was Everest, the tallest, most potent and most

19. Private conversation.

20. Private information. One Cabinet minister has spoken only twice, briefly, in over two years of Blair Cabinet meetings.

21. Previous Press Secretaries were allowed admittance in exceptional circumstances.

majestic of all the peaks. But there have always been others of size and significance. Tony Blair's Downing Street is like a single enormous mountain, surrounded by foothills.[22]

This new structure of government has handed over an overwhelming amount of power in Whitehall and Westminster to the tiny group of men around Tony Blair, among them chief of staff Jonathan Powell, the Downing Street Policy Unit head David Miliband, and Alastair Campbell. But no one in Whitehall is in the faintest doubt that Campbell carries far more clout than either of the other two individuals.

This, too, is a change from past regimes. Thatcher's government was the most centralising of all administrations before Tony Blair arrived. And yet when John Redwood was head of the Downing Street Policy Unit, he carried greater weight than Bernard Ingham. Charles Powell, Margaret Thatcher's Private Secretary, was a more senior figure than Sir Bernard. In Tony Blair's inner circle, the spin-doctor carries more weight than either the policy boss or the chief of staff. No government has ever been as conscious of the importance of presentation as New Labour. No Prime Minister has ever been as aware of the media as Tony Blair. It is perhaps inevitable, therefore, that his most powerful courtier and adviser should be a spin-doctor. But, of course, there is more to it than that. For Campbell's power in Downing Street is not merely a function of his job. It is a function of the strength of his personality, his prodigious capacity for hard work, the quality of his advice and his immensely strong personal relationship with the Prime Minister.

It is hard to think of an unelected politician this century who has had such sweeping powers at his command as Alastair Campbell has. It is necessary to consider now how he has used them. His first target was Gordon Brown, the Chancellor of the Exchequer, and his highly engaging spin-doctor, the remarkable Charlie Whelan.

---

22. The best guide to this impressive, rapidly imposed, though far from irreversible process has been Professor Peter Hennessy, Professor of Contemporary History at Queen Mary and Westfield College, University of London. Professor Hennessy has devoted the past thirty years to analysing Whitehall. Senior officials entrust him with confidences they would not dream of granting to conventional political journalists. Hennessy is therefore in a unique position. Though not a civil servant himself, he is in a position to see what civil servants see. Hennessy's contention is that British government has undergone, in the words of one of Tony Blair's innermost circle, 'a change from a feudal system of barons to a more Napoleonic system'. He compares Blair's system of government to an elected monarchy, with the Prime Minister at the centre of a court, though he himself does not put it as simply as that. See *The Blair Centre: A Question of Command and Control?* (1999). See also Hennessy's lecture *The Blair Style of Government: An Historical Perspective and an Interim Audit* (1997).

Chapter Ten

BLAIRITES AND BROWNITES

Two households, both alike in dignity,
In fair Verona, where we lay our scene,
From ancient grudge break to new mutiny,
Where civil blood makes civil hands unclean.
William Shakespeare,
Romeo and Juliet, *Prologue*

A little local difficulty at the Treasury

Charlie Whelan is one of the most improbable and, in his way, appealing figures ever to have strutted his stuff on the Westminster stage. Even at the time, it seemed extraordinary that this hard-drinking, foul-mouthed, ex-Communist bruiser was able to play his full part in government. He was certainly the most implausible figure to hold influence and sway at the Treasury since Winston Churchill chose the twenty-six-year-old Bob Boothby to become his Principal Private Secretary in 1926. Churchill later said of Boothby that he possessed 'much capacity but no virtue', a remark which applied to Whelan as well.

For eighteen months, Charlie Whelan, as Gordon Brown's Press Secretary, was one of the tight little group of men and women who governed Britain. The manner of his departure was thoroughly in keeping with what went before. He hated Peter Mandelson with every sinew of his body and when Mandelson went, Whelan went with him. It was almost as if he felt that his job was now complete. The French have a term for it, coined from the battlefield – *le coup des deux veuves*. Mandelson and Whelan died together, locked in mortal combat. It was politics at its most raw, human passion at its most destructive.[1]

Civil servants, eager to ingratiate themselves with the barbaric creature they found in their midst, since they correctly believed that he carried great sway with his master, presented him with a capacious office on the first floor of the

---

1. Barely two weeks after Mandelson was forced out of his office when his £373,000 home loan from Geoffrey Robinson became public, Whelan's departure was announced (4 January 1999). Explaining his departure, he said: 'The job of press secretary becomes extremely difficult if the press secretary and not the department he serves, becomes the story and the subject of excessive attention' (*Daily Telegraph*, 5 January 1999). Later he warned that the same fate could befall Alastair Campbell.

splendid Treasury building on the corner of Parliament Square and Whitehall. The office accurately conveyed Whelan's status and importance, but he preferred not to use it. Opposite the Treasury was a public house known as the Red Lion. When the Red Lion became too hot for him, he would repair to the Two Chairmen by Queen Anne's Gate. Perhaps he felt most at home at the Victoria Club, a smoky drinking den frequented by trade unionists; it was just a few hundred yards in physical distance but several thousand miles in spirit from Millbank Tower, from where Peter Mandelson masterminded New Labour's media operation before the 1997 General Election.

At these various drinking establishments, Whelan would do his business. Unlike Campbell – but like Mandelson, another former member of the Communist Party – he preferred to operate with a few trusted intimates. Kevin Maguire, the political editor of the *Daily Mirror*, was one. Patrick Hennessy, political correspondent of the *Evening Standard*, was another. Much time was devoted to cultivating Richard Littlejohn, the renowned newspaper columnist and television presenter. Sometime in the dim and distant past, Littlejohn had been an industrial correspondent and Whelan a union official: they had done business with each other then. Littlejohn and his wife were invited to dinner parties in the flat above No. 10 Downing Street along with the Chancellor and his girlfriend, Sarah Macaulay. Paul Dacre, editor of the *Daily Mail*, was also cultivated. Dacre had remained impervious to the charms of Tony Blair: Brown made a determined effort to capture him for himself. One night, the two men stayed up till 2 a.m. drinking whisky. This was fêted as a triumph at the Treasury. It was held that the two men were bound together by a common gargantuan work ethic, an impossibly strong moral sense and a joint unease in social situations.

All this was promptly reported back to Alastair Campbell, who hated it. The existence of Whelan was a direct affront to his own authority in Whitehall. All other government departments, with their associated spin-doctors and other specialists, were under his direct control. But Whelan was allowed to range freely about London and medialand as if he owned it. Campbell ordered his staff to monitor Whelan's activities and report back. Anji Hunter, a key Downing Street aide, was just one of those who found themselves under the suspicion of spying on Whelan. Invited to the wedding of Ed Balls, Gordon Brown's special adviser, and the Labour MP Yvette Cooper, she at one point detached herself from proceedings to talk on her mobile phone. It was immediately assumed that she was talking to Alastair Campbell, then accompanying Tony Blair on a trip to Japan. The wedding was a key Brownite event and

Hunter was one of a handful of Blairites invited to it. Relations between the two camps were at an especially rocky stage: the episode did nothing to improve them and was held against Hunter ever after.

Cherie Blair was also blamed, whether fairly or unfairly it is hard to tell, for stirring up difficulties between Gordon Brown and Tony Blair. At the Treasury, she was sometimes called 'Lady Macbeth'. It is likely that news of this fresh insult, too, was swiftly relayed back to Downing Street.

Campbell kept a capacious file of Whelan-related cuttings in his office and would painstakingly sift through it, working out what stories Whelan had given to whom and why.[2] Whelan would very often get blamed for stories that were absolutely nothing to do with him. Once Hennessy – a known Brownite and therefore distrusted in Downing Street – picked up the information that Peter Mandelson was to put his name forward as a candidate for the National Executive Committee. He approached Whelan who, knowing nothing of the plan, denied it. Hennessy ran the story anyway, having ascertained through other sources that it was true. Whelan got the blame for giving it to Hennessy. 'He didn't just get it wrong,' a bemused Hennessy recalled later. 'He got a bollocking for something he didn't do.'

In the Downing Street Press Office, journalists were not divided up according to whether they were Tory or Labour or accounted good or bad. They were classified as Brownite or Blairite.[3] The destruction of Charlie Whelan became a primary objective of Downing Street policy. For many months, Campbell plotted to weaken Whelan at the 9 a.m. meeting. He wanted to force him to bring his deputy, a civil servant called Peter Curwen, as chaperone, a move that was intended to undermine Whelan's authority. Curwen was placed in a delicate situation, becoming so concerned that at one stage he went to see the Permanent Secretary about the dilemma. But there was nothing Campbell could do about the Whelan problem without the active permission of Gordon Brown. Campbell spent hours over the phone to Brown trying to drive home the message that Whelan, his mischievous freelance operator round Whitehall, must go.[4]

Whelan was merely the symbol, though an important one, of a much greater power struggle. He had been hired shortly before the death of John Smith by, of all people, Peter Mandelson. Whelan told Mandelson that he would work only

2. Campbell disclosed the existence of this file to political correspondents.
3. Government information officers were staggered and alarmed that the distinction should loom so large.
4. Private information.

for Gordon Brown or Tony Blair. The fact that Mandelson placed Whelan in Brown's office as his press adviser is yet another indication that he was backing Brown rather than Blair as party leader right up to the end. At that point, he would have viewed Whelan, for whom he had secured a job, as one of his own creatures and therefore placed him in the office of the man whom he rated more highly.

Something seems to have gone terminally wrong with the relationship between Mandelson and Whelan even before John Smith died. It may well be that Whelan resented Mandelson's proprietorial attitude. They fell out almost at once, and after the feuding started between Mandelson and Brown, the ill-feeling became yet more bitter, rancorous and destructive.

But it is wrong to see the vendetta between the Blair camp and the Brown camp, which became such a dominant theme of the first eighteen months of the New Labour government, as being mainly about personalities. It wasn't. It is certainly impossible to underestimate the depth of the hatreds which the individuals involved felt for one another. To a normal person, conversant with the proprieties of everyday life, unfamiliar with the various ways that ambition and lust for power can alter the human character, it is quite shocking.[5] Be all this as it may, the underlying battle was a power struggle between Downing Street and the Treasury.

What made this contest unusually difficult to solve was the deal struck by Tony Blair and Gordon Brown at Granita restaurant in Islington at the height of the Labour leadership contest in 1994. Gordon Brown reluctantly agreed to stand down, but he insisted on conditions which Blair, guilt-stricken at the turn events had taken, was weak enough to concede. Brown demanded complete control over the economy and sweeping powers over other areas of policy as well. He demanded the ability to place his own people in key posts. In effect, he demanded, and got, something approaching a dual premiership.

There were many manifestations of this in the government formed by Tony Blair after May 1997. Tony Blair abandoned his right to chair the Economic Affairs Committee of the Cabinet, the first Prime Minister to leave it to his Chancellor since the disastrous early Wilson period of 1964–6. Nick Brown, a close ally of his namesake Gordon Brown, was permitted to become Chief Whip. Most alarmingly of all to Blairite eyes, the Chancellor was allowed to run his own briefing operation independently of the Downing Street machine.

5. See, for example, Paul Routledge, *Gordon Brown* (1998); Pym and Kochan, *Gordon Brown: The First Year in Power* (1998), etc., as well as numerous press accounts.

All of these decisions amounted to a recipe for grotesque instability at the heart of government, threatening to undermine the kind of Presidential operation that Tony Blair and his advisers were determined to impose from Downing Street. That is why the cheerful, jaunty presence of Charlie Whelan, with his freedom to tell journalists whatever he wanted, a freedom he availed himself of to the full, antagonised Downing Street so much. He became, for eighteen months and whether he liked it or not, a symbol of rebellion against the ever tighter control from the centre. He had to be destroyed if Campbell, and therefore Blair, was to run his own show.

The process of destruction was very slow. The first attempt to undermine Whelan had come before the General Election. It was masterminded by Peter Mandelson, who had his own personal motives.[6] Campbell kept out of it. The attempt failed. The second bid came at the time of the 1997 General Election. On the first Friday in power, basking in the joy of their landslide victory, Gordon Brown and Tony Blair went for a walk in the Downing Street garden. They wandered in and out of the shrubbery for forty-five minutes, relishing the sweet feeling of victory as well as the scents and sounds of the glorious sunlit afternoon. Fifteen minutes of that discussion were taken up with the Chancellor's imminent plan to grant independence to the Bank of England. The remaining thirty minutes of this first conversation between the two most powerful men in Britain on Labour's first day of power in two decades was devoted to the vexatious subject of Whelan. The new Prime Minister hinted to his old friend that Whelan's ferocious reputation for briefing against certain members of the new Cabinet would end by harming Brown's own position.[7] The Chancellor was deaf to this suggestion. The proposition was aired at one stage that Whelan could be made welcome as Alastair Campbell's deputy in the Downing Street Press Office. This, too, was repudiated. In the end, the Prime Minister shrugged his shoulders and gave up. When Campbell bumped into Whelan later, he professed no knowledge of the conversation. 'What was that about?' he muttered.

For the first few months after the General Election, both Downing Street and the Treasury did their best to make sure that the relationship worked out. There was an awkwardness in midsummer when the sheer verve of Gordon Brown led commentators to contrast his hard work and energy with Tony Blair's more

6. A key player in this early attack on Whelan was Tim Allan, technically Campbell's deputy in Tony Blair's Press Office. In practice, however, journalists were unclear whether Allan reported to Campbell or Mandelson.

7. Private information.

relaxed style of doing business. Comparisons were made between Blair, the laid-back company chairman, and Brown, the dynamic chief executive. Brown basked in these comparisons. Blair did not. Campbell sniffed danger. It is hard to say whether these ideas were spread about by the Treasury or not. The important thing is that Downing Street believed they were. After a friendly conversation, both sides agreed to play the notion down and emphasise Blair's forceful, proactive role. This was an example, and not a rare one, of the two sides working helpfully together during the first months of the Blair premiership.

The first crisis to hit the relationship between the Treasury and Downing Street came over European Monetary Union. With the start date for EMU set for 1 January 1999, the single currency was always going to be the biggest issue facing the government in its first year of office. It is a striking commentary on the Blair administration that when the problem hit, precipitated by Robert Peston's story in the *Financial Times*,[8] that the government would shortly be joining EMU, the government was found without a policy. The following three weeks, as Blair and Brown endeavoured to sort themselves out, were a shambles, the dénouement even worse. Whelan and Campbell attempted to bring the messy saga to an end by planting a story clarifying the government position. This was New Labour spin-doctoring at its worst, cynical, clumsy and deceitful. The techniques used repay close examination.

First, a friendly journalist, who it was hoped could be relied on not to make a nuisance of himself, was chosen in the shape of Philip Webster, political editor of *The Times*. Webster was promised an 'interview' with Gordon Brown. Only what he got wasn't a full interview at all; the most important part of it was a prepackaged quote. Even the quote, suggesting caution about immediate entry into EMU, was anodyne and hardly newsworthy. The story that created the front-page headline was in the spin handed down the phone by Campbell and Whelan, which gave *The Times* licence to go much further than Gordon Brown's carefully chosen platitudes. The aim was twofold. First, Campbell and Whelan wanted to present a picture to the outside world of a bold and tough New Labour administration coming down hard against immediate entry to the single currency. Second, they were determined to take the utmost care not to make any irrevocable commitments of any kind. It was a delicate balancing act and certain conditions needed to be met for this plan to work. *The Times* needed to be an accomplice in the deception of the British public. Also, elementary

8. See *Financial Times*, 26 September 1997.

competence in execution was required. Neither was forthcoming. First, the Eurosceptic Murdoch paper took the story one stage further than New Labour spinners had intended, and splashed that Labour was ruling out EMU until after the next election. Then, the plot was exposed when Whelan was overheard briefing journalists on his mobile phone in his favourite Red Lion. The result was mayhem.

Peter Mandelson strongly pressed for Whelan to be sacked in the wake of this episode. But Campbell – who later said that the EMU débâcle was the scene of his own biggest mistake – stood by him: he himself was too strongly implicated in the fiasco to allow Whelan to become a victim. So the effect of it all, so far as Whelan was concerned, was limited. A month later, Robin Mountfield, the Permanent Secretary at the Office of Public Service, produced a report on the government information service whose recommendations were designed, at least in part, to limit Whelan's freedom of action. Whelan never showed much sign of being bothered by Mountfield. He did, however, temporarily move his centre of operations to the Two Chairmen rather than the Red Lion, a not insignificant change in his pattern of life. Otherwise, things carried on as before. But, as it soon emerged, Campbell was merely biding his time.

'Psychological flaws'

The battle royal between No. 10 and No. 11 Downing Street began three months later, in January 1998. This heavyweight confrontation began with the publication of a biography of Gordon Brown by the journalist Paul Routledge, now chief political commentator of the *Daily Mirror*. It reached its peak with the revelation in the *Observer* that a very senior and well-placed figure close to Tony Blair believed that the Chancellor possessed 'psychological flaws'. It was a week which seemed to reveal that Campbell's Downing Street machine would stop at nothing in order to damage Gordon Brown and cut down his freedom of action. It was also a week which raises a question mark about Campbell's claim, made to a Commons Select Committee in June 1998, never to have briefed against Cabinet ministers. For there are grounds for believing that it was Campbell himself who coined that deadly phrase.[9]

Paul Routledge was a close personal friend of Charlie Whelan. The two

9. See Select Committee on Public Administration, Sixth Report: *The Government Information and Communication Service* (29 July 1998), p. 56. Campbell told MPs: 'I have not briefed against any member of the Cabinet.'

would meet once a week, or more, for lunch. Known to their friends in the lobby as 'four bottlers', these lunches would often intrude upon the afternoon, and the two would end up at some stage at the Victoria Club. No one knew exactly what was discussed. It is perfectly likely that most of the conversation was innocent stuff, as the two friends mulled over old times and engaged in innocent gossip. It was widely assumed within Downing Street, however, that Routledge was being made privy to Treasury inside information and bile.[10]

The widespread assumption that Whelan lay behind the Routledge book may have put Downing Street on a short fuse. For, rereading it today, it is hard to see what all the fuss was about. It was mainly a reiteration of material that had already entered the public domain, rather than anything strikingly fresh or new. It contained a handful of 'revelations'. One was the suggestion that Gordon Brown still nurtured a resentment against Tony Blair for the events that took place at the time of the leadership contest. But this, if anything, placed Brown in an unfortunate light, suggesting that he was unable to come to terms with life, preferring to brood helplessly on alleged past injustices. In any case, Brown's belief that he had been hard done by was already familiar territory at Westminster.

The Routledge book was a competent and readable piece of work, which contains much of value, but it was nothing like a full frontal and provocative attack on Tony Blair by the Brown camp. It did not go close to justifying the outburst of rage and spleen that it provoked in Downing Street.[11] It would have been perfectly possible, and more realistic, to have laughed off the book and the intense speculation that accompanied it. It was Downing Street, not the Treasury, that opted not to take this course of action. Things were made much more difficult by the departure of Tony Blair that week on an official trip to Japan. When in a foreign country, it is always difficult to assess the mood back home at Westminster. But there is no need to look for excuses. This was the opportunity Campbell had been waiting for.

The frenzy of apparently Downing Street-inspired briefing against the Chancellor reached a climax in the famous *Observer* front page of 18 January, with its headline: 'Blair reins in flawed Brown'. But the *Observer* story was

10. Of the two men, Routledge was probably – at this time – the heavier drinker. Despite a reputation for serious toping, Whelan normally ensured that he remained sober enough to cope with a conversation with, say, Gordon Brown without risking it going disastrously wrong. Though always reported to drink beer or whisky, he was careful to stick to spritzers in the afternoons.

11. Even bearing in mind the mischievous manner in which Routledge's work was first released to the public, in a front-page *Guardian* splash headlined 'How Blair broke secret pact' (*Guardian*, 9 January 1998). The author was Seamus Milne, the *Guardian* labour editor.

merely the strongest of a series of brutal attacks on the Chancellor of the Exchequer, all of which originated in the Blair camp. The *Express on Sunday* that same weekend produced an exclusive story that Blair had given Brown a full-scale dressing down at the Cabinet meeting that week. Today the author of the report, the paper's feared political editor Simon Walters, remembers that he was given the story by 'a middle-ranking member of the Blair inner circle, who was very keen for me to use it.' John Williams, then political editor of the *Daily Mirror*, received a similar briefing. He wrote a piece for the *Daily Mirror* which, say those who saw it, was strikingly similar in tone to the notorious article by Andrew Rawnsley in the *Observer* a few days later. Williams' article, which is important fresh evidence that a concerted Downing Street operation was being mounted against the Chancellor, never appeared. It was spiked by his editor, Piers Morgan.[12] Nor was this all. Lance Price, BBC political correspondent, reported on the day the Rawnsley story appeared that 'close allies of the Prime Minister are furious at the Chancellor for, as they see it, reopening old wounds.' He went on to say: 'Some within Whitehall have warned that, while Mr Brown is in a very strong position politically, that may not last for ever, and nobody is indispensable.'[13]

Lance Price was regarded within the parliamentary lobby as a friend of Peter Mandelson, who therefore got the blame – whether fairly or unfairly – for the BBC attack.[14] There can be no question, however, that the monster operation to smear Gordon Brown in the second and third weeks of January 1998 was sanctioned by Alastair Campbell. He was Press Secretary, an exceptionally powerful and commanding one at that. No operation as high-level and potentially dangerous as a full-frontal assault on the Chancellor of the Exchequer can possibly have taken place without his direct authority. That the offensive against Gordon Brown was authorised by the Prime Minister is possible, but doubtful. Campbell was confident enough to mount an independent operation of his own.

Campbell was subsequently asked about the 'psychological flaws' comment

12. Williams believed that Morgan had downgraded the *Mirror*'s political coverage to an unacceptable level. Morgan's decision not to run Williams' well-informed piece – which had to do with pressure on space in his paper and not the frenzied manoeuvrings at Westminster – was the final straw which provoked his columnist into resignation. John Williams, a loyal Labour man, was then hired as head of the Foreign Office press department, from where he set about rescuing, not without success, the battered image of Robin Cook.

13. BBC Radio 4 *News*, 18 January 1998, 6 p.m.

14. Price soon afterwards accepted the job as Campbell's deputy in the Downing Street Press Office, another bracing moment for Gordon Brown.

about the Chancellor when he gave evidence to the Select Committee on Public Administration six months later. He was asked the wrong question. The Tory MP David Ruffley, displaying the lack of attention to detail for which the Conservative Party became legendary before the last election, asked Campbell whether he knew who had called the Chancellor 'psychologically flawed'. The phrase used in the *Observer* was that the Chancellor 'has psychological flaws.' Campbell was thus able to profess ignorance instantly, even if he did know the answer: Ruffley had let him off the hook.[15]

The problematic question is this: if Campbell was not the 'someone who has an extremely good claim to know the mind of the Prime Minister' and expressed his or her doubts about the Chancellor of the Exchequer's mental equilibrium, who was? There are very few other candidates. Andrew Rawnsley is a respectable, extremely well-connected journalist, and the *Observer* a respectable newspaper. It is inconceivable that either would be prepared to run a front-page splash on the basis of the remarks unless they had been made by a very close member of the Blair circle. Peter Mandelson is certainly one who falls into that category. But he has denied the allegation vigorously. Tim Allan, Campbell's Downing Street deputy at the time the comments were made, is another. He too denies the charge. There are other senior figures in Downing Street who qualify: but it is very hard to imagine Jonathan Powell, David Miliband or Anji Hunter speaking to a journalist in such a fashion.

On the other hand, it is easy enough to imagine a senior Labour spin-doctor such as Campbell letting his hair down a little in conversation with Rawnsley of the *Observer*. Rawnsley is a columnist and broadcaster, with no recent record for dabbling in news stories. He gives a doubtless illusory air of taking things easy, of being something of a New Labour boulevardier. Someone like Campbell would have felt able to say things to Rawnsley which he could not have done to a news reporter, however friendly. The intention, of course, would have been to prod Rawnsley into expressing his own grave doubts about Gordon Brown's mental stability rather than to embarrassingly place those doubts in the mouth of an unnamed Downing Street aide. It is greatly to Rawnsley's credit that, if such was indeed the intention, he neglected to oblige.

According to Hugh Pym and Nick Kochan, the authors of an illuminating book on Gordon Brown's first year in office, Campbell answered questions from journalists the day after the *Express on Sunday* and *Observer* stories appeared. According to them, Campbell threw cold water on the *Express* story.

15. Select Committee on Public Administration, Sixth Report, p. 57.

'"No such thing was said", he told journalists, "the report was nonsense." His reaction to the *Observer* story was noticeably more muted and there was no attempt to disown it.'[16]

There have since been two public claims that Campbell was the source of the story. The following Sunday, Joe Murphy, political editor of the *Mail on Sunday*, stated categorically that Campbell was the mystery man.[17] A few months later, Paul Routledge, who had sparked off all the trouble, brought out a revised edition of his Gordon Brown biography in paperback. He lightly fingered Campbell.[18]

Nor was that all. The Prime Minister was angry and embarrassed enough by the messy affair to take Campbell aside and tell him off. According to one well-placed Whitehall source, the rebuke was peremptory – mainly handed out so that Blair could later tell Gordon Brown that he had indeed disciplined Campbell rather than being motivated by genuine fury.[19] Nevertheless, the episode showed that Blair held Campbell responsible for the vicious and personal attack on the Chancellor, whether or not he felt that he had personally carried it out. There is no suggestion that Campbell tried to wriggle out of the blame.

No one can know for sure whether Alastair Campbell was the source of the 'psychological flaws' remark unless Andrew Rawnsley or whoever was the other party to the conversation chooses to come clean about it. Two things can be said with certainty about this unsettling episode, however. The first is that the remark was just one of a battery of charges laid against the Chancellor in a campaign that can have been authorised only by the Prime Minister's Press Secretary. The second is that, even if Campbell did not say it, almost everybody connected with the episode believes that he did. Above all, Gordon Brown's friends feel certain that he did so. Campbell's relations with the Chancellor have never been warm. Since January 1998, they have been close to freezing. Subsequent events have done nothing to improve relations. Campbell was a key adviser to Blair on the 1998 Cabinet reshuffle which moved Brown supporters from key positions. One senior Labour MP who is very close to Brown says that 'Gordon hates him.' That may be going too far. But Gordon Brown is a man who remembers insults, and as insults in the political arena go, that was a sharp one.

16. Hugh Pym and Nick Kochan, *Gordon Brown: The First Year in Power* (1998), p. 180.

17. *Mail on Sunday*, 25 January 1998.

18. Paul Routledge, *Gordon Brown: The Biography* (revised edition, 1998), p. 347. Routledge is more measured than the *Mail on Sunday* and makes no definitive statement, merely stating that 'most political correspondents' believed that Campbell was the source.

19. Private information.

Chapter Eleven

MANAGING THE MEDIA

Explain to me just why I should waste my time with a load of wankers like you
when you're not going to write anything I tell you anyway.
  Alastair Campbell to the Sunday lobby, May 1997

There were journalists who adapted themselves to the new circumstances that
prevailed after 1 May 1997 – and there were those who did not. Michael
Brunson, political editor of ITN, had always made it his business to get on with
the old John Major regime: colleagues marvelled at the ease with which he did
so. Now he made it his business to get on with Tony Blair. With dazzling sleight
of hand Brunson converted himself, at any rate in the minds of his colleagues,
from a Tory loyalist to a New Labour loyalist. Much the same could be said of
the BBC political editor Robin Oakley.

There were others who felt a warm and enjoyable sense of coming in from
the cold. The political editor of the *Independent*, Tony Bevins, had viewed the
Thatcher and Major governments with cold antipathy. Tory grandees like Alan
Clark surmised that he was taking revenge for slights alleged to have been
handed out to his father, Reginald Bevins, who served with distinction in the
governments of Eden and Macmillan. Though a minister of high competence,
his middle-class origins meant that he was never fully accepted by the Tory
establishment of the day.[1]

These speculations were wrong, however: there was no vendetta. The Clark
analysis failed to take into account the high principle of this self-appointed
Savonarola to the political establishment of the 1990s. Tony Bevins hounded
the Tory Party with unspeakable ferocity, and he played a modest part and took
a deep personal pleasure in the downfall of John Major's government.
Thereafter, this angular, uncomfortable but curiously warm-hearted man

---

1. Reginald Bevins served as Postmaster-General, 1959–64. He was MP for Toxteth from 1950 to
1964. Bevins once attended a high-powered Chequers meeting and observed that, of the company
present, only he and Ernest Marples did not possess landed estates (see A. J. Davies' history of the
Conservative Party *We, the Nation*, 1996).

collapsed with a sigh into the embrace of New Labour.[2] He and Philip Webster of *The Times* became the two most promising cheerleaders for New Labour among the ranks of political editors.

Peace with Murdoch

Others travelled the same sort of journey, only in the opposite direction. For more than a decade George Jones, the distinguished political editor of the *Daily Telegraph*, had been the favoured recipient of whispered confidences from Cabinet ministers. These dried up on 2 May 1997. Any attempt Jones may have made on his own behalf to ingratiate himself with the new administration was rendered hopeless by the adamantine stand of his editor Charles Moore. Moore could see no good in Blair: correspondingly, Campbell could see no good in Jones. So poor Jones found himself in the wilderness, starved of the oxygen of information which alone can sustain the dedicated political reporter. This state of deprivation turned to torment as he was compelled to watch Philip Webster, his *Times* rival and his closest competitor, drink deeply from the very same sources that had been taken away from him.

Webster was prodigious. An ace reporter with the finest shorthand note in the lobby, his skill and craftsmanship had long been held in high respect by colleagues. *The Times* has always been a paper enjoying a promiscuous relationship to power: its habit of taking marching orders from Downing Street dates back to the 1930s and beyond. Now Webster turned its political news pages into Fleet Street's closest equivalent to a noticeboard for the government. His efforts were richly appreciated. Stories – such as the change of policy on EMU – started to fall into his lap.

Webster is an extremely talented amateur sportsman, but his knowledge of modern poetry is limited. Nevertheless, he scooped the world with the identity of the new Poet Laureate, infuriating the Palace, which felt that the decision to leak the news was a discourtesy.[3]

On trips abroad Campbell started to treat Webster as one of the official party rather than as a travelling hack. Before briefing reporters, he would take

2. Although his old indignation did not entirely die away. Bevins roused himself to lead a brilliant and successful campaign against Paymaster-General Geoffrey Robinson in the pages of the *Express*. Some observers felt, however, that this attack on a notable Brownite ally might have served Campbell's purposes well.

3. See *Daily Telegraph*, 20 May 1999. Campbell denies being the source of the leak.

Webster to one side and try out the official line, rather like a medieval king employing a food-taster at a banquet. If Webster spat it out, Campbell would try a different spin. There have been occasions when Campbell, unable to be physically present to brief the lobby, has to all intents and purposes employed Webster to do the job on his behalf. Philip Webster is the most scrupulous and honourable of reporters, and would never abuse this privileged position. Nevertheless, it caused mumblings of resentment among the travelling pack.

At Westminster the *Times* political team was cleansed of Tories.[4] The process was not replicated, however, at the paper's Wapping headquarters. There Tory thinkers, mainly of the Eurosceptic persuasion, thrived: it was New Labour that struggled to make itself heard. Readers of the top people's paper were presented with a schizophrenic menu. The political news pages endeavoured to place the best possible construction on government policy, while on the comment pages Gove, Kaletsky, Rees-Mogg, Parris and others – a brilliant constellation – were all capable of placing the worst. This disjunction reflected the ambiguity of the Murdoch press. On the one hand, it was accepted that Tony Blair was as fine a Prime Minister as Thatcher. On the other, it was accepted that the Prime Minister's support for Europe – held by *The Times* to be the decisive issue of our day, the vital matter at stake in the 1997 election – was an abomination.

This dilemma also faced *The Times*'s stablemate, the *Sun*. Its readers were starkly presented with two contradictory propositions. On the one hand they were informed that federal Europe presented an apocalyptic menace which had to be fought with ceaseless vigilance. On the other they were reminded daily that Tony Blair, the man set on leading Britain towards that feared destination, was not merely a genius of outstanding gifts but also a secular saint. *Sun* readers were asked to stomach one further fact: the one British politician alert enough to share the paper's alarm about the European menace, William Hague, was a contemptible buffoon. At the Conservative Party Conference of 1998 they portrayed him on their front page as a dead parrot. David Yelland, the paper's new editor, had to be dissuaded by senior staff from hiring an actor to put on a parrot outfit, dash up to the stage as William Hague made his annual conference speech, and then theatrically expire.

4. This process was in part tempered by the appointment of Tom Baldwin, formerly political editor of the *Sunday Telegraph*, as Webster's deputy. Such political sympathies as Baldwin possessed lay in a New Labour direction. These were, however, overshadowed by a predilection for the creation of mayhem. To this extent, he made an admirable foil to Webster.

Campbell was not bothered about the complexities of the *Sun* editorial line. He was simply happy to have the paper in his pocket. Having got it there he would do whatever was necessary to keep it there. Favours flooded in. *Sun* journalists continued to get special treatment. The *Sun* itself suddenly became the favoured vehicle of communication with the British people, not merely for Tony Blair but for foreign leaders as well. This new craze started with the Japanese premier Ryutaro Hashimoko's letter to *Sun* readers ahead of the Emperor's trip to Britain on 14 January 1998. Hashimoko's article was drafted, at least in part, by Alastair Campbell during Tony Blair's trip to Japan. The *Sun* claimed, in its front page splash, that the premier was apologising for the war, a claim that was later challenged by the Japanese. This operation was considered to have gone off so well that it was followed, in October that year, by an identical stunt ahead of the visit by the Argentine president Carlos Menem to the United Kingdom. This was also arranged and drafted by Campbell: the Argentinian, too, vainly protested that he had never apologised either.

The *Mirror*, the *Sun*'s mass-market rival, stayed loyal to Labour for eighteen years of opposition only to see the benefits of victory fall into the lap of its deadly rival – which had spent those eighteen years smashing Labour to pulp. Some *Mirror* journalists were convinced that Campbell took a special pleasure in leaving them out in the cold because of the particular circumstances of his own departure from the paper. But this was no long-delayed revenge: it was merely an icy cold appreciation of the realities of the situation. Campbell grasped that he could take the *Mirror* for granted because, like Old Labour, it had nowhere else to go.

Ironically enough, it took the arrival of Kelvin MacKenzie, the brilliant populist editor of the *Sun* during many of those years of Tory dominance, to jerk the paper out of its lethargy. That and the episode of the Clinton letter, which demonstrated the complete cynicism with which Campbell and the Downing Street machine was prepared to treat the *Mirror*.

It was the inspired idea of the *Mirror*'s political editor, Kevin Maguire, that President Clinton should make a personal intervention in the Irish peace process. Maguire spotted that Clinton's presence in Britain for the G-8 economic summit in May of 1998, just days before the Irish people voted on the Good Friday agreement, could be put to good use. He put up the proposition to Campbell that the President should use the pages of the *Mirror* to write an open letter to the Irish calling on them to 'say Yes to Peace.' Campbell, after consulting with the US embassy, readily agreed. But he had one stipulation:

Maguire must write the piece himself and then submit it for approval. Maguire dutifully rattled off the words he considered President Clinton might have wished to write, and submitted them for inspection.

He swiftly received a reply from Downing Street. His piece was sound, but redrafting was required. The *Mirror* was asked to hold its fire for 24 hours. Maguire was happy to agree, but not so happy to see the first editions of the following day's *Sun*. For there, splashed all across the front page, was Clinton's dramatic appeal for peace, much of it Maguire's own handiwork.[5] Campbell would appear to have handed over the *Mirror*'s idea, written up by the *Mirror*'s political editor, to the paper's deadliest rival. It was by any standards – even those of Westminster and Fleet Street – an incredible act of betrayal.

Maguire was incandescent. He rang Campbell, who tried to wriggle his way out. He explained that the British embassy, which had been approached separately by the *Sun*, was responsible. It was all an innocent mistake. Maguire's call was followed up by his editor. 'Piers [Morgan] gave Campbell both barrels,' records a *Mirror* executive. 'It lasted ten minutes. It ended with Campbell grovelling, saying: 'Look Piers, I did this for peace.'

'Sure, peace with Murdoch.'

After this brazen moment the *Mirror* had no choice but to change tack. The paper gave up taking the Downing Street line. It hired Paul Routledge, fresh from wreaking destruction with his biography of the Chancellor, and turned itself into the voice of the Brownite faction and the Old Labour left. But Campbell didn't care. He had the *Sun*. And *Mirror* readers weren't going to vote Tory at the General Election.

Campbell should have been content with the press New Labour enjoyed for its first two years in government – but he was not. The mass-market tabloids were Labour, the *Mirror* albeit reluctantly. In the middle market the *Express* had converted itself from Tory to Labour. The *Mail*, however, the paper of middle England, refused to come across: this was a cause of great distress to New Labour. Intimates revealed that Tony Blair was 'heartbroken' about the *Mail*. The failure to win the paper was not from any lack of effort. Before the General Election enormous strides had been made. David English, the

5. *Sun*, Wednesday 20 May 1998. It is believed at the *Mirror* that Rupert Murdoch was in London at the time, and that his presence played a part in the decision to give the story to the *Sun*. There was a stroke of poetic justice to this tale. That night nurses Lucille McLaughlan and Deborah Parry were freed from jail in Saudi Arabia. By the final editions, only the *Sun* was not leading on this dramatic story. See Nick Cohen, *Cruel Britannia* (1999), pp. 147–8.

newspaper genius who chaired the group, had come close to falling – platoni-
cally – in love with the young leader of the Labour opposition.

The handling of English is another example of the ineptitude of the last Tory
government. John Wakeham, the Conservative leader of the Lords, twice urged
on John Major the wisdom of converting English's knighthood into a peerage.
On each occasion Major rejected the proposal on the grounds that he was not
prepared to reward a man whose newspapers had attacked his government so
brutally. It fell to Tony Blair to effect the elevation. He felt no Majorish qualms.
The fact that English's newspapers had been the bitterest enemy of the Labour
Party for three decades, and played a large part in keeping it out of power for
two of them, did not put him off in the least. Sir David English died just a few
days before his elevation was due to be publicly announced.

Blair's charm and skill worked just as well on Viscount Rothermere, the
great newspaper baron who with English had saved Associated Newspapers
from terminal decline in the 1960s. They are currently being applied, with
equal dexterity and – so Downing Street believes – success to the young
Jonathan Harmsworth who has been chairman of the *Daily Mail* and General
Trust since the death of his father in 1998. The tragedy, as far as New Labour is
concerned, is that Paul Dacre, now editor-in-chief at the *Mail*, is unimpressed.

Bashing up the lobby

Such was the British tabloid mood as the nation prepared to embrace the
Millennium. By the standards of previous political epochs, even including the
high noon of Thatcherism fifteen years earlier, New Labour received an extraordinarily good press. In many ways it deserved to. The media had to acknowledge that Tony Blair had won a ringing endorsement in the 1997 General
Election. His achievements were generously celebrated, nobody apart from a
handful of malcontents dwelt too long on his failures. The contrast with the
coverage of John Major's doomed administration was striking. The nation
urged on the New Labour government to succeed, just as it had willed the
Tories to fail, and the media reflected that novel mood of benevolence.

The peculiar thing is that this was not the mood in Downing Street. At the
court of Tony Blair there was a sense of siege. Well-meaning critics were seen
as hostile, and balanced assessment was understood as an attempt to damage
the reputation of the Prime Minister. It is the central paradox of New Labour
that never has there been a political movement that stretched out so far,
enjoyed such national popularity, and broke down so many traditional political

boundaries. And yet rarely has any government felt itself to be so beleaguered as New Labour's.[6] This wholly irrational sense of isolation found its outward manifestation in the person of Alastair Campbell and in his daily encounters with parliamentary journalists.

Upon entering Downing Street Alastair Campbell dropped any remaining pretence that he had any fondness for his old craft. He had made little enough attempt to ingratiate himself with the press even during the pre-election period. Now he made none. His first briefing to the lobby, given the day after the election, set the tone. It was only with a show of great reluctance, which started with a failure to return pager messages and was followed by a claim that he had better things to do, that the No. 10 Press Secretary agreed to meet the press at all. When a time was finally agreed, Campbell turned up late. He strode to the front of the briefing room, followed by a gaggle of his Downing Street civil servants. 'OK, you bastards,' Campbell kicked off genially. 'Explain to me just why I should waste my time with a load of wankers like you when you're not going to write anything I tell you anyway.'[7]

The officials seated behind him looked on stupefied. They, unlike the lobby men at the receiving end of the assault, had never heard anything like it before. This had not been the tone adopted by Sir Christopher Meyer, Campbell's distinguished predecessor. Campbell was setting a style which he clearly intended to maintain for the remainder of his term of office. Everyone who knows him at all, either as a reporter or a colleague within Downing Street, agrees that he dislikes – some people say hates – journalists. In particular he dislikes the parliamentary lobby. He regards it as corrupt, deceitful, untrustworthy, morally worthless and depraved. He expects no good ever to come of it. His attitude, interestingly enough, is similar to the one invariably taken by former journalists when they became Press Secretary at No. 10. Sir Bernard Ingham and Joe Haines both scorned journalists, though neither with anything quite like the passionate disdain which Campbell sometimes communicates. Trained civil servants, by contrast, feel none of this hostility. Gus O'Donnell, John Major's first Press Secretary,

---

6. Anji Hunter, a senior member of the Prime Minister's staff, remarked at a reception in spring 1999: 'They all hate us out there, don't they?' At the time the government's popularity stood at over 50 per cent in the polls, close to a record for any government in peacetime.

7. I am grateful to Sunday paper colleagues for this account. It should be remembered that Campbell was addressing the Sunday lobby. This group of accredited correspondents from Sunday papers is a smaller and less influential group than the daily lobby, which meets Campbell or one of his deputies twice a day. Campbell's contempt for the Sunday lobby, of which he was once a prominent member, is even greater than his contempt for the daily lobby.

liked and respected the lobby and the lobby in return liked and respected him. This did not prevent them, however, turning over his boss whenever they felt like it, which was very often indeed and in an especially nasty way.

So there was some good sense in the Campbell approach. He was only being realistic. Since lobby journalists were beyond salvation, it was preposterous to treat them like civilised and decent human beings. If you did, they would only take advantage. Campbell is a walking demonstration of Joe Haines' old adage that the Press Secretary is there for the sole purpose of defending the Prime Minister, never to help the press. If it is necessary to obstruct, bully or even on occasion mislead reporters in the course of his duties he will do so, for his over-riding loyalty lies with Tony Blair. Ever since Campbell has been in Downing Street, he has stopped at nothing to protect the Prime Minister. His defenders argue that his behaviour simply reflects the moral code of the world at Westminster in which he lives and breathes.

Campbell possesses the skills of a playground bully – mimicry and an uncanny insight into his victim's weaknesses – and he puts them to good use. This is one of the things that make lobby meetings, on the increasingly rare occasions that Campbell takes them, such arresting events, the best spectator sport in town. For a long time he targeted Robert Peston, political editor of the *Financial Times*. Peston is an able journalist, with an ability to pick up stories which distress the government. In the lobby, Campbell would mercilessly mock and mimic Peston's mannerisms. Peston had the habit of stroking the hair at the back of his head, which could be taken as a sign of vanity. Campbell got that perfectly. His imitation never failed to raise a laugh.

He also singled out Peston's junior, a bright young reporter called Liam Halligan, for special abuse. Campbell was warmly welcoming when Halligan, now economics correspondent for *Channel Four News*, turned up in the lobby. But he turned nasty after Halligan produced a few awkward stories. He called him 'gel-boy' or the 'Derek Draper of the lobby', a reference to Peter Mandelson's assistant who had gained a reputation for playing fast and loose. When Halligan spoke, Campbell would welcome 'another question from the Peston school of smartarse journalism'. He rubbished his stories.

Halligan hit back, always the best way with Campbell. 'He just thought I was going to be scared of him. I wasn't. I told him: at least I didn't run away from Oxbridge; at least I'm my own person; at least I don't follow other people around; at least I'm not a coat-tails merchant.'[8]

8. Conversation with the author.

Campbell enjoyed bullying women journalists. On a trip to the Middle East in the early summer of 1998, he picked out Rachel Silvester, a young reporter on the *Telegraph*. He mocked her interventions and referred to her throughout the trip as 'Rachel Silvester of the venal *Daily Telegraph*'. At the end of the trip, somewhat to Silvester's mortification, Charles Moore sent a sharply worded complaint to Campbell. But that did not stop him handing out the same sort of treatment to a woman reporter from the *Scotsman*, Joy Copley, when she accompanied Tony Blair and Campbell on their trip to South Africa in January 1999. Copley's crime was to challenge Campbell too openly in a lobby briefing. Their clash came shortly before Blair made his keynote speech of the trip. The day before Campbell had briefed that Tony Blair would signal unspecified 'harsh and authoritarian' measures for the welfare state. This line duly appeared in morning papers. When the speech was handed out all mention of these harsh measures had disappeared. Copley accused Campbell of peddling a false line. Campbell's response was typically robust. 'The lobby all write garbage anyway.' Copley was not to be deterred. 'You fed us that garbage,' she said. 'You made us write a story that wasn't true.' Campbell's response was contemptuous. 'I wouldn't wet your knickers about it', he said. To his credit, he later apologised to Copley for the remark.

There are very few journalists in the lobby whom Campbell has not attempted to abuse or humiliate at some stage. His only rule is that he leaves the *Sun* well alone. Once he forgot to obey this precept and pinpointed George Pascoe-Watson, the deputy political editor of the *Sun*, who had written an unhelpful story on Labour's attitude towards the single currency. Campbell beat him up verbally for a good five minutes. It was a splendid sight, Campbell in full flow, and a group gathered round to watch Campbell front up Pascoe-Watson and point his finger at his chest. The following day Campbell took Pascoe-Watson gently aside and thrust an envelope into his hand. It contained a fulsome apology. Campbell apologies are rare things: almost never handed out after a routine piece of thuggery such as the one he had dished out to Pascoe-Watson, who in any case was perfectly capable of looking after himself. That Pascoe-Watson got his letter was less evidence of contrition on Campbell's part than testimony to the respect owing to his newspaper, the *Sun*. Pascoe-Watson is said to keep Campbell's note in a drawer by his bed, a unique and valued item.

Insults are deliberately targeted at what Campbell sees as the weak spots of his victim. When the Scottish journalist Ian Hernon – a familiar figure round the bars of Westminster – left a lobby briefing early, Campbell sneered as he left: 'Need a drink, do we?' Hernon was a constant thorn in Campbell's flesh, one of the most mischievous of a school of Glasgow correspondents who caused Downing Street intense grief in the months leading up to the elections for the Scottish Assembly in the summer of 1999. At one stage Campbell fired a letter off to John Scott, the editor of Hernon's paper the Glasgow *Evening Times*, which accused Hernon of inventing a story. Pending an explanation, said Campbell, 'further action will be taken.' This was taken as a threat to get Hernon's lobby status removed, thus destroying his livelihood. Like many of Campbell's threats, it was never followed up. Even friendship is no bar to a Campbell assault. During the 24-hour period on 22 December 1998 when Downing Street was officially backing Peter Mandelson to survive as Trade Secretary after the revelation of the Robinson loan, *Sky News* political editor Adam Boulton asked Campbell for an interview with the Prime Minister so that he could publicly throw his weight behind the beleaguered minister. 'Oh fuck off,' came the reply from Campbell. Boulton immediately went on air and conveyed to Sky viewers the flavour of this exchange. Campbell was infuriated, called Boulton on his mobile phone, and informed him that personal relations between Sky and Downing Street had been severed. The following day, when Mandelson did resign, Sky TV was frozen out of interviews with the fallen minister.

New Labour has never hesitated to destabilise journalists by going behind their backs to their bosses.[9] Numerous reporters have had the experience of being run down behind their backs to their editors or proprietors by New Labour spin-doctors. This weapon could be used even against close allies who strayed from the party or government line. Very shortly before the 1997 election, Andrew Marr, then editor of the *Independent*, wrote a critical piece about Labour's European policy. The Marr attack was sparked by some palpably dishonest and disingenuous remarks by Tony Blair in the *Sun* in which he invoked the shade of St George against the European dragon.[10] It was all too much for the fastidious, pro-European Marr, who launched into a rare attack on the Labour leader. Marr said that Blair had backed himself into a corner and

9. *Observer* columnist Nick Cohen, *Mail* deputy political editor Paul Eastham, and *Independent* political correspondent Colin Brown are among those who have suffered in this way. Normally, such attacks merely serve to strengthen the position of the intended victim. Trevor Kavanagh of the *Sun* and his deputy George Pascoe-Watson were once at the receiving end of an incompetent Brownite attempt to dislodge them. Kavanagh, the acknowledged doyen of the parliamentary lobby, is safe as houses anyway. Rupert Murdoch gave David Yelland three conditions when he appointed him editor of the *Sun*. One of them was on no account to move or interfere with Kavanagh.

10. *Sun*, 22 April, headlined 'We'll see off Euro-dragons'. This famous conversion to Euroscepticism was not, as has repeatedly been claimed since (for instance Macintyre, p. 329), a first person piece by the Labour leader. It was actually an article by George Pascoe-Watson, the *Sun*'s deputy political editor. It arose by accident.

that in future he would either be 'betraying the whole emotional tone of his *Sun* piece or betraying our nation's better future.'

It was a sensitive piece of journalism and, looking back on the turn events have taken since, quite certainly correct. It is highly unlikely that, appearing where it did, it will have cost New Labour a single vote. Marr's article, in the rarefied air of the *Independent* newspaper, had no bearing on the General Election campaign. The criticism was made, in dulcet tones, by a man who was one of the closest and most valued allies of the future New Labour government. Campbell's response to this thoughtful piece of writing was quite out of proportion, so strange that it suggests that his judgement was impaired by the strain of the campaign. He rang up David Montgomery, chief executive of Mirror Group Newspapers, which owned the *Independent*, and suggested that Marr should be sacked.[11] Even taking into account the emotions generated in the cauldron of an election, Campbell's actions were those of a man who was incapable of distinguishing true friend from foe, or fair criticism from hostile attack. It was an alarming portent for the future, and a trait that he was to take with him into Downing Street.

Six of the best for Alan Rusbridger

About a year before the election Alan Rusbridger, editor of the *Guardian*, was invited to a private meeting with Tony Blair in the Leader of the Opposition's office in the House of Commons. It was suggested that he should bring with him Martin Kettle, the *Guardian*'s chief leader-writer, and his political editor, Michael White. The *Guardian* editor happily accepted. He hardly knew Tony Blair, having met him only once before, at a dinner party given by mutual friends. The *Guardian* team arrived at the Commons under the impression that they had been invited for a friendly chat with the Prime Minister.

They realised they had been mistaken. Besides Blair the Labour team

During the election campaign Blair, inspired by Campbell, made a practice of ringing up political correspondents during dull moments for a chat. Others to be favoured with a sudden, unannounced call included Patrick Hennessy of the *Evening Standard*, Roland Watson of the *Express* and Simon Walters of the *Express on Sunday*. Pascoe-Watson was quick-witted and adroit enough to take the opportunity to steer the future Prime Minister towards the xenophobic remarks to which Andrew Marr took such exception.

11. Campbell's attempt to get rid of Marr was first described by the *Observer*'s Nick Cohen. An account appears in *Cruel Britannia*, pp. 153–4. Some mystery surrounds this episode. Today Montgomery says he has no memory of Campbell demanding that Marr should be fired. But Marr remembers Montgomery telling him so at the time.

comprised Alastair Campbell and David Hill, Director of Communications. This was no social event. The Leader of the Opposition wanted to read the riot act. After perfunctory greetings he brought out a sheaf of cuttings, and went through them all. At one stage the future Prime Minister demanded to know why the word 'Blair' appeared in a headline. 'I imagine because it was shorter and fitted better than Labour,' came Rusbridger's reply.

'It took me back to public school,' recalled Rusbridger later.[12] 'This sense of being in the senior prefect's study. Campbell said nothing, just looked on. Blair gave this imperious speech about how the *Guardian* was behaving. It was as if he was saying: "It's your attitude I object to."'

The meeting ended frostily. A few days later a version of the events was leaked from the Blair camp to the gossip column of the *Evening Standard*. This conveyed the information that a furious Campbell regarded Rusbridger as a 'public school twat'.[13] Rusbridger wrote a letter demanding an explanation. Peter Mandelson then arrived in the role of mediator, and arranged a private dinner between Rusbridger and Blair at the Labour leader's Islington home. Here warm personal relations were restored, though on a professional level the problems persisted.

It is difficult to know what Campbell and Blair thought they could achieve. The technique used could hardly have been more counter-productive. Campbell and Blair might have had some success in changing *Guardian* policy had they confronted Rusbridger on his own. Doing so in front of two senior colleagues made it impossible for him to climb down, even if he had wanted to, without losing face.

In the months that followed, every technique was used by Campbell in attempts to bring the *Guardian* round. 'He used to ring up to cajole, plead, shout and horse-trade,' says Rusbridger. 'Stories would be offered on condition that they went on the front page. I would be told that if I didn't agree they would go to the *Independent*. They would withdraw favours, grant favours, exclude us from stories going elsewhere.' Gradually, Campbell woke up to the fact the *Guardian* simply wasn't interested in the Downing Street approach to news management. 'Now we have almost no contact,' says Rusbridger.

Even after abandoning the full frontal approach, Campbell and Blair continued to find other ways of getting at the *Guardian*. The newspaper became a ritual object of attack at meetings of the Parliamentary Labour Party, the

12. Interview with the author, May 1999.
13. Rusbridger was educated at Cranleigh.

National Executive Committee and even, at times, the Cabinet. 'I don't read the *Guardian*. I prefer to read a Labour paper,' became a standard Blair remark. At one point he is supposed to have urged Labour MPs to read the *Sun* instead. The real preference, however, was for *The Times*. Downing Street found the political reporting in the Murdoch broadsheet gratifyingly reliable. The *Guardian* lobby team, by contrast, produced shudders of distaste.

Part of Campbell's hostility to the *Guardian* was simply the tabloid man's contempt for the complexities and irreverence of good broadsheet journalism. The urbane wit and irony of Michael White was never going to fit Campbell's taste – and it is not impossible that a lingering enmity survived from their fist-fight a decade earlier. White's deputy Ewen MacAskill was also regarded with dark suspicion by Downing Street. He was seen as too Scottish, too Old Labour and, worst of all, a Brownite.

The real object of Campbell resentment was the cheerful and bucolic figure of David Hencke, the *Guardian* Whitehall correspondent. To look at, Hencke is nothing much. A beard, a mop of hair, a badly cut suit. He does not have an office and operates out of a tiny desk in a sweaty and overcrowded room just off the Commons Press Gallery. Those who know him best record that he lives in constant fear (completely unjustified) of being given the sack. And yet there is a strong case for the claim that this dilapidated figure is the greatest jour-nalist of his generation. In the Media Class age where shallow celebrity colum-nists stand at the peak of their profession, Hencke is a throwback. In defiance of fashion he has industriously carried on doing what real reporters ought to do – ferret out wrongdoing and corruption. Singlehandedly – though with the loyal and courageous support of his newspaper – his stories have been respon-sible for the downfall of two Cabinet ministers, one for each political party, Jonathan Aitken and Peter Mandelson. Throughout the Tory years, Hencke was responsible for a series of brilliant scoops which were deftly exploited by Labour when the Tories were in government – Hencke can claim the credit for the downfall of Neil and Christine Hamilton. But Campbell smelt danger. He sensed that the same man who had been so invaluable to Labour in opposition could wreak havoc to Labour in government. The existence of Hencke, and his ability to prise out damaging stories, has been one of the major bones of contention between Rusbridger and Alastair Campbell. A correspondence exists on the subject. Recently Campbell bumped into Hencke in the lobby corridor of the Commons and barked at him: 'You're just completely insane' before marching on.

Campbell believes that the best way to get back at the *Guardian* is by hitting the paper commercially. Returning to London from Blackpool after the Labour Party Conference of 1998, Ewen MacAskill found himself sharing a railway carriage with the Downing Street Press Secretary, who soon went on the offensive. He listed several recent atrocities carried out by the *Guardian* – an opinion piece by Jonathan Freedland, one of the paper's star columnists, on Labour's maladroit handling of the annual elections to the National Executive Committee appeared especially to have infuriated him – and then made an extraordinary threat. 'If you carry on in this vein,' Campbell calmly told him, 'We are going to tell our people not to buy you.' Campbell indicated to MacAskill – who subsequently sent a memo to his editor about this bizarre train conversation – that 10–20,000 readers could be knocked off the circulation of the *Guardian* if the Prime Minister sent out an edict to Labour Party members to boycott the paper.

This troublesome relationship shows Campbell at his worst. His numerous letters to the newspaper, both the ones that appear on the correspondence page and those written for the private perusal of the editor and others, display a ponderous solemnity. They have very much the same tone as the letters Harold Pinter writes to the press when confronted with the latest outrage of American capitalism – humourless, self-righteous, incapable of understanding the other side's point of view.

The feud with the *Guardian* shines a most illuminating light on Alastair Campbell's Downing Street machine. Part of it is the sheer unreality of it all – the weird belief that Labour Party members could be ordered to give up reading their daily paper, the deluded notion that the *Sun* and even the *Mail* could be true, rather than merely fair weather, friends of the Labour Party. Most worrying of all is Campbell's belief that the *Guardian* is hostile to New Labour. It is not. To think that it is is to misunderstand the paper's role. There are two ways that a friendly newspaper can behave when its side is in power. It can either act as house journal, repeating the government line in a slavish way. Or it can play the role of candid friend. The *Guardian*'s entire history and character compels it to choose the latter, more complicated route. All previous leaders of the Labour Party have complained about the *Guardian*. Michael Foot, in the early 1980s, used to plead with its political editor Ian Aitken not to disclose the proceedings of the PLP. There are plenty of columnists who are thought to be Blairite – Hugo Young, Polly Toynbee, Jonathan Freedland, Martin Kettle. Roy Greenslade, the paper's media writer, is the most devout follower of the Downing Street line in all Fleet Street, reflecting the alarms and preoccupations of Campbell himself with an uncanny accuracy. Few would dispute that the

Guardian has been, on the whole, supportive of the New Labour government rather than not. None of this counts with Campbell. His view is that you are either with him or you are against him. And because the *Guardian* produces the occasional story that highlights the rifts in Labour ranks or an editorial that pours scorn on government incompetence, he thinks it is against. That attitude is an inheritance from the days when he shared Neil Kinnock's bunker. It is strikingly similar to Margaret Thatcher's approach to the media during the 1980s.

Thatcher had a series of big and bloody battles to fight. She had powerful enemies who needed to be destroyed. She needed a praetorian guard to stand by her in a hostile world. But Blair, in many ways, is the opposite of Thatcher. Where she brought division, he is a healer. Where she polarised, he unifies. As a political leader it is his mission to reach out and break down the boundaries that divide British society rather than create new ones. And yet the Downing Street Press Office retains and even fosters the narrow, paranoid, sterile mentality of the 1980s. It could hardly be less appropriate for the new world ushered in by Tony Blair's great election victory of May 1997.

New Labour's culture of concealment

One important expression of the bunker mentality that Campbell brought with him to Downing Street was his attitude to revealing the truth. It was the view of Campbell's immediate three predecessors as Press Secretary that, all things being equal, Downing Street should disclose as much as it could. Campbell took a different approach. He believed that he should release as little as he could get away with, and ideally a little less than that.

This sparing approach to the release of information was evident long before he entered Downing Street, indeed before he formally took up the reins as Tony Blair's press spokesman. The first reporter who formed the impression that Campbell's account of events could be partial and not wholly reliable was Nicholas Jones, the BBC political correspondent. After Tony Blair dropped his Clause 4 bombshell at the Labour Conference of 1994, Jones suggested on air that 'John Prescott was only on board a week ago and did advise against it.'

This was, for New Labour, a damaging suggestion. The Clause 4 announcement could not have been more sensitive or more potentially explosive. Any notion that the Deputy Leader of the Labour Party had reservations about dropping it was inflammatory. After the broadcast, according to Jones's account, Campbell asked to see him. He told Jones that Prescott had been aware of the move for several weeks and had been 'fully on board every step of the way.'[14] Campbell used the episode to publicly humiliate the BBC man and demonstrate the muscle and firepower of his own press machine.

Jones's original broadcast may very possibly have been wanting in some respects. But Campbell's assertion that Prescott was 'on board all the way' is simply wrong. Prescott's biographer, Colin Brown, provides a detailed account of his conversion to the proposal that Clause 4 should be abolished. He makes plain that it was a laborious process in which Campbell himself played a prominent role. Brown records that the 'deputy leader maintained his opposition right up to seeing the first drafts of Blair's speech for the conference. Then, like a reluctant craftsman, drawn into a project to make it work, Prescott relented.'[15]

Another episode before the last election showed how obstructive Campbell and New Labour were capable of being. In early 1996 the *Sunday Express* ran a story that a close and intimate political friendship had sprung up between Tony Blair and Roy Jenkins. With Blair facing dissent on the left of the party, the report highlighted the sensitive issue of New Labour collaboration with the old Social Democrats who had broken away from Michael Foot's Labour Party in the early 1980s. When the *Express* rang Campbell for confirmation the story was comprehensively rubbished. The denial was specific. It was claimed that the two men had met only once since Tony Blair had become Labour leader, at a dinner with a number of others present. The *Express*, confident of its sources, went ahead and ran its account anyway. The *Sunday Times* tried to follow up the *Express*. Michael Prescott, the paper's political correspondent, rang Peter Mandelson for confirmation, but he too denied it. A month later a television programme made by Michael Cockerell showed that the *Express* story was even truer than its reporters had realised. It proved that Jenkins and Blair had become personally and politically close, and showed that Blair had even been a welcome visitor at Jenkins' country home.

When this programme appeared the *Express* rang Campbell to complain. He said that he 'understood how you might think that you have been misled.' Other papers reported similar episodes with Campbell, but not too much was made of them. It was understood that politics was a tough old game.

When Tony Blair appointed Campbell his Press Secretary he already knew that Campbell had a reputation as a man who could not be relied on to tell the

14. See Nicholas Jones, *Soundbites and Spin Doctors* (1996) pp. 164–5.
15. Colin Brown, *Fighting Talk: The Biography of John Prescott* (1997), p. 255.

whole truth. In May 1996 the then Tory MP Rupert Allason took Campbell and Mirror Group Newspapers to court on a charge of malicious falsehood. The case resulted from a long-running feud between Allason and the *Mirror*, which dated back to the days when Robert Maxwell controlled the paper. The details of the case were complicated, and Allason narrowly lost, though the decision was later reversed on appeal. In his summing up the judge, Sir Maurice Drake, was scathing about Alastair Campbell. He said: 'I did not find Mr Campbell by any means a wholly satisfactory or convincing witness', adding that 'Mr Campbell was less than completely open and frank, he did not impress me as a witness in whom I could feel 100 per cent confident.'[16] It is a sign of the media goodwill towards Campbell and towards New Labour at the time that this striking judgement was mainly reported on inside pages. Had a Tory spokesman been the victim of a similar attack by a judge, he would have been most unlikely to have survived the ensuing uproar.

John Major's Press Secretaries, Gus O'Donnell, Sir Christopher Meyer and Jonathan Haslam, were all civil servants. They all owed their loyalty, in the last resort, to the crown and not to John Major. This is not so with Alastair Campbell. Though technically he is a civil servant, with a salary paid by the state, he owes his overriding loyalty to Tony Blair. And it is a ferocious loyalty. 'Loyalty, that is what I am about,' he once told Benjamin Wegg-Prosser, Peter Mandelson's young assistant. For pressmen dealing with Campbell this brings one huge advantage. When they deal with the Prime Minister's Press Secretary, it is like dealing with the Prime Minister himself. It also brings one disadvantage. Campbell is more knowing, and more bashful, about the information he releases than anyone who has gone before. Robert Peston, political editor of the *Financial Times*, puts the difference like this: 'With previous press secretaries one always felt that if one asked the right question one would get the right answer. Not necessarily with Alastair. He is more obsessed with controlling the flow of information.'

Many lobby journalists have their own stories of this kind of obstruction from Campbell or his team. A year after the 1997 election, the *Mail on Sunday* learnt that special in-flight beds were being built so that Tony Blair could sleep on long-haul journeys overseas. It was an eminently sensible idea, and the main question it raised was why British Prime Ministers, who often faced fraught

16. See the Judgement by Sir Maurice Drake on Allason *v.* Alastair Campbell, Andy McSmith and MGN Ltd., Royal Courts of Justice, 2 May 1996. The judge compared the way Campbell gave evidence unfavourably with the testimony of his former colleague Andy McSmith, who was singled out for praise.

and complex negotiations at the end of their journeys, had not been provided with beds years before. But the government information machine put up a smokescreen. At first it denied that the beds had been ordered at all, then claimed, inaccurately, that the order had been placed by the Tories before New Labour gained power.

This was routine obstruction. Liam Halligan of the *Financial Times* faced the same kind of difficulty in November 1998 when he ran a story that the government welfare reform programme had run into difficulties. He reported that ministers had dropped plans, announced the previous March, for compulsory saving for pensions, adding that the government pensions review had been delayed.[17] Campbell dismissed the story, says Halligan, as 'crap'. Two months later, when the pensions review was finally published and the compulsion element was missing, Campbell was asked in open lobby why he had rubbished Halligan's story. He replied that he could not remember having done so.

At times Campbell, when under pressure, appears simply to have made information up. During the height of the problems facing the government over the Ron Davies resignation, there was suddenly a spate of stories highlighting fears that the former Welsh Secretary might kill himself. They made good headlines, and deflected attention from a growing row about Downing Street's handling of the affair. The only trouble was that they had no basis in fact. Looking back on the febrile coverage of his resignation, Davies later commented: 'Alastair was under pressure at the time and he made a throwaway comment: "Leave off him, you guys, in case he tops himself." That was without any discussion with me or my psychiatrist – not that I have a psychiatrist – or with my wife, who is better equipped than anyone to judge my mental state. Of course I was concerned. I saw this headline about suicide and it was dreadful. I'm not that sort of person. I'm certainly not a manic depressive and I'm not suicidal.'[18]

In June 1998 a furious row broke out following Ulster Secretary Mo Mowlam's decision to invite both Prince Charles and Sinn Fein leader Gerry Adams to the annual summer garden party at her official residence in Hillsborough Castle. The Prince was deeply irritated and upset, partly because he felt that the Sinn Fein invitation had been deliberately kept from him. A group of the Prince's aides had visited the province three weeks before on a reconnaissance ahead of what was always expected to be a very sensitive trip.

17. *Financial Times*, 3 November 1998.
18. *Daily Mail*, 18 February 1999.

They had been told nothing. The Prince found the whole episode particularly disturbing because his great-uncle Lord Mountbatten was blown apart by an IRA bomb, and he himself is Colonel-in-Chief of the Parachute Regiment. On the Monday after the story broke, the Prince's office was alerted that Downing Street was briefing journalists that the Prince of Wales had been made aware of the meeting some time before and had approved it. The Prince was so angry about this that Mark Bolland, a senior member of his private office, rang up Alastair Campbell personally to complain. In a heated exchange, he informed Campbell that unless he himself set the record straight, the Prince's office was ready to publicly contradict the Downing Street version of events.

These were all everyday incidents in the rough and tumble of lobby combat. What was perhaps more striking was how questions about the integrity of the government machine were often highlighted during moments of acute political crisis. It began to look as if the first reaction of the government when put under pressure was to cover up and to dissemble rather than come clean. This syndrome quickly emerged when the new and squeaky clean Blair administration was first put to the test with the Bernie Ecclestone affair. The government failed that test, though Campbell himself emerged with flying colours.

The Ecclestone affair started to crackle on Guy Fawkes Day 1997, when it emerged that Tessa Jowell, the Health Minister, was planning to grant Formula One a special exemption from the government ban on tobacco advertising. This news caused a great deal of rumbling on the left, but the problem only really began when Tom Baldwin, then of the *Sunday Telegraph*, was informed that Bernie Ecclestone, the owner of Formula One, was a giant donor to Labour Party funds. He rang Downing Street for corroboration of this story on the afternoon of Thursday 6 November.

There followed a great soul-searching within the government machine. Campbell strongly urged that the press should be informed not merely that Ecclestone was a donor, but that he was a very large one indeed, having contributed £1 million to Labour's accounts. It seems to have been Tony Blair, after talking the matter over with Gordon Brown, who ran scared of coming clean. He decided on an alternative course of action. A letter should be written from the Labour Party to Lord Neill, chairman of the Committee of Standards in Public Life, enquiring about the propriety of the donation. That way the government would be seen to have acted properly. In the meantime instructions went out that the donation should not be confirmed to Tom Baldwin or any other member of the press.

This tactic did not work. Baldwin wrote the story anyway. The situation got

out of control. In the end Tony Blair made the decision to go on national television for a soul-bearing interview to protest his own innocence. *On the Record*,
John Humphrys' Sunday lunchtime political show, was deliberately chosen as
the vehicle. It was decided that it was important to show that Blair was prepared
to face up to Britain's toughest interviewer.

The Ecclestone affair confirmed Campbell's reputation for good judgement.
His advice to come clean was based just as much on his sound strategic sense of
how to handle a story as on any belief in open government. But his general
aversion to telling the truth in anything like an open and straightforward way
was demonstrated by the row that blew up over a lobby briefing given on the
morning of 24 March 1998. It followed a front-page story in that day's
Financial Times by Campbell's old tormentor Robert Peston. Peston wrote that
Blair had 'intervened on behalf of Rupert Murdoch . . . by speaking to Romano
Prodi, the Italian premier, about the media magnate's attempt to acquire an
Italian television network.' This was a sensitive story. The government's close
relations with Murdoch have always been unpopular with great tranches of the
Labour Party. Just a month earlier the government had been defeated in the
House of Lords over an amendment to the Competition Bill aimed at outlawing
predatory pricing. This was directly aimed at the News International policy of
reducing the cover price of the *Times* in order to gain readers from less well-
endowed rival broadsheets.

There is no absolutely authoritative account of what happened at that lobby
briefing. A Downing Street tape was taken of it: it was subsequently, as usual
with all such tapes, deleted. Lobby journalists took notes: no one has come
forward with a word-for-word account. Perhaps it was simply not possible to
make one in the mayhem and confusion.

Campbell was asked why the British Prime Minister was asking Prodi
questions on behalf of Rupert Murdoch. He was not eager to answer. Lobby
correspondents persisted in their chosen line of attack. There are various techniques that Campbell uses when he is in a tight corner and wants to change the
subject. He stonewalls, evades the question, answers a different one from the
one that has been asked, puts up a smokescreen of confusion by launching a
savage attack on his adversary. On this occasion he settled on bluster and abuse.
While not denying that a conversation had taken place, he described the
Financial Times story as a 'complete joke'. Just to make his meaning even more
clear he proclaimed that 'it's balls that the Prime Minister "intervened" over
some deal with Murdoch. That's C–R–A–P.'

Two days later the *Financial Times* revealed that Murdoch had told colleagues the previous week 'that he would ask Tony Blair for help in ascertaining whether the Italian government would block his £4 billion acquisition of Mediaset, Italy's leading commercial television network.' When this conversation was confirmed by Ray Snoddy, the media editor of the Murdoch-owned *Times*, Campbell was exposed.

But Campbell did not lie over the Prodi business. For him, much hinges on the definition of the word 'intervention'. He continues to this day to defend, in the pugnacious, no-nonsense manner he has made his own, his stance that morning in Downing Street. Three months later, grilled by MPs on the episode, he was sticking to his guns: 'I described that story as a joke and I happen to think it was a joke. I think it is the oddest form of intervention to sit in your office waiting for a phone call from the Italian Prime Minister.' He has his defenders in the press. Roy Greenslade, former editor of the *Mirror*, pronounced afterwards that 'Campbell didn't lie to journalists, though he was economical with the truth because he and Blair were punctiliously observing the protocol of protecting the confidentiality of a private conversation between government leaders.'

Most journalists involved in the episode would not accept this gallant defence from Campbell's old friend, at any rate not in its entirety. Robert Shrimsley, the political correspondent of the *Daily Telegraph*, puts this point of view in no uncertain terms:

Campbell has mastered the trick of conveying a message which conveys the direct opposite of the truth without telling a lie. A good example is the Prodi story. He informed the lobby that the story was C–R–A–P. It later turned out that the only thing that was wrong was that he [Blair] had not actually instigated the telephone call himself. Strictly speaking he can probably defend the position that he did not lie. But any rational person attending that briefing would have drawn only one conclusion from what he was saying and that conclusion would have been wrong. And that was his specific intention, that they should draw the wrong one.[19]

The episodes mentioned above were spread over a period of years. The great majority of Campbell's dealings with the press are straightforward and rewarding for both sides. One example of Alastair Campbell's superlative service and attention to detail came on the day bombing started in the Kosovo War. Campbell was with the Prime Minister at the Berlin Summit. Even though

19. Conversation with the author, April 1999.

mainstream media were clamouring for Blair to talk on the war, Campbell made sure that West Country TV, in Berlin specially to cover a funding matter of concern to local farmers, got their Prime Ministerial soundbite.

Occasionally the fourth estate and the government clash angrily: it is right and proper that they should. Campbell was brought up in a rough old world. But there is still no question that somewhere in the heart of New Labour there is a culture of concealment. It is not Campbell's alone. Political journalists find Peter Mandelson just as tricky a customer to deal with, some claim more so.[20] Tony Blair has a spectacularly clean public image. It is not wholly deserved, as his biographer Jon Sopel's riveting account of the denials, evasions and falsehoods involved in the release of the information that the Prime Minister was once a member of CND demonstrates.[21] But it is an important part of the New Labour appeal. He has maintained that image, in part at least, thanks to the readiness of others to do his dirty work for him. And, for Alastair Campbell, that is what loyalty is all about.

Taming the press

Alastair Campbell was profoundly affected, well before he became Downing Street Press Secretary, by two visceral experiences. One was the way the media destroyed Neil Kinnock as a credible Leader of the Opposition. The other was the Media Class's destruction of John Major as Prime Minister. He is determined that the same fate should not afflict Tony Blair.

Everything he has done as Press Secretary is designed to prevent that – including the bullying, the manipulation, the distortion and above all the cultivation of News International. There is nothing new about many of these techniques. Campbell learnt his strong-arm tactics and his reverence for the *Sun* on the lap of Sir Bernard Ingham.

20. Trevor Kavanagh, political editor of the *Sun*, says: 'I was writing a story in which Peter Mandelson featured. When he got wind of it he called me and categorically denied a number of facts which I had good reason to believe were true. As a result of his denial the story collapsed. It subsequently emerged that the story was completely true. I have told him to his face that he dissembles.'

Paul Eastham, deputy political editor of the *Mail*, recalls: 'It came my way that the Prince of Wales and Peter Mandelson had formed a friendship. I checked this with Mandelson and he denied it so I left the story alone. It subsequently emerged that the story was true and that Mandelson was helping the Prince in some way with presentation.'

Even Donald Macintyre, Mandelson's broadly sympathetic biographer, comments critically on the accuracy of an answer given by Mandelson when interviewed on LWT's Dimbleby's *Question Time* about the Ecclestone Affair (Macintyre, p. 379). See also p. 188.

21. See Sopel, p. 65.

But New Labour is also set on achieving something far more ambitious. It is determined to change the nature of the media itself. It wants to change what Peter Mandelson and Alastair Campbell both call, in an elegant phrase, the 'grammar of reporting'. Downing Street believes that British political writing is focused to the point of obsession on the manufacture and elaboration of rifts, rows and controversy and is guilty of failing to cover the real issues that affect the ordinary people of Britain. It wants, in effect, to take British journalism back to where it stood forty years ago. Then newspapers were happy to report what politicians did and said on the terms in which politicians wanted their actions and speeches to be reported. They had not yet got ideas above their station. The Media Class had not yet emerged.

Since New Labour lacks even a sense of recent history, it can be assumed that Alastair Campbell does not consciously want to drag reporting back to where it was a generation and a half ago. His model is the Clinton White House. In the United States, with its strong culture of regional newspapers, an élite political corps lacks the strength to impose its interpretation on the nation at large. New Labour is deeply impressed by the way the President communicates direct with the American people either through personal appearances on television or through a relatively unsophisticated regional press. It watched, fascinated and absorbed, as President Clinton sustained his popularity with the American people throughout the Starr investigation.

Campbell set out these ideas in a Fabian Society seminar on government and the BBC. He accused the writing press of creating 'cynicism about politics, about politicians, about people who work in public life.' The speech is worth quoting from at some length:

As a public sector broadcaster, the BBC does have a special duty to give most coverage to the stories and issues that most affect people's lives. This will often mean having a different agenda from newspapers and often going against the flow. It means accepting that conflict is not the only source of news. It means that just because businesses are not, as predicted, attacking the National Minimum Wage, people are still interested in and have a right to be informed about it. It means that policy success stories – such as the New Deal and the part it has played in cutting youth unemployment – should be covered just as much as policy rows which may emerge from a leaked memo. This is not a political point. Such an approach should not mean that the Government secured more coverage or that opposition criticism was muted. Indeed, oppositions are more vulnerable than governments to the tendency of only being covered when there is a row.

This is a plea to the broadcasters not always to wait for the leak, the row, the scandal, before deciding to examine a particular Government or Opposition proposal. Because if they do, like as not they'll be travelling in the press's wake. That journey is a one-way road to cynicism, and while cynicism is an essential part of politics and journalism, when it dominates most judgements, the media's dominant role becomes the erosion of politics.[22]

Campbell was immediately denounced by the Media Class: he was an easy target.[23] Even at Westminster, there have been few more shameless examples of hypocrisy than Campbell's speech to the Fabian Society. He was effectively asking listeners to ignore his previous career as a journalist and polemicist which had been devoted to coverage precisely of the 'leak, the row, the scandal'.

They were also being asked to ignore New Labour's behaviour in opposition. Between 1994 and 1997 Tony Blair's Labour opposition was the most brilliant in history. Its campaign against sleaze, which was masterminded by Campbell and a handful of others, cleverly seized on a few individual cases to give the impression that the majority of British public figures were in it for the quick buck. No opposition has ever done more to foster cynicism about public life than Tony Blair's. It was, of course, acting hand in hand with the Media Class.

Now, having won power through the cooperation of the broadcasters and the press, Campbell was turning his back on his old allies: no wonder the denunciations rang out so fiercely and strongly. Tony Blair had seized power by using the media in the most flagrant way imaginable to undermine confidence in the government of the day. Having done so, his Press Secretary was doing his best to make it impossible that the same should not be done to him.

The speech was a demonstration of the confidence Campbell was coming to feel in Downing Street. It marked the beginning of his campaign to change the way that politics is reported. He started on the parliamentary lobby.[24] That was

22. Fabian Society pamphlet, March 1999.

23. See, for example, Kirsty Scott, *Glasgow Herald*, 3 February 1999; and Andrew Rawnsley, *Observer*, 14 February 1999.

24. Few have described the lobby system better than Ben Pimlott, writing about the Wilson years: 'Political journalists do not normally seek to be objective. This is partly because they are often employed by people who do not understand the meaning of the word. It is also because they do not see it as their job. Their first aim is to write copy that will be read, or make programmes that will be watched; and this is achieved by conveying a strong and consistent message, not a subtle or balanced one. It is also achieved by being predictable. Though people quite like to be shocked, they do not like to be puzzled or disturbed. Hence, in journalism, the quest is not for originality but for fashion: to be abreast of it, if possible to lead it, but not to be behind or out of tune with it. For three years Wilson had benefited greatly from this pack-like aspect of the press, perhaps more than he realised. Now the fashion changed: and for the rest of his career he suffered immeasurably because of it' (*op.cit.*, p. 448).

because he knew how dangerous it is. The Press Gallery is sweaty and over-crowded, like a Bombay slum. It is also, collectively, immensely influential. Its unsurpassed physical squalor sets the tone for national political debate. It is capable of paralysing and even, as the case of John Major showed, destroying governments as an effective force. Campbell's aim was to reduce the capacity of the parliamentary lobby to wreak havoc and destruction. Partly he attempted to achieve this by taming its most powerful figures through the cultivation of News International, and partly by diminishing the importance of the institution itself.

Lobby correspondents garner their information in two principal ways. First, they attend formal briefings with the Press Secretary or his deputy. Second, they make use of their lobby privileges to frequent areas of Parliament where MPs and ministers are most likely to be found – above all the Members' Lobby at the entrance to the Commons chamber.

Campbell set about reducing the value of both sources of information. Chance encounters – indeed encounters of any kind – between ministers or MPs and journalists were discouraged. Ministers and MPs were urged to spend as little time as possible in the Members' Lobby.[25] A very small category of Labour MPs were trusted enough to speak on a one-to-one basis to journalists without disgracing themselves. Like good SAS soldiers they were deemed capable of independent operation when cut off from headquarters. These select few were permitted to fraternise with reporters, apparently free with interpreta-tion and gossip, in practice putting about the approved Downing Street line, sticking in the knife in the approved Downing Street fashion and all the while gathering intelligence. The most effective representative of this group has been Fraser Kemp, a North-Eastern MP.[26]

The clampdown on the gathering of unofficial information was paralleled by a change in the style of official briefings. Shortly after the General Election, Robin Mountfield, a civil servant known for his expertise in financial regulation of the City, produced a report on the complicated subject of the government

25. Private information.

26. Kemp frequently used to appear on television and radio to defend the government when it was in trouble. In February 1999, he woke up shaking after a vivid dream. 'In my dream,' he later recalled in a conversation with the author. 'Tony Blair had just called an election. I was standing in front of the TV cameras saying: "This is a bold, courageous and correct decision." And then I was turning away in my dream and saying to myself: "We're only 18 months into the Parliament. What an ass. What a crass and stupid thing to do." And then I turned back to the cameras and said: "This is a brilliant and statesmanlike move."' Fraser Kemp's dream is a metaphor for the plight of the loyal back-bench MP under New Labour or, for that matter, any other government.

information service. Campbell to all intents and purposes oversaw the report, which was partly aimed at establishing the authority of his Downing Street briefing machine at the expense of competing centres, above all Gordon Brown's freelance briefing operation at the Treasury. All briefings were put 'on the record'. Campbell, all too well aware of the hazards of too public a profile, refused to let in cameras and signalled his desire to be known not by his own name but as the Prime Minister's Official Spokesman – or PMOS, as he is known all over Whitehall. The lobby system, and the anonymity it gives him, is still too valuable to lose.

The system is based on two daily lobby briefings,[27] and it is important to distinguish between the two. The 11 a.m. briefing takes place in Downing Street and Campbell is host. He can invite whom he likes and, in an attack on the exclusivity of the lobby, has widened the guest list to include foreign correspondents.[28] Campbell has an agenda and finds it relatively easy to set the tone. The second takes place in Parliament, only this time Campbell is technically a guest of the lobby. This subtly changes the balance of power and furthermore takes place later in the day, when the news cycle has moved on, sometimes away from Campbell's control. This more hidden event takes place in the mysterious little lobby briefing room up in the eaves of the Houses of Parliament: besides serving its purpose for political reporters it is rumoured to be used for meetings by the parliamentary masons.[29] Historically, this has been the meeting that political editors have preferred to attend. It has tended to generate the more lively discussion.

Campbell would like to get rid of the second lobby briefing, and he made subtle approaches to John Deans of the *Daily Mail*, the long-serving and respected lobby secretary, to do so. These approaches were rejected. Wary of any unilateral declaration, Campbell has responded with a partial boycott: he attends these more dangerous 4 p.m. briefings less than any previous Press Secretary. He frequently sends along his deputy Godric Smith, a civil servant, in his place.

At the same time as attempting to reduce the status of the lobby, Campbell has pursued a policy of bypassing it altogether. Fascinated by the White House

27. Except Friday afternoons.
28. The representative from Agence France Presse was a woman of quite exceptional good looks. Without effort she reduced Campbell and every male lobby reporter to a state of quivering imbecility. She got treated with almost as much friendliness as *Sun* reporters and *Times* political editor Philip Webster.
29. The furniture, when journalists arrive for briefings, has often been inexplicably rearranged, with some chairs and tables facing the back of the room.

example, Downing Street tried to develop much closer links with regional papers in Britain. Regional papers still have many pre-Media Class characteristics. They do not try to impose their slant or spin and are extremely grateful to be given a piece of the Downing Street action. In one spectacular stunt in 1998 Campbell managed to foist an identical exclusive article by Tony Blair on more than a hundred regionals, each distinguished only by an individual paragraph which acknowledged the local audience.

For Downing Street the great point was that the 'message' had gone out unmediated by journalists. It was in this sense, too, that Campbell discovered the merits of the foreign and the ethnic press. Foreign journalists – and this applies to Americans as much as Europeans – are as a general rule more earnest, serious and dull than their British counterparts. They lack British irreverence, humour and scepticism. They can, however, be relied upon to deal with the issues in an extremely thorough, if ponderous way. They lack, in short, the defining attributes of the Media Class.

Before entering Downing Street Alastair Campbell shared the contempt felt by all British political journalists for pompous and pedantic foreign journalists. Once, when Campbell was still at the *Mirror*, John Major's Press Secretary Gus O'Donnell returned from a trip to a European capital to face a barrage of hostile and angry questions from lobby journalists. At length he plaintively declared, 'All the European papers are saying that the trip was a great success. Why can't you be more like them?' Campbell, sitting at the back of the room, took it upon himself to answer for the lobby. 'Because they are all so bloody boring,' he declared.

Campbell carried with him into opposition this contempt for the foreign media. To their considerable anguish, they were ignored by the Millbank juggernaut, where they were known as the 'No Votes Press'. But in government his attitude slowly changed, and the dullness which seemed so contemptible when Campbell was a journalist suddenly seemed attractive and worthwhile: something to be cultivated. Little groups of foreign journalists were given special access to Downing Street, where they diligently took notes about the success of the New Deal and the finer points of the Third Way. London's foreign press corps is now close to Campbell's model of how all press corps ought to behave.

His final stroke was to cultivate the ethnic press. In January 1998 two black journalists, Paul Macey from *Voice* newspaper and Steve Pope from *New Nation*, were invited to join the travelling press corps accompanying the Prime Minister to South Africa. It was an inspired idea which originally came not from Campbell or even within Downing Street but from the British Council.

The parliamentary lobby is mainly white, male and middle-class: it is also exclusive. Macey and Pope were not made welcome by the press party on the trip. Talking to Campbell, they mentioned this sense that they were outside a closed shop. Immediately spotting an opportunity, he went out of his way to encourage them to write about it.

Pope went ahead and produced a powerful piece. It drew attention to the cliquiness and exclusivity of the lobby. 'A bigger bunch of middle-class, public school, ego-tripping, arrogant, smug, patronising, cynical, nasty, self-important merchant bankers you'd be hard pressed to find this side of a Pall Mall gentleman's club,' proclaimed Pope. He took the side of Downing Street: trying to show how its brave attempts to get its message across were blocked by political journalists intent on scoring points and reporting trivia. He drew attention to the lobby's obsession with domestic politics and its pathetic lack of interest in the tragic realities of a country finding its feet at the end of the Apartheid era. 'At the end of it,' he announced,' I actually started to feel sorry for Tony Blair.'[30]

It was a valid and interesting piece of writing. Downing Street understand-ably seized upon it, punting it around as a damning commentary on British political reporting. This was the view, commentators were told, of 'two black journalists' exposed to the British lobby for the first time.[31] Only it wasn't.

The second black journalist on the trip, Paul Macey of the *Voice*, refused to write an attack on the lobby. His reasons are interesting. He shared many of Steve Pope's perceptions about British political reporting. He too was vividly struck by the lobby's parochialism and obsession with the domestic agenda. But he felt that there were criticisms to be made of Downing Street as well. Macey noted Campbell's arrogance and refusal to answer questions. 'If reporters asked an awkward domestic question,' he said,

Campbell would brush it aside, saying: 'We're in South Africa, can't you report on what's going on out here?' But if there was good news back home he was the first one to make the most of it. And Tony Blair's big speech in the South African Parliament wasn't about South Africa. It was his big Third Way speech and aimed at the audience back in England . . . Steve Pope said he felt sorry for the government, under siege from a negative press. I didn't agree. One thing that the government did very well was manip-ulate the press coverage.[32]

30. See *New Nation*, January 1999.
31. Downing Street briefing, February 1998.
32. Interview with the author, July 1999. A year before, Macey applied for a lobby pass. It had still not been granted when this book went to press.

Chapter Twelve

'DEPUTY PRIME MINISTER'

That fatal drollery called a representative government.
Benjamin Disraeli, Tancred, *1847*

The Mandelson eclipse

No one who was there will ever forget the press briefing that Campbell gave on Wednesday 23 December 1998. He dragged himself into the room to meet the waiting journalists, all hungry for news of Trade Secretary Peter Mandelson's next move following the revelation of his undeclared £373,000 loan from Geoffrey Robinson, the Paymaster-General. When Campbell eventually sat down in his chair in the front of the press, he looked terrible. He was pale and shaking. There were great rings under his eyes. An emotional man, he had wept when he had realised that Mandelson would have to resign.[1] Normally pugnacious and confident, Campbell had no fight left in him that day.

Like every other member of the Blair close circle, he feared that the disgrace of Mandelson would mark the effective destruction of the Tony Blair government, in the same way that John Major was to all intents and purposes destroyed by sterling's eviction from the Exchange Rate Mechanism in September 1992. He felt lost, purposeless, alone. New Labour's inner circle must have spent Christmas in rather the same spirit as an apocalyptic sect awaiting the end of the world on a mountain top.

Returning ten days later from the Christmas break, they had a spring in their step. With a growing sense of exhilaration, they realised that the worst had happened – and nothing had changed. The turning point was a Gallup Poll at the beginning of January. It showed Labour support was practically as strong as ever. When Campbell brought news to the lobby early in the New Year that his old enemy Charlie Whelan had quit, the contrast with his appearance a week

1. Private information. Despite his hard and manly appearance, Campbell weeps regularly. His friend Roy Greenslade asserts that he wept during the film *The Full Monty*. Witnesses also record that his eyes filled with tears when he left the *Daily Mirror*, and when he heard of Robert Maxwell's death, though he stopped short of actually crying on both occasions.

before could hardly have been greater. The colour had returned to his cheeks, the gleam to his eyes and Campbell spat out the news of Whelan's demise with whole-hearted relish.

The cataclysmic events of Christmas 1998 marked a change of mood and pace in the Blair administration. It gave it, after the initial onslaught, a new poise and confidence. For the first eighteen months in government, all decisions had been taken in acute anticipation of the likely press response. Now the press had done its worst to Peter Mandelson, and the foundation-stones were still standing. From now on, the Prime Minister and his aides would feel a little more certain of their own capacity. It was no coincidence that just six weeks later, in a statement to the Commons, the Prime Minister found the courage to defy the Murdoch press and make by far the most pro-European statement of his premiership. The government's refusal to give in to the media-driven clamour for a ban on GM foods was another sign of this new assurance. So, later on, was Tony Blair's strong and decisive posture throughout the Kosovo War.[2]

For Campbell, the consequences of the Mandelson calamity were immense. They established him as the guv'nor. In one single stroke two of his biggest rivals in Whitehall – Peter Mandelson and Charlie Whelan – were removed from the political stage. The departure of Whelan on 4 January, which Campbell had sought so assiduously since the first day of the Blair government, took away much of Gordon Brown's ability to deal independently with the press. Whelan's successor Peter Curwen was a conventional civil servant, unfamiliar with and disapproving of the special operations which his predecessor had carried out with such panache. In any case Curwen enjoyed none of the instinctive trust that the Chancellor had placed in Whelan. From January 1999 Campbell was to all intents and purposes able to control Gordon Brown's press machine: a spectacular victory in the running power struggle between No. 10 and the Treasury.[3]

The eclipse of Peter Mandelson was just as important for Campbell, though – one would have expected nothing else from this complex and tortured soul – a very much more complicated matter. Campbell had gained what he really wanted when, in the summer of 1998, Tony Blair gave Mandelson the post of Trade Secretary. That was the critical moment. Until then Mandelson, as

2. See Alice Miles, 'The Impotence of the Press', *Spectator*, 27 February 1999.

3. In the high summer of 1999 Gordon Brown appointed a new special adviser, Ian Austin. Though a former researcher for Geoffrey Robinson he was suspected of having a foot in both the Blairite and Brownite camps.

Minister without Portfolio, had been based in the Cabinet Office and right at the heart of government. Campbell had no alternative but to defer to him. It had been Mandelson, for instance, who took the 9 a.m. daily meeting which gave ministers their marching orders. He even sat on the committee, alongside Treasury Minister Helen Liddell and Civil Service Minister David Clark, which set Campbell's salary and terms of employment. Mandelson would taunt Campbell about this from time to time. There were claims from within this committee – never proven – that Mandelson had tried to keep Campbell's salary as low as possible, so as to emphasise his subordinate status. One civil servant who frequently attended meetings with both men remembers: 'There was a definite rivalry but equally no question who was in charge – Peter Mandelson.'

Campbell inherited the bulk of this power when Mandelson went off to run a Whitehall department. Mandelson's Cabinet Office successor, with responsibility for government presentation, was Jack Cunningham. Cunningham, however, took a notably more relaxed role than his predecessor. He turned up at two or three of the 9 a.m. meetings, then stopped attending on a regular basis. It was assumed that he did not like the early hours. They suited Campbell, with his inexhaustible appetite for hard work, and he promptly seized control of this vital instrument of government and made it his own. It was Peter Mandelson who, long before Labour won power in May 1997, had understood that Labour would govern by agglomerating power to the centre. A year before the election, he set out some of his ideas in a book he wrote jointly with Roger Liddle.[4] At the end of the day it was Campbell who inherited the machinery of government whose inventor and midwife had been Peter Mandelson. That is just one of the innumerable ironies of their absorbing relationship.

So it was the summer 1998 reshuffle that passed power at the heart of government from Mandelson to Campbell. But it was 23 December 1998 when Campbell finally secured the upper hand in the battle for the heart and mind of the Prime Minister. For nearly five years Campbell and Mandelson had been colleagues, friends, comrades – and rivals at the court of King Tony. But until the matter of the Robinson loan reared its head, Mandelson had always been the favoured and senior courtier.

For Mandelson, one of the most painful moments of the whole terrible business must have come on Thursday 18 December when, after a meeting with his Permanent Secretary Sir Michael Scholar, he realised that he would have to inform Tony Blair of the secret he had kept from him for so long. That meant

4. Peter Mandelson and Roger Liddle, *The Blair Revolution* (1996).

telling Campbell of his dereliction, thus putting himself in the hands of his most feared and powerful rival. Not surprisingly, he could not bear to do so, and delegated the heart-rending task to his assistant, Benjamin Wegg-Prosser. It was Campbell who then interrupted a meeting to tell the Prime Minister, who was preparing to make a Commons statement about the previous night's bombing in Iraq, about the 'big bad story' that was going to present the government with its worst crisis and remove Mandelson from government ranks.[5]

When Alastair Campbell accepted the post of press spokesman to Tony Blair five years before, numerous people had been as close or closer to the party leader: Blair's old mentor Derry Irvine, his friend Charles Falconer, his rival Gordon Brown, his chief of staff Jonathan Powell, his close aide Anji Hunter, Philip Gould and Peter Mandelson. Campbell had had the sense not to take on the existing hierarchies around Blair all at once. He waited. By 1999, partly through his own ability and hard work, and partly through the weakness of others, he had established himself as Blair's principal adviser. After the Prime Minister himself, he was the most powerful man in the country. It was at the beginning of 1999 that well-informed people started calling Campbell 'Deputy Prime Minister.'[6]

Battle honours in Kosovo

The Kosovo crisis showed what an accomplished figure Campbell had become. At the time the Press Secretary's luminous role in the affair was scorned by commentators who sneered at 'war by spin-doctor'. These sneers could hardly have been wider of the mark. The West's military superiority was total. The battle was for public opinion. Milosević gambled that support in the NATO countries would fade, and splits would open in the Western alliance. In the first two weeks of the campaign that began in March 1999, he came within an inch of success. Military misjudgements were greatly magnified by the weakness of the NATO media operation in Brussels. The role played by Campbell and Blair in ensuring those rifts never came into the open was vital. An example of their skill came very early in the war, when Milosević made his first peace offer. This was designed to cause allied disarray, and nearly succeeded. It was essential not only that the response was firm but also that the nineteen members of the

---

5. See Macintyre, p. 439.

6. David Miliband, head of the Downing Street Policy Unit, likes to joke: 'He hates that. He hates being called deputy. That's terrible.'

coalition showed a public unity. The British team played a very large part in ensuring a common response.

In April 1999 Campbell took his Downing Street team to the NATO HQ. The manner in which he transformed the way the NATO briefings worked was masterly. The office of NATO press spokesman Jamie Shea, who now pays a most generous and heartfelt tribute to Alastair Campbell, was in a parlous state. He was under-resourced, overworked and had no media strategy. He had only three support staff and was obliged to write up his own notes before each press conference. There was no system for monitoring each day's press; Shea was vulnerable to being caught off-guard and unprepared for running news stories.

Shea, though liked by defence correspondents, lacked the level of access to NATO bosses that Campbell was able to take for granted in Downing Street: one reason why NATO's initial reaction to the bombing of the civilian convoy in Kosovo on Wednesday 14 April was so muddled. The first day that Campbell attended the briefing at the NATO summit in Washington to celebrate its 50th birthday, there was a rambling 25-minute statement from Shea about the war, followed by 15 minutes from a NATO general. Watching the performance, Campbell turned at one stage to a colleague and said: 'He stands there and says too many different things.'

Afterwards, Campbell took Shea outside. He asked: What was the top line? What did you want the story to be? The following day's press conference was transformed. Shea delivered a short five-minute statement, with a clear message. Afterwards – as Campbell had previously arranged – both Tony Blair and President Clinton congratulated Shea in person. 'It was a masterly perform-ance,' says one well-informed observer. 'Alastair could have humiliated Shea and stepped forward and taken the credit for himself. But he didn't. He handled Shea with enormous tact and sensitivity, turned around the whole thing.'

By the end Campbell was one of a handful of people intimately involved in running the war. Tony Blair often left it to Campbell to hammer out important and delicate matters with the US President directly. He was on the way to becoming a significant and even celebrated figure not just on the national but on the world stage. Once, on a visit to Washington, Clinton is said to have been so impressed by Campbell's abilities that he jokingly offered him a job. The Kosovan War showed how effective the New Labour media machine had become. The lessons from the Clinton White House had all been learnt and absorbed. Now Downing Street was going out and teaching some of its own. It resembled in some ways a superb international media consultancy. After the NATO mission there were reports that Campbell was being drafted in to sort out the disaster-prone European Commission. Most telling of all was the moment when New Labour aid was sought to help Hillary Clinton's campaign for the Senate.[7]

Kosovo illustrated one other powerful theme in Blair and Campbell's Downing Street: their strategic theory about how to handle the media. In public Campbell rubbishes media talk as 'navel-gazing' and 'self-obsession'. Actually Downing Street has given it the deepest thought. Sometimes Campbell will talk about it in private. The basic strategy is this: New Labour has four or five big policies; it will stick firm on them and never be blown off course, never show any signs of losing control. That is why, in its third year, Downing Street became more relaxed about trivial and subsidiary issues, believing that come the next election, the voters would judge it on its performance on its high-level commitments.

Kosovo was a case study of this. At the beginning of the war NATO was a shambles, clear neither about its objectives nor how they could be achieved. Then Blair and Campbell moved and set the minimum requirements that the West demanded: the refugees must return to Kosovo and Serbian troops must get out. Having set those requirements, they refused to weaken. Even two weeks before Milosević climbed down the NATO war effort appeared to be crumbling. But it has become ever more apparent since the end of the war that Britain was prepared to see it through, even to the extent of providing the bulk of the ground troops if necessary. There is no doubt that Kosovo was one of Campbell's and – more important to him – Tony Blair's finest hours. In the end, Campbell deserves to be judged by how he rose to the great challenges. He rose to this one.[8]

Perhaps inevitably, the war yet again brought to the fore Campbell's short-tempered intolerance of hostile or inconvenient press comment. On 16 April the *Times* political editor Philip Webster wrote a front-page story recording government anger at John Simpson, the BBC correspondent in the Serb capital Belgrade. Webster's well-informed piece described how senior government figures were accusing Simpson of being too credulous of claims coming from the Serb propaganda machine. This article produced a heated public controversy, with Downing Street coming away battered and bruised. At the end of it

7. New Labour spin-doctors were reportedly present along with President Clinton at the June 1999 meeting in Florida where Hillary Clinton finally decided to run for the Senate.

8. The above account of Campbell's role in the Kosovo War is based on private conversations with senior figures involved.

all, Campbell dispatched a conciliatory letter to Simpson.[9] In an attempt to clear himself of the charge that he had briefed harshly against the famous BBC war correspondent, Campbell included a 'contemporaneous record' of his briefing to journalists.

The problem was that Campbell's angriest and most intemperate attacks on Simpson did not take place at any formal briefing. Two days before the Webster story about Simpson, British journalists were with Campbell at NATO's Brussels headquarters. After the official briefing he wandered over to the press area and chatted to a group of reporters. They included the *Daily Mirror*'s Nigel Morris, *Mail* man John Deans, the *Sun*'s Bill Coles and Philip Webster. He left these reporters absolutely clear about his view that Simpson was far too uncritical of Serb war claims. He let his views rip and left nobody present in any doubt about the scale of his irritation with the BBC reporter.'[10]

Strains on family life

All this has come at some personal cost. Alastair Campbell is a devoted family man. Even though he is not technically married, the term 'uxorious' might have been invented for him. Having invited the Campbell-Millars to dinner, one hostess was surprised to receive a phone-call from Campbell saying he'd 'like to check a few things first.' He demanded a read-out of the guest-list and insisted on changing the placing so that he could sit next to Fiona. Even at this late stage in proceedings, Tony and Cherie Blair still nag at the Campbell-Millars to tie the knot. To the perplexity of observers Fiona Millar does from time to time wear a wedding ring.[11] But the demands of Campbell's job, with its late hours, intermittent crises and relentless travel, have taken him away from his children very much more than he would like.

The demands on Fiona Millar have grown too. After the last General Election she agreed to take on the part-time job of press adviser to Cherie Blair. As time has gone on she has assumed more responsibilities. In addition to the

9. See the report by Andrew Alderson, *Sunday Telegraph*, 9 May 1999. Campbell was replying to a letter from Simpson claiming that Campbell had made 'highly defamatory criticisms of my professional abilities.'

10. Campbell returned to the attack after the war was over. In a speech on 9 July 1999 to the Royal United Services Institute, he accused war reporters of being duped by 'the Serb lie machine'.

11. I am grateful to Charles Moore, editor of the *Daily Telegraph*, for this information. Moore, punctilious about this sort of thing, spotted the ring instantly upon meeting Ms Millar. Campbell's failure to make an honest woman of Millar is a source of distress to Moore as to other right-wing newspaper editors.

work carried out for the Prime Minister's wife, she is now Downing Street reception secretary, heavily involved in organising Downing Street social functions. All this weighs heavily upon the couple. Their life would not be possible without endless help and loving care from Fiona's mother Audrey. Even so, Campbell often confides to friends his worries that he is letting his children down by being away so much.

Few fathers in such a position as Campbell's, in fact, would spend nearly so much time with their children. He is constantly to be seen on the touchline of football matches cheering on his son. He tries to take Fridays off in order to be with his family. Lobby correspondents who ring him on Saturday mornings are likely to be given a running commentary on whichever game he happens to be watching. On Sunday afternoons the Campbell-Millars sometimes take their children skating with North London friends. This élite group hires the entire rink at the Michael Sobell Leisure Centre near Finsbury Park, to the irritation of other residents who are therefore excluded from their afternoon's pleasure.[12] So there is no doubt Campbell takes his duties as a father with high seriousness. One of the great sadnesses of his life is that his son refuses to let him teach him the bagpipes, as his own father did for him in the back garden of the family home in Leicester 25 years ago.

An unelected official

In one sense it was absurd to call Campbell Deputy Prime Minister. His power is not his own. He does not have a political base. He is not an elected politician. As he himself is well aware, the day that Blair leaves politics, he himself will leave Downing Street. He is merely the creature of Tony Blair, nothing more.

Nevertheless, there was something novel – and quite extraordinary – about the way that Campbell came to wield such power from Downing Street as the Blair government found its feet. Campbell could stand eyeball to eyeball against the great political figures of the day. He fought, and won, battles against Gordon Brown and John Prescott, the man who carries the nominal title of Deputy Prime Minister. Other members of the Cabinet carry out his

12. These select Media Class events are organised by the broadcaster Jon Snow. Others who attend or have been invited include Lord Falconer, Will Hutton, Anna Coote, and Sky political editor Adam Boulton. Campbell's presence at these events is evidence that the workerist image he affects is at least partly bogus and that Gordon Brown is correct to pigeonhole him as a member of the North London Media Set. The Campbells are also attenders at the traditional Christmas period party given by Helena Kennedy, an important North London social event.

instructions. There have been powerful officials in previous governments – Charles Powell under Margaret Thatcher, Marcia Williams under Harold Wilson, Tom Jones under Stanley Baldwin or Sir Maurice Hankey under Lloyd George. But none of them was half as feared or wielded a fraction of the influence across so many areas as Campbell. This is what made it understandable, even if far from correct, to call Campbell 'Deputy Prime Minister'. The fascinating question to ask is this: what is it about Tony Blair's style of government that has given such sweeping power to an unelected official?

The answer is that several factors have come together to present Campbell with his unique opportunity. The first is what Professor Peter Hennessy calls Tony Blair's 'Napoleonic' style of government. Blair rules from the centre: the feudal barons are kept under control. All governments in living memory have contained a number of 'big beasts' thundering around the jungle. With the possible exception of Gordon Brown, and perhaps John Prescott, New Labour has no big beasts.[13] There is no room for them. All previous Labour Prime Ministers have had, in addition, the party's ruling National Executive Committee to contend with, with its overall control over so much, including press management. It is one of Tony Blair's many immense debts to Neil Kinnock that the NEC is now an atrophied body with a mainly symbolic existence. This autocratic style of rule presents huge opportunities for officials like Campbell to acquire power at the expense of politicians. In this sense he is directly comparable to the advisers to the French crown who gained such prestige and power in the age of French absolutism at the expense of the old aristocracy, Cardinals Richelieu and Mazarin.

The second factor is the rise of the media. Tony Blair has put the media at the heart of his operation from the very beginning. He is himself, to a prodigious extent, a creation of the Media Class. It is no coincidence that his strongest and closest adviser is a spin-doctor. That is because the media is what New Labour thinks about and fears most. It is occasionally claimed – sometimes by Campbell himself, when he wisely tries to play down his own vast sphere of influence – that the Prime Minister's Press Secretary does not influence policy. To concede that claim is grievously to misunderstand the nature of this government. For Tony Blair and the tiny group of men and women around him, policy and presentation are identical, part of the same process, carried out by the same people. Blair's brilliance has been to recognise the importance of packaging

13. Foreign Secretary Robin Cook's decision to play the pussycat rather than the tiger is symptomatic.

and presentation. Blair in politics is a follower of the classical tradition. For him (a very modern thing this) form matters more than content. That is why – in a direct reversal of the balance of power under Thatcher – the Press Secretary counts for very much more in Downing Street than the Head of the Policy Unit or the Chief of Staff.

The third factor that has created Campbell is the precipitate decline in the power and status of Parliament, which is in danger of turning into nothing more than a sectional interest group. New Labour is instinctively hostile to representative institutions: they are messy, they take up time, they want to discuss things. It prefers to govern in other ways, through the use of the plebiscite and by handing power to unelected figures. The unexpected landslide victory in May 1997 has given it an opportunity to put much of that into practice. With Parliament quiescent, politics now predominantly takes place in the Media Class arenas of the television studio and the printed page. That carries it into the domain of Alastair Campbell and the control mechanism of Millbank. In all previous administrations this century, whether Labour or Tory, the post of Chief Whip has carried great power and mystique. It has been the Chief Whip who has exercised control over MPs, possessed secret forms of knowledge, brutalised, carried a hidden menace. That is why the bestselling writer of political novels, Michael Dobbs, made his main protagonist Francis Urquhart a Tory Chief Whip.

Under Tony Blair the post has been to all intents and purposes downgraded into that of an administrative drudge. Its occupant in the summer of 1999, Ann Taylor, was a worthy and respected figure but carried none of the power and menace of her predecessors. That had slipped away from the House of Commons and towards Downing Street and Alastair Campbell. Among his many other qualities, he is the nearest in spirit and in presence to the mysterious Francis Urquhart. The opportunity has been there, and Campbell has seized it and converted himself into the dominant presence of the Blair administration.

All these factors – the Blair autocracy, the eclipse of Parliament, the rise of the Media Class – have come together to create something that has never been met with before in British political life. It is a completely novel constitutional development, and needs to be appreciated as such. There are no meaningful parallels in recent history, at least not since the autocratic principle was wiped away in 1688. Before the power of the throne was stripped away by Parliament, it is indeed possible to discover powerful, brooding figures close to the executive who bear cautious comparison with Campbell. Thomas Wentworth, Earl of Strafford, advised Charles I in his attempt to impose personal rule.

Popularly known as Black Tom, he was one of the earliest casualties in the King's battle against Parliament. Wentworth went to the scaffold at Tower Hill.

Like Wentworth, Campbell is not a character who can ever coexist easily with representative democracy. The stronger he is, the less power elected politicians enjoy, and vice versa. That may very well be what Tony Blair is straining towards: a direct and unalloyed communication with the British people, unmediated by Parliament, the press or the Labour Party. Campbell himself, in exercises like his Fabian Lecture of February 1999, is pushing him in that direction. Personal rule would suit his purposes well.[14]

A dangerous future

The elected politicians know this, and they are beginning to stir. Campbell now occupies an exposed position. He has always been skilful at handling his personal relations: he will need all of that skill in the years to come. He is, at last, beginning to make enemies: not least among dispossessed and humiliated ministers and former ministers. And even well-disposed MPs are beginning to ponder the propriety of his position. At a heated meeting of the Parliamentary Labour Party in June 1999 Tam Dalyell spoke up angrily against the influence of a tiny circle of favourites in Downing Street. Above all, and Campbell must know this well, the Chancellor Gordon Brown and perhaps the Deputy Prime Minister John Prescott would be happy to see his power and influence sharply diminished.

His enemies haven't come in the night with knives for Campbell yet. Things are going too well, and Campbell is playing too skilful a game. But he knows that the moment Tony Blair falters they will come, not for the Prime Minister himself, but for the all-powerful and unelected official who stands behind him in the shadows. King Charles I had to hand over Wentworth in 1640 in order to save his own skin: there may come a time when Tony Blair is asked to do the same.

Campbell's ambitions are uncertain. There are times when he has talked of following in the footsteps of Peter Mandelson and going into Parliament. That way he could answer the charges that he lacks the courage to be a politician in his own right. A seat could be found for him: New Labour has become very

---

14. So long as Labour's constitutional plans stay on course, Tony Blair will have called more referenda or plebiscites than all previous Prime Ministers put together. Peter Mandelson is said to have remarked that the age of representative democracy is coming to a close.

accomplished at managing these things just as the Tories have lost the knack of doing so. Burnley would be ideal: Campbell has reportedly been obliged to give assurances to the Labour MP for Burnley, Peter Pike, that he is not after his job. It is easy to imagine the Prime Minister's Press Secretary as a capable and bruising performer in the Commons chamber, a pugnacious defender of government policy on television, and a tough, competent government minister. Some Campbell supporters believe that he could be in the Cabinet within two or three years of the next General Election and a candidate for Tony Blair's job not long after that. Nothing is impossible. But it would be a long, perilous and above all uncertain journey. Campbell would be exchanging the certainty of absolute power and total access for the lottery of Parliament: an institution for which, from the high ground of Downing Street, he feels a certain lofty disdain.

Another possibility for him would be to return to Fleet Street and the punditry which he abandoned so reluctantly in 1994: a big editorship with salary to match would fall into his hands. And Campbell has a meal ticket for life, if, as is often reported, he keeps a daily journal.[15]

But there is no need for the Prime Minister's Press Secretary to ponder his future. Just at present he lords it in Westminster and Whitehall as no one has ever done before. There is – as Professor Marquand has highlighted[16] – a burning paradox at the heart of New Labour, and Alastair Campbell is poised at the centre of it. On the one hand the government is embarking upon the most profound package of constitutional change for three centuries. Much of this is about giving up power and handing it back to the people, through devolution in Scotland and Wales, mayors for the big cities, the rapid shift towards

15. He has never publicly denied repeated assertions in the press that he does so. This document, if it exists, would be of enormous value for future historians of the epoch. It would be like no other diary that has ever been written before. Alan Clark's diaries, though beautifully written, came from a man on the periphery of power. Even the Crossman diaries in the Wilson years came from a Cabinet minister circling anxiously and at times contemptuously around Downing Street, trying to second-guess the Prime Minister's intentions. Campbell's, by contrast, would have come from a man who had been active at the very heart of power. Not merely that, he is a trained writer, with an eye for a story.

Some Cabinet ministers are surprised that the Prime Minister might allow his Press Secretary to keep a written account of events. The suspicion that confidences exchanged behind closed doors could in due course be published disturbs the nature of his relationship with colleagues. Donald Dewar, who left the Cabinet in the summer of 1999 to become First Minister of Scotland, told a journalist (*Sunday Times Magazine*, 18 April 1999) that he could never keep a diary because it would be a 'betrayal'.

16. David Marquand, *Must Labour Win?* (ESRC Annual Lecture, 1998). Marquand argues that: 'New Labour has been torn between two alternative statecrafts, each a legacy from the party's past and each manifest in current government policy.' He argues that one is 'essentially top down and dirigiste' and the other 'civic pluralist'. There is no question which of the two traditions Campbell finds more sympathetic. See also Marquand's *Populism or Pluralism? New Labour and the Constitution* (Mishcon Lecture, 1999).

proportional representation. On the other hand New Labour has imposed a culture of control on Westminster and Whitehall on a scale that has rarely been experienced before. The resolution of this absorbing conflict will be decisive in determining what kind of government the New Labour administration turns out to be and whether in the end it is a real and permanent force for good.

It is neither absurd nor impertinent to relate Campbell's intolerance of dissent to the unusual and fractured circumstances of his own life. Few men and women entering politics these days have quite so rich and engaging a past. From his early days Campbell was a vivid and colourful figure, a dangerous man. Before he met Fiona Millar he was a womaniser. Before and afterwards he was a drinker and a pub brawler. In his late twenties, for reasons that are hard to understand, he suffered a breakdown. To his enormous credit, and thanks to the love and loyalty of those around him, he survived and emerged a stronger and better man.

But there was a cost. He would seem to have survived only by the suppression of large tracts of his own personality. That prodigious effort must somehow have released large amounts of dormant energy in Campbell's own character and opened the way to his extraordinary rise through British politics. But those demons are lurking there somewhere. They will never go away. Somewhere in Campbell's own mind there might well be a link between the dissident voices on the Labour benches and those drinking afternoons that he renounced so long ago. The link with the political reporters he bullies, obstructs and insults is still more direct. The clever, irreverent, irresponsible, anarchic lobby journalists whom Campbell hates so much: they are his old self, the one that he could not live with and that drove him to his breakdown.

Now Campbell is in control; he knows it, and so does everybody else. People who see a great deal of him say that he is a man who sometimes gives the appearance of being frightened of himself, what he might do or what he might become.

NEW LABOUR AND THE CIVIL SERVICE

After the General Election of 1997 New Labour made no secret of its belief that the Government Information and Communication Service (GICS) should be transformed. In opposition Peter Mandelson and others had pioneered the most sophisticated media machine in history. Once New Labour had secured power it was only natural to compare the expertise, ruthlessness and sheer commitment of the pre-election Millbank office with the somewhat cumbersome and lacklustre government equivalent. In almost every way the GICS was found wanting.

Soon after the General Election Peter Mandelson, then Minister Without Portfolio in the Cabinet Office, and Alastair Campbell called a meeting of heads of government information departments in 10 Downing Street. Drinks were served, though neither Mandelson nor Campbell drank. Campbell spoke first. He was, in the words of one present, 'very kindly and friendly'. He explained that New Labour intended to place government communications right at the heart of policy-making. He insisted that New Labour would want to maintain control of the media agenda in the same way as it had done in opposition. He insisted that he wanted a 24-hour service and that he needed to know 'tomorrow's news' rather than what had already appeared in the papers. He said that if first editions got the story wrong, he wanted the failure corrected at once. He called on government information departments to be more interventionist and proactive. He spoke of the importance of reiterating the central government messages. 'When you and I are heartily sick of repetition, that is when we are getting through to the outside world,' he insisted. Campbell made reassuring noises that New Labour had no intention of using the government information service for party political advantage and he gave assurances that no great purge of Civil Service jobs was planned.[1]

1. The above account is based on conversations between the author and several of those present at the meeting.

There is no reason whatever to believe that Campbell's last assurance was not honestly meant, but that is not how things worked out. Between 1 May 1997 and 1 June 1998, no less than 25 heads of information or deputy heads were replaced, a turnover of more than 50 per cent.[2] That attrition continued. By August 1999, all but two of Whitehall's seventeen directors of communications had been replaced since May 1997, a staggeringly high and completely unprecedented turnover.[3] Some of the changes were entirely routine career moves, but others were forced moves and effective sackings which gave cause for unease.

The one head of information to speak out at the Downing Street meeting was Steve Reardon at the Department of Social Security. When Mandelson and Campbell had stopped talking there was what one witness refers to as 'an uneasy silence'. Then Reardon began a passionate defence of his profession: 'You see in front of you in this room a set of people generally reckoned by the outside world to be the *crème de la crème.*' Reardon was one of the earliest casualties of the new regime. Some of those present believe that Reardon did himself no good with this stance; within six months he was gone, so was Andy Wood from the Northern Ireland Office, Liz Drummond of the Scottish Office, Gill Samuel from the Ministry of Defence, Jonathan Haslam from Agriculture, Jill Rutter from the Treasury, as well as a number of others.

Two charges could never be made against these people. First: incompetence. They were all highly respected within the Civil Service. One or two of them were high-flyers recognised for their outstanding qualities, and most of them were snapped up by the private sector. Second: political bias. As a group they were simply not open to the charge of being anti-Labour. If anything the reverse was the case. Much of the Civil Service had looked forward keenly to a Labour victory. Wood, for instance, had been a party member before entering government service.

Wood was informed by the Permanent Secretary at the Northern Ireland Office that 'personal chemistry' in his relationship with the Ulster Secretary Mo Mowlam meant that he had to be moved from his post. Reardon clashed with Harriet Harman and her two Special Advisers, accusing them of improper interference in the work of his department. In an important piece of evidence to the Select Committee on Public Administration, Reardon claimed that: 'In particular the drafting of departmental press releases was closely scrutinised to the

2. See Appendix I to the Select Committee on Public Administration Report on the GICS (HC 770, 29 July 1998).
3. See *The Times*, 17 August 1999.

point of obsession by the Special Advisers who frequently issued instructions about drafting and re-drafting directly to junior press office staff without my knowledge. There were frequent arguments about the proper language to be employed in a departmental draft and Special Advisers sought to reproduce the tone of the Labour manifesto and repeat its election commitments as emerging news.'[4]

The most disturbing case of all was that of Jill Rutter, whom Gordon Brown inherited as his Treasury Press Secretary from Kenneth Clarke. Rutter was an outstanding civil servant who had made her career at the Treasury. The arrival of Charlie Whelan and Ed Balls as the new Chancellor's Special Advisers cut the ground from under her. They took a vigorous interest in press handling and it was often all too obvious that they were better briefed than she was. Rutter asked her Permanent Secretary Sir Terence Burns for a transfer. She complained that three-quarters of her job had been taken away. He told her to carry on with the other quarter 'for the sake of the service'. Eventually life became impossible and she left the Treasury altogether.

New Labour set about not merely changing the personnel within the GICS; it also set about changing its structure. Campbell wisely decided not to follow the example of his predecessor Sir Bernard Ingham and head up the GICS himself. He left that role to Mike Granatt, all the while retaining and strengthening the mechanisms of central control of the GICS as a whole. Within weeks of the Election victory the Cabinet Secretary, Sir Robin Butler, was prevailed upon to commission a report into the GICS. Sir Robin commissioned the Permanent Secretary at the Office of Public Service, Sir Robin Mountfield, to undertake the task. His report was received in November 1997.

Press attention at the time of publication of the Mountfield Report focused upon its least interesting and most conservative recommendations: these concerned the attribution of statements by Alastair Campbell. In the past there was a fiction that Downing Street spokesmen, like the Secret Service, did not exist. This convention had already been breaking down: Mountfield did away with it altogether. After the publication of his report a new entity emerged: the Prime Minister's Official Spokesman – or PMOS as Campbell has come to be known around Whitehall. The Mountfield Report stopped short, however, of permitting Campbell to be identified by name or broadcasting lobby briefings. This was the key decision: the secretive lobby system has been too useful to the government for it to be done away with altogether. Furthermore, the Prime

---

4. Appendix 5 to the Select Committee Report.

Minister's Press Secretary was well aware of the dangers of allowing himself to become a public figure in his own right.

More important were Mountfield's other recommendations. They brought many of the innovations of the Millbank system into the heart of Whitehall. His report recommended a new body to coordinate departmental announcements and government initiatives. Thus the Strategic Communications Unit was born. This small cadre, made up of a mixture of Labour appointees and civil servants, was given an office in 10 Downing Street formerly used for the appointment of bishops.

Mountfield announced the creation of a central media monitoring unit 'to provide 24-hour monitoring of emergency stories, and immediate warning to Departmental Press Offices and the centre.' This was a direct lift from Millbank and, according to those who saw its product, not as accomplished as the original version. Mountfield also referred to plans for a new computer to replace the Cab-E-Net electronic information system which had served the Tories. Cab-E-Net had been constantly dogged with technical difficulties; not so its replacement. Given the name Agenda, it listed forthcoming events, lines to take and ministerial speeches. It became a vital tool of government.

Most of these changes were pure common sense, designed to lift the government out of the media stone age. New Labour was not content merely with these improvements, however. A hugely enhanced role was also given to Special Advisers in government. Special Advisers have a unique, and in some way contradictory, status in Whitehall. They do not have to abide by Civil Service rules of neutrality. On the other hand, they are paid for by the taxpayer. New Labour in government has seized on the freedom offered by Special Advisers, increasing the numbers from 35 at the end of the last government to nearly 70 at the last count. Many of these Special Advisers are given a purely media relations role. The most notable example of this was Charlie Whelan at the Treasury, who to a large but informal extent took on the role of Press Secretary. But he was merely the best-known and noisiest example. More unobtrusive and typical was Joe McCrea, Frank Dobson's Special Adviser at the Department of Health.

In 1998, McCrea wrote an account of his first year in government for *Progress*, a magazine for Labour Party members. It was clear from McCrea's article that his work was overwhelmingly concerned with the media. 'My overriding impression of the first seven months is one of having to battle to bring the government standards of briefing up to those which we developed in the run-up to May 1997.' McCrea went on to explain how he had told civil servants: 'you can't win 21st century political battles with techniques and technology from 30 years ago.'[5] McCrea appears not to ask himself whether it is the role of government departments to fight and win political battles. He cheerfully accepts the equivalence between the Millbank fighting machine and the domestic Civil Service. His article shows little awareness of the distinction between a neutral Civil Service and an election-fighting political machine. It highlights a distinctive feature of Tony Blair's New Labour government, which is its apparent lack of respect for the traditional detachment of the British Civil Service.

The claim of 'politicisation' has been made against all recent governments. It was made against the Wilson administration, against Margaret Thatcher's government and against John Major. In the final years of the last-named government the New Labour opposition was reckless with charges of politicisation against the Tories.[6] Yet the transgressions which Tory ministers were accused of were minor compared to New Labour's cull of government information officers or its doubling of the number of Special Advisers.

Campbell's own appointment, as a party political man placed in a key government role, raised huge questions about the neutrality of the Civil Service. Previous occupants of his post have been civil servants. Tony Blair's decision to lift the restrictions on civil servants in Campbell's case created problems. The Civil Service Order in Council 1995 created an obligation that all Home Civil Service appointments should be made 'on the basis of fair and open competition'. One exemption was allowed, for Special Advisers. But they were forbidden to exercise executive authority over civil servants, and so the exemption was useless for either Campbell or the Downing Street Chief of Staff Jonathan Powell. That was why, acting on the advice of officials, the incoming government changed the Order in Council to allow up to three posts at No. 10 to be both party political and to carry executive responsibilities.

Senior officials say that they welcome the new formula. Sir Richard Wilson, the Cabinet Secretary, made a virtue of it when questioned by the 1998 Select

5. *Progress* magazine, Winter 1998.

6. See the *Scotsman*, 15 November 1995. George Robertson accused Scottish Secretary Michael Forsyth of treating government north of the border as a 'wholly owned subsidiary of the Tory party'. Forsyth's crime seems to have been the insertion of the phrase 'Tartan Tax' in a press release, even though he sought and was given Civil Service sanction before doing so. John Prescott accused Deputy Prime Minister Michael Heseltine of being 'out to politicise the Civil Service' (quoted in the *Daily Telegraph*, 12 November 1996). The supporting evidence here was Heseltine's plan to use Whitehall departments to identify individuals prepared to support the government. It was dropped after Cabinet Secretary Sir Robin Butler said it would jeopardise Civil Service neutrality. A Civil Service mole subsequently leaked the plan. In April 1994 David Blunkett, then Shadow Health Secretary, attacked the 'creeping politicisation of the Civil Service' (quoted in the *Guardian*, April 1994).

Committee on Public Administration, saying that 'everybody knows where he [Alastair Campbell] is coming from'.[7] Senior Tories are also supportive. Tim Collins, now a Tory MP and formerly the party Director of Communications, says that the politicisation of the Press Secretary role, is a 'welcome, sensible and entirely legitimate change.'[8] Another former Tory Director of Communications, Shaun Woodward, goes further still. He says that 'criticising the Blair machine is a bit like attacking Sainsbury's for having a PR Department. What Campbell and others have done is to professionalise a department which until then was run by amateurs.'[9]

Critics, however, note the dangers of an erosion of the distinction between the political party and the Civil Service. The government machine in Britain has not been the servant of a single political party since the reforms of the mid-nineteenth century aimed at rooting out nepotism and corruption. Under New Labour the Civil Service is coming to bear a closer resemblance to the American system, where Civil Service jobs routinely change hands with an incoming administration.

7. Select Committee Report, p. 36.
8. Conversation with the author.
9. Conversation with the author.

BIBLIOGRAPHY

Bayley, Stephen, *Labour Camp: The failure of style over substance* (B. T. Batsford, 1998)

Brown, Colin, *Fighting Talk: The Biography of John Prescott* (Simon & Schuster, 1997)

Cohen, Nick, *Cruel Britannia* (Verso, 1999)

Davies, A. J., *We, the Nation* (Little, Brown, 1996)

Gilbert, Martin, *Winston S. Churchill*, vol. 8: *Never Despair 1945–1965* (Abacus, 1995)

Gould, Philip, *The Unfinished Revolution: How the Modernisers Saved the Labour Party* (Little, Brown, 1998)

Greenslade, Roy, *Maxwell: The Rise and Fall of Robert Maxwell and his Empire* (Birch Lane, 1992); UK edition published as *Maxwell's Fall: An Insider's Account* (Simon and Schuster, 1992)

Haines, Joe, *The Politics of Power* (Coronet, 1977)

Harris, Robert, *Good and Faithful Servant: The Unauthorized Biography of Bernard Ingham* (Faber and Faber, 1990)

Healey, Denis, *Time of My Life* (Penguin, 1990)

Hennessy, Peter, *Whitehall* (Fontana, 1989)

— *The Blair Style of Government: An Historical Perspective and an Interim Audit* (Leonard Schapiro Lecture, London School of Economics, 2 December 1997/ included in *Government and Opposition*, vol. 33, no.1, Winter 1998)

— *The Blair Centre: A Question of Command and Control?* (Public Management Foundation, February 1999)

— *The Importance of Being Tony: Two Years of the Blair Style* (Guy's and St Thomas's Hospital Trust, July 1999)

Jones, Nicholas, *Sultans of Spin* (Victor Gollancz, 1999)

— *Campaign, 1997* (Phoenix, 1997)

— *Soundbites and Spin Doctors* (Phoenix, 1996)

Kampfner, John, *Robin Cook* (Victor Gollancz, 1998)

Kinnock, Glenys and Millar, Fiona, *By Faith and Daring* (Virago Press, 1993)

Koss, Stephen, *The Rise and Fall of the Political Press in Britain* (Hamish Hamilton, 1981)

Leonard, Mark, *Britain: Reviewing Our Identity* (Demos, 1997)

Macintyre, Donald, *Mandelson: The Biography* (HarperCollins, 1999)

Mandelson, Peter and Liddle, Roger, *The Blair Revolution: Can New Labour Deliver?* (Faber and Faber, 1996)

Margach, James, *The Abuse of Power* (W. H. Allen, 1978)

Marquand, David, *Must Labour Win?* (ESRC Annual Lecture, 1998)

— *Populism or Pluralism? New Labour and the Constitution* (Mishcon Lecture, 1999)

McSmith, Andy, *Faces of Labour* (Verso, 1997)

— *John Smith: A Life 1938–1994* (Mandarin, 1994)

Pimlott, Ben, *Harold Wilson* (HarperCollins, 1993)

Pym, Hugh and Kochan, Nick, *Gordon Brown: The First Year in Power* (Bloomsbury, 1998)

Rentoul, John, *Tony Blair* (Little, Brown, 1995)

Rosenbaum, Martin, *From Soapbox to Soundbite: Party Political Campaigning in Britain since 1945* (Macmillan, 1997)

Routledge, Paul, *Gordon Brown: The Biography* (Pocket Books, 1998)

Seaton, Jean (ed.), *Politics and the Media: Harlots and Prerogatives at the Turn of the Millennium* (Blackwell, 1998)

Sopel, Jon, *Tony Blair: The Moderniser* (Michael Joseph, 1995)

Williams, Hywel, *Guilty Men* (Aurum Press, 1998)

Broadcasting Politics (Fabian Special 42, March 1999)

Ministerial Code: A Code of Conduct and Guidance on Procedure for Ministers (Cabinet Office, July 1997)

Select Committee on Public Administration, Sixth Report, The Government Information and Communication Service (HC 770, House of Commons, 29 July 1998)

INDEX

INDEX

INDEX